INSIGHT GUIDES

The world's largest collection of visual travel guides

Rio De Janeiro

Project Editor Edwin Taylor

Photography by John Maier Jr. and Vange Millet

Editorial Director: Brian Bell

Part of the Langenscheidt Publishing Group

INSIGHT GUIDES

Rio De Janeiro

First Edition 1988
Updated 1999

Distributed in the United States by
Langenscheidt Publishers Inc.
46–35 54th Road, Maspeth, NY 11378
Fax: (718) 784 -0640

Distributed in Canada by
Prologue Inc.
1650 Lionel Bertrand Blvd., Boisbriand
Québec, Canada J7H 1N7
Tel: (450) 434-0306. Fax: (450) 434-2627

Distributed in the UK & Ireland by
GeoCenter International Ltd
The Viables Centre, Harrow Way
Basingstoke, Hampshire RG22 4BJ
Fax: (44) 1256-817988

Distributed in Australia & New Zealand by
Hema Maps Pty. Ltd
24 Allgas Street, Slacks Creek 4127
Brisbane, Australia
Tel: (61) 7 3290 0322. Fax: (61) 7 3290 0478

Worldwide distribution enquiries:
APA Publications GmbH & Co. Verlag KG
(Singapore branch)
38 Joo Koon Road, Singapore 628990
Tel: 65-8651600. Fax: 65-8616438

Printed in Singapore by
Insight Print Services (Pte) Ltd
38 Joo Koon Road, Singapore 628990
Fax: 65-8616438

This guidebook combines the interests and enthusiasms of two of the world's best known information providers: Insight Guides, whose range of titles has set the standard for visual travel guides since 1970, and Discovery Channel, the world's premier source of nonfiction television programming.

The editors of Insight Guides provide both practical advice and general understanding about a destination's history, culture, institutions and people. Discovery Channel and its Web site, www.discovery.com, help millions of viewers explore their world from the comfort of their own home and also encourage them to explore it firsthand.

The guides are carefully structured: their first section covers the destination's history, and then analyzes its culture in a series of magazine-style essays. The main Places section provides a run-down on the things worth seeing and doing. Finally, a listings section contains useful addresses, telephone numbers and opening times.

To maintain this consistent high standard, for each book Insight recruits a project editor who coordinates the work of the best local writers and photographers.

Edwin Taylor, project editor for this guide, is an American journalist-writer who has written extensively about Brazil from all its varied angles – politics, economics, history, and culture as well as travel. Taylor moved to Brazil in 1979 to become managing editor of the *Latin America Daily Post*, an English-language daily newspaper that Taylor helped found. Four years later, Taylor started the first English-language information service on Brazil, called *Brasilinform*, which publishes what is recognized as one of Brazil's most authoritative and influential newsletters. Taylor has written dozens of articles and was co-author and editor of *Fodor's Guide to Brazil*, editor of *Fodor's South American Guide* and in 1988 launched the first English-language travel newsletter on Brazil called *Brazil Travel Up-*

Taylor

Murphy

Maier

Pickard

Ashford

Emert

date. Over the years Taylor has written for such prestigious publications as T*he Wall Street Journal, The New York Times, Newsweek* and *The Miami Herald.*

Tom Murphy, an American journalist from New Jersey, wrote about Rio's lesser known attractions – the historical downtown area, the charming Santa Teresa neighborhood and the city's out of the way viewpoints. Murphy spent long hours researching his portrait of Rio's romantic past plus his all-inclusive look at the greatest show on earth, Carnival in Rio. Murphy is a former UPI correspondent for Brazil who has written for numerous publications including *The Wall Street Journal, The International Herald Tribune,* and *The Christian Science Monitor.* He has also researched the *Berlitz Guidebook to Rio* and currently writes for the *Brasilinform* newsletter and the *Knight-Ridder Financial News Service.*

The task of capturing the spirit of Rio's famed neighborhood, Copacabana, went to **Christopher Pickard**, who left his native England for Rio in 1978. As Brazil correspondent for *Screen International, Down Beat, Cash Box* and *Music Week*, Pickard is a bona-fide expert on Brazilian song, dance and film. He is best known for *Insider's Guide to Rio*, winner of a Thomas Cook award for excellence. In 1988, Pickard published *Insider's Guide to São Paulo for the Business Executive* and joined Taylor in launching *Brazil Travel Update*.

Another expatriate British journalist, **Moyra Ashford**, drew on personal experience to describe the unique sensation of dancing down the avenue in a Rio samba school and to write her well-documented piece on Rio's Guanabara Bay. Having written for *Euromoney,* London's *Sunday Times, Macleans* magazine and *The Chicago Sun-Times*, Ashford went on to become Brazil correspondent for the *Daily Telegraph* of London.

A world traveler, journalist and professional musician, ex-New Yorker **Harold Emert** has been chronicling his love affair with Rio de Janeiro since 1973. Emert, author of the features on the Beach Lifestyle and the Girl From Ipanema, left New York in 1969, oboe in hand, to discover the world, an adventure that took him to South Africa, Israel and Germany before he accepted a job as first oboist in Rio's Brazilian Symphony Orchestra. Since then he has combined music and journalism, freelancing for a variety of publications including the London *Daily Express, New York Post, USA Today* and *Compass News Features.*

In theory, photographing a city as beautiful as Rio should be easy. In reality, however, Rio-based photographer **H. John Maier Jr.** faced an enormous problem – finding new, unusual and spectacular shots in a city that is among the most photographed in the world. Over a four-month period, he trekked across the seashores and mountains of Rio as well as surrounding locations, searching out the majority of the book's photos.

Maier, who is an American by birth but has lived most of his life in Europe, Asia and South America, works out of the South American bureau of the Time-Life News Service in Rio where he handles writing assignments as well as photography. He contributed the Green Coast feature. His photos have been published in *Geo Magazine, Time, Fortune, Asia Magazine, USA Today* and *Runner's World.*

No guide book can succeed without painstaking research, a responsibility that fell to **Kristen Christensen**. An American from Minnesota, Christensen abandoned the cold winters of her hometown Duluth for the tropical sun of Rio in 1971. She has worked as a journalist, translator and teacher. For *Rio de Janeiro*, Christensen researched and wrote the fact-filled Travel Tips and the Sugarloaf box story. She also served as editorial assistant to project editor Taylor.

The updating of this edition was done by **Ricardo Librach Buckup**, based in São Paulo, who also helped in the updated of the latest edition of Apa's *Insight Guide: Brazil*. Revision and re-editing of this edition was done by Insight editors **Huw Hennessy** and **Rachel Parsons**.

C O N T E N T S

TRAVEL TIPS

WHAT IS A *CARIOCA*?

Sprawling in majestic disarray across a strip of land between granite peaks and the South Atlantic, Rio de Janeiro is the final victory of fantasy over fact.

Each day, Rio's streets and sidewalks support some eight million persons transported by some one million cars, trucks, buses, motorcycles, scooters and bikes all competing for room in a space designed for one-third their number. This spectacular chaos does nothing to dampen the enthusiasm of the *cariocas*, Rio's imperturbable native sons and daughters. For the *carioca*, all things are relative except for one – the wonder and beauty of Rio de Janeiro.

The *carioca* lifestyle is a mixture of hedonism and irreverence. They respect nothing and no one, yet are always searching for someone and something to provide them with pleasure. He or she is, of course, a Brazilian, but above all each is a *carioca*, an individual of immense resourcefulness, of keen wit, of engaging conversation, of stunning beauty and of worldly knowledge – or so they claim. The *cariocas'* unflagging optimism, boundless confidence and utter self-absorption might be seen as conceit. Nevertheless, *cariocas* are as their legend says they are, charming.

Altogether, there are 5.7 million *cariocas*, residents of Rio proper, but an additional four million live in suburbs ringing the city. As many as 70 percent are poor by American or European standards. But there is the beach and the samba and there is Carnival and the comforting presence of Rio's extraordinary beauty.

All *cariocas* are passionately in love, 24 hours a day, with their city, the *Cidade Maravilhosa* or "marvelous city." The beach is their playground, *samba* is their music and Carnival is their party, a *carioca* party where the poor parade as if they were the rich and the rich parade with the poor.

Each day, the *cariocas* sit and stare at their beautiful city, at the sea, the forested mountains, the granite monoliths and concoct their dreams. For these tropical Walter Mittys, there could be no better place. Romantics lose their hearts in Rio. Social scientists lose their minds. This is the ultimate land of yellow brick roads.

Preceding pages: tiny bikinis and beautiful bodies; view from Sugarloaf at sunset; spectacular Carnival float; Sugarloaf guards the entrance to Guanabara Bay. **Left,** Christ the Redeemer statue.

The first tourists arrived in Rio on January 1, 1502 as part of a Portuguese exploratory voyage by Amerigo Vespucci. Vespucci entered what he thought to be the mouth of a river. Hence the name Rio de Janeiro or January River. Vespucci's river was in reality a 147-sq. mile (380-sq. km) bay, known today by its Indian name, Guanabara ("arm of the sea").

Vespucci's voyage was one of a series launched after Portuguese explorer Pedro Alvares Cabral discovered the east coast of Brazil in 1500. Portugal laid claim to the territory, including Rio, but concentrated its colonization in the northeast, where sugar plantations were set up. Seeing no immediate economic value in Rio, the Portuguese put off settling in the region, an opening that was seized upon by the French.

French colony: In 1555, a French fleet arrived at Guanabara Bay intending to found France's first colony in the southern half of South America. Under Admiral Nicolas Durant de Villegaignon, some 500 French settlers disembarked on an island in the bay that today bears Villegaignon's name. A fort was built on the island and the French proceeded with their grand scheme to found Antarctic France for settlement by Calvinists brought from Europe.

Another 1,000 settlers arrived but problems broke out when the Calvinists discovered that the religious freedom they sought in the New World was less than what they had expected. Rumors of religious persecution in the colony reached Europe, bringing further immigration to a halt. Meanwhile, Portugal took interest in the southern part of its colony, resolving to drive out the French.

In 1560, a Portuguese fleet entered the bay, and after a week of fighting the French were defeated. But when the Portuguese left,

the French returned, leading to a second expedition in 1565. This time, the Portuguese were determined to rid themselves of the French and win Rio. After two years of intermittent fighting, Portugal destroyed the French dream of Antarctic France.

City founded: From then on, Rio received increasing attention from Brazil's Portuguese masters. In 1567, the city of São Sebastião do Rio de Janeiro was founded. Named in honor of Saint Sebastian on whose feast day the founding occurred, São Sebastião do Rio de Janeiro soon became simply Rio de Janeiro. Initially confined to what is today the downtown area facing the bay, Rio's growth was determined by the importance of its port to the colony. By the end of the 16th century, Rio became one of the four main population centers of Brazil. But its port remained secondary to those of the sugar-growing northeastern provinces, particularly the colony's capital of Salvador.

All of this changed when gold was discovered at the end of the 17th century in the neighboring province of Minas Gerais. Thousands of prospectors and fortune hunters, many of whom came from Portugal, flocked to Minas to participate in the largest gold rush of its time. Rio, the only port city close to Minas, benefited immediately. A road was built to link Rio to the gold fields while in the city's port, gold seekers disembarked daily. The enormous wealth uncovered in Minas made Portugal the world's largest producer of gold in the 18th-century. Gold became the colony's main export item and all of Brazil's gold went through Rio to Portugal, thus shifting Brazil's economic center from the northeast to Rio.

Boom days also brought problems. Twice, in 1710 and 1711, the French attacked Rio. On their second try, they broke through its defenses and sacked the city. Blessed with the seemingly unending flow of gold from Minas, the city was soon rebuilt. In 1763, Portugal at last recognized Rio's new status as the colony's leading city and transferred the capital from Salvador to Rio. ➡ *28*

Preceding pages: nineteenth-century panorama of Guanabara in oil painting by Nicolau António Facchinetti. **Left,** portrait of Maria Leopoldina of Hapsburg with her children (the future Emperor Pedro II on her lap) by Domencio Failutti.

Visitors to Rio de Janeiro's stunning **Copacabana Beach** at the mouth of **Guanabara Bay** might spare a moment to consider that, had a few events been different, they would instead be sitting on world-famous Sacopenapã Beach in the heart of São Sebastião near the azure waters of Santa Luzia Bay.

In the year 1502, a Portuguese fleet under the command of Admiral André Gonçalves dropped anchor off what was to become Rio

most residents had accepted the more logical name for the bay that came from the Indians – Guanabara. The name São Sebastião would fall away too, for reasons that are obscure, and residents came to call their city simply Rio de Janeiro.

Since 1565, the residents of Rio de Janeiro have been called *cariocas*. The name is known to come from the Tamoio language and it probably means "house of the white man" or perhaps simply "white man."

de Janeiro. The Tamoio Indians who lived there called the vast bay *Guanabara*, which in their language meant "arm of the sea."

But the Portuguese believed that they had discovered the mouth of a wide river. Because they sailed into the waters in January, they called the place January River, or **Rio de Janeiro**. They named the bay Santa Luzia, in honor of the favorite saint of fleet navigator, Amerigo Vespucci.

The city that was founded on the site years later was called São Sebastião do Rio de Janeiro because Saint Sebastian's feast day coincided with the founding. But by then,

Cidade Maravilhosa or "marvelous city," is Rio's nickname among Brazilians. This nickname was first used in 1908 by the Northeast writer Coelho Netto in his novel, *Os Sertanejos*. The author described the "urban marvels" of Rio, which was then the nation's capital, and showed how they attracted the poor from Brazil's hinterland.

The word *favela* is also derived from events in the Northeast of Brazil. At a place called **Morro da Favela**, a battle was fought which ended a bloody war in the late 19th century between Brazil's federal government and the fanatically religious settlers of Canudos in

Bahia. When the victorious federal troops were discharged, many made their way to Rio de Janeiro where they settled on the **Morro da Providência**. They called their community Favela and, because of their low pay and the lack of urban facilities on the hillside, Favela gradually declined into a slum. Rio's mountainside shantytowns from then on have been called *favelas*.

The name **Copacabana** has its origin in the Quechua language of the Indians living around Lake Titicaca on the border between Peru and Bolivia. In the Quechua language, *Copa* means "luminous place" and *Caguana* means "blue beach." When the Spanish stumbled across the site – and thus the chapel – as Copa Caguana. This name later corrupted into its modern form – Copacabana.

Decades later an itinerant silver merchant had a copy of the Lake Titicaca image made and donated it to the diocese of Rio de Janeiro. The image was placed in a tiny church on a remote fishing beach called **Sacopenapã**. Soon the image attracted the devoted from all over Rio. At first, pilgrims would say "I'm going to Sacopenapã to see Nossa Senhora de Copacabana." Later, they shortened it to "I'm going to see Copacabana" thus saving what is probably the most famous beach in the world from being forever known

Lake Titicaca in the 16th century they discovered a spot called Copa Caguana which the Indians regarded as sacred. The Spanish erected their own chapel on the site, a common technique for supplanting pagan religions with Christianity. Within the chapel they placed an image of Nossa Senhora da Candelária. However, the Indians who were converted to Christianity continued referring to

Left, view of Niterói, as seen by Henri Nicolas Vinet in the 19th century. **Above**, the view of Rio from the hills of Santa Teresa in an 1883 oil painting by Jorge Grimm.

as Sacopenapã, a Tupi Indian name meaning "the noise and the flapping of the herons."

Ipanema has a less elaborate origin. It is a Tamoio word meaning "dangerous waters." **Leblon** is named after the area's first important land owner, Frenchman Charles Le Blon.

Flamengo, on the other hand, received its name following the war to expel the Dutch from the colonial Northeast. Dutch prisoners-of-war, most of them Flemings, or *Flamengos* in Portuguese, were brought to prison camps in the then outlying district. For years, the neighborhood was known as Campos dos Flamengos, later shortened to Flamengo. ■

Brazil's pre-eminent city: For the next 200 years, Rio was to be Brazil's pre-eminent city. When the Portuguese royal family fled from Napoleon's conquering army in 1808, Rio became the capital of the Portuguese Empire. With Brazil's independence in 1822, Rio became the capital of the Brazilian Empire, changing again in 1889 to capital of the Republic of Brazil. Throughout these years, Rio was the economic, cultural and political center of Brazil, home to the pomp of the monarchy and intrigue of the republic.

Among the events that shaped Rio during these years, the most remarkable was its sudden and unexpected elevation as the capital. Over the next decade, Rio Europeanized more than any other New World capital. Schools, parks, newspapers, banks and various imperial government organizations sprouted. Then the emperor opened up commerce which previously had been restricted to Portugal. By stressing trade relations with Napoleon's enemies, principally England, Portugal gave a giant boost to Rio's economy and ended its previous isolation. Rio became not only the capital of an empire but an important center of world trade.

During Dom João's 13-year residence, Rio's population tripled to 100,000. The emperor left his son Dom Pedro behind as

tal of a European empire. The flight of Portuguese Emperor Dom João VI, with an entourage of over 15,000 noblemen, created the unprecedented situation of a colony becoming the seat of government for the mother country. The arrival of the emperor in 1808 thrust Rio into a world of courtly manners and elegance which hardly fitted its backwoods character. More unusual still was the insistence of the transplanted nobles on maintaining their European court dress in a fetid port city in the midst of the tropics.

Determined to make the best of the situation, the emperor set about to change his new prince regent of Brazil, but Pedro came under the influence of Brazilian nationalists, declaring the colony's independence from Portugal in 1822. Rio then became the capital of the independent nation of Brazil, formally entitled the Brazilian Empire although it had no territorial possessions. Brazilian noblemen replaced Portuguese dukes and counts. But the capital, and the empire itself, was about to go through its most tumultuous period. For the next 20 years, Brazil was nearly torn asunder by constant revolts and regional challenges to the central authority in Rio. The first disappointment of independence was the emperor himself. Rather than adopting the liberal policies his subjects wanted, Pedro maintained the privileges and power of an absolute monarch.

Dom Pedro finally abdicated and turned the empire over to his five-year-old son, Dom Pedro II, who ruled through a regency. For the next 48 years, Pedro II reigned as emperor, using his extraordinary talents to create domestic peace and giving Brazil its longest continuous period of political stability. A humble man, Pedro was blessed with enormous personal authority which he used to direct the nation. During the American Civil War, Abraham Lincoln remarked that

the only man he would trust to arbitrate between north and south was Pedro II of Brazil. Under this scholarly monarch, regional rivalries were kept in check and Pedro's own popularity extended the control of the central government over the nation. It was out of desperation that the country's political leadership agreed in 1840 to declare Pedro of age and hand over rule of the

Left, the old Carioca Aqueduct can still be seen in Lapa near the downtown business district. Above, the "Pedra da Gávea" or "Crow's Nest Rock" before the city spread out to São Conrado.

country to a 15-year-old monarch. But the decision proved to be sound – it was in the 1840s that Pedro II was able to silence the separatist movements and unite the nation.

What followed were four decades of domestic peace, marked by steady progress and increasing contact with the outside world. Pedro II, a scholarly, well-traveled man, made his capital a South American showcase of the latest marvels of modern science. The city was lit by gas in 1854 and was linked with London by telegraph in 1874. Pedro's greatest coup was the construction of the first telephone line outside of the United States of America, between Rio and his imperial retreat, Petrópolis, in the mountains outside the capital.

Military revolt: The tranquil reign of Pedro came to an abrupt end in 1889 when the military, expressing growing republican sentiment, overthrew the monarchy and sent Pedro into exile, scattering the nobility and bringing to a halt Rio's days of titled elegance. In place of emperors and princesses, the capital of the newly formed Republic of Brazil became the battleground of civilian politicians as Brazil embarked on the first of several attempts at democracy.

In reality, however, the Republic amounted to little more than an exchange of elites. In place of Rio's nobles were the wealthy landowners of the states of São Paulo and Minas Gerais. These new power brokers quickly became the nation's political establishment, deciding amongst themselves the vital issues of the day, including the choice of the president. Their authority remained unchallenged until a 1930 coup brought to power Getulio Vargas, a defender of the urban working class. Under Vargas, populism and nationalism became dominant political themes with the nation's politicians fighting for influence over the masses. As the capital and the country's industrial center, Rio was soon caught up in the urban turmoil that marked Brazil's industrialization.

During these years, the city underwent rapid urbanization. Its swelling population forced the government to find creative solutions to overcome Rio's chronic lack of space. Establishing a trend that has continued throughout this century, city planners looked south, following the contour of the beaches. At the start of this century, tunnels were drilled through granite mountains to open up the beachside neighborhood of Copacabana and to prepare the way for the later development of Ipanema, the lagoon and the beaches further south. The first beach front drive was built running from downtown along the bay to Sugarloaf.

Dramatic facelift: Downtown itself was given a dramatic facelift with the construction of Rio's most elegant avenue. Inaugurated in 1905, Avenida Central was built in response to President Rodrigues Alves' vision of a tropical Paris. Unfortunately, Alves overlooked the fact that downtown Rio, unlike Paris, had no room to grow other than vertically. Through the years, the elegant three and five-story buildings of Avenida Central, the Champs Élysées of Rio, were replaced by 30-story skyscrapers. In the process, the avenue suffered a name change, becoming today's Av. Rio Branco. Of the 115 buildings that flanked Avenida Central in 1905, Rio Branco has preserved only ten.

Construction booms were important for the modernization of Rio, but the city paid a heavy price in the loss of architectural heritage. With space severely limited by topography, the wrecking ball did away with much of old Rio. Modern-day landmarks of the city such as the wide Copacabana beach and the splendid Aterro, the giant park that flanks the bay, were made possible by landfill from downtown hills. The most tragic example of this was in 1921–22 when the downtown hill of Castelo was carted off for landfill together with most of Rio's remaining 16th- and 17th-century structures.

Expansion alternative: While Rio was struggling to find room to expand, its rival to the south, São Paulo, was enjoying a surge of economic and population growth. By 1950, the city of São Paulo had surpassed Rio in population and economic importance, a lead that it has never relinquished. In 1960, Rio suffered the final humiliation when President Juscelino Kubitschek formally moved the nation's capital to the city he had built in the center of the country, Brasília.

To civil servants used to the physical beauty, lax formality and non-stop pleasures of Rio, the move to Brasília was seen as a life sentence to Devil's Island. All struggled against it and while most were forced in the end to move, Rio remains home to thousands of federal government employees whose *carioca* creativity won them last-minute pardons. Many forced to make the move have retained their Rio bases, spending four days a week in Brasília and three in Rio.

Since it lost its status, Rio has floundered about, losing also its ranking as the country's leading industrial and financial center, to the upstart São Paulo. Adding to Rio's troubles was government indecision on what to make of the former federal district after the capital

was moved to Brasília. At first, the city of Rio was transformed into the state of Guanabara, but in 1975 Guanabara and the existing state of Rio de Janeiro were combined to join into Rio state, with the city of Rio becoming its capital.

Loss of prestige: This decision solved the question of Rio's administrative identity but did nothing to compensate for the loss of prestige and revenue occasioned by the creation of Brasília and the consequent mass exit of government bureaucrats and foreign diplomats. Unfortunately for Rio, while the city continues to lose industry and jobs to the fast growing south, it remains a mecca for poor Brazilians from the northeast and the interior states. The steady influx has swelled Rio's infamous shantytowns, the *favelas*, as well as the slums of the northern suburbs.

During the 1980s and early 1990s, with the country strapped by its foreign debt, Rio was unable to make the investments needed to maintain public services and resolve the housing problem. Downtown Rio, in particular, suffered a steady deterioration. Visible signs of decay are still apparent in the downtown and near-downtown neighborhoods. Even Copacabana has been affected, as shown by the pot-holed streets and littered

federal funding. In a country where the federal government controls the majority of the nation's public sector purse strings, this meant ten straight years of austerity for Rio.

In recent years, however, Rio has begun to make a comeback. Major oil finds off the coast of the state of Rio will provide both the city and state with substantial royalty payments for the foreseeable future. The oil has also generated plans for a major petrochemical complex. The promise of growing tax receipts has encouraged the city government to unveil an ambitious plan to revitalize downtown Rio, turning it into a landscaped area of shops, offices and culture centers.

sidewalks of the famed beach neighborhood.

The problems of today had their origins in the last ten years of the 1964–85 military regime, when Rio suffered a form of political ostracism. In two consecutive administrations, the state of Rio was governed by politicians in opposition to the military rulers in Brasília. Although the military did not interfere directly in the administrations of these two governors, it did hold back on

Left, the Rua do Ouvidor, the heart of 19th-century business Rio. **Above**, a rustic bridge in the gardens of the presidential Catete Palace.

Rio has also been the main beneficiary of a boom in tourism. Although Rio's upper crust refuse to admit it, the city has become increasingly dependent on the tourism trade, the state's biggest money maker today.

For diehard *cariocas*, however, economic gains can never replace the lost glory of the days when Rio was the political eminence of Brazil. But even in the still uncomfortable role of number two, Rio remains a major force in the nation's unending political intrigue. As *cariocas* proudly note, decisions may be made in Brasília and São Paulo, but plots are hatched in Rio.

Once upon a time, poker chips circulated in Rio de Janeiro like coins of the realm. World-famous stars such as Maurice Chevalier, Tommy Dorsey and Josephine Baker performed on stage while the brother of Brazil's dictator plotted and drank in the back rooms. International show business celebrities like Jayne Mansfield and Orson Welles gambled with their love lives and their reputations.

Once upon a time... The time was the mid-1930s to the late 1950s. The locale was a string of casinos, nightclubs and hotels which gave Rio de Janeiro an international reputation for exotic and sometimes excessive fun.

The map of that exotic Rio still exists. And so do most of the former pleasure domes, some refurbished, others dilapidated like overused Hollywood movie sets.

The map begins at the ice-cream cake facade of the **Copacabana Palace Hotel**, halfway down the famous beach. Then it runs down Avenida Princesa Isabel, makes a detour to Urca, continues around downtown to the Rio-Petrópolis Highway, and finally stops at the Grand Ballroom of a spectacular palace called Quitandinha.

When it was inaugurated in 1923, the Copacabana Palace was one of the few luxury hotels in South America.

In those days, luxury meant something. "Guests had everything – pool, theater, gambling casino, the best restaurants in South America and the best service," says Gabriel Catena, a Copa waiter for 39 years. "We weren't allowed to say 'no' when a guest wanted something."

Casino gambling – black tie only – was permitted from the early 1920s until the games were outlawed in Brazil in 1946.

"Some people came to the Copa just to gamble," says Catena, "and some played too much. Portugal's the Marquês de Pombal came over just to gamble. Then there was an Argentine millionaire, whom everyone knew as Dodeiro, and a Madame Seabra. Nobody ever knew her first name. But the biggest gambler was a landowner from Rio Grande do Sul who came just to drink and gamble. Over the years he sold off more and more of his property to cover losses until he ended up with nothing."

The Copa had several game rooms, including one that was called the Morgue which featured the lowest bet in town and

was near the main entrance so the croupiers could expel poor losers. But even the Morgue was a black tie affair.

The gambling rage was so great during the 1930s that one columnist wrote "respectable women – really of the very best society – hock their jewelry to pay gambling debts."

But the Copa didn't stop in 1946. In fact, some people say the 1950s were its heyday. Hardly a celebrity who came to Brazil in those years failed to stay at the Copa – the Copa was Rio high society, what they called "café society." "To be a waiter in those days," Catena says, "you had to have person-

Left, enjoying the spectacular view of Sugarloaf and the bay from Corcovado. **Above**, a tropical interlude in a hammock.

ality and speak languages. I was a sad case – I only spoke three. We had a head waiter who spoke 14. At the Golden Room we had the best shows in Brazil – black tie only. Everybody who came to the Copa had class."

John F. Kennedy ("when he was in his 20s, right after the war"), Lana Turner, Tyrone Power, Eva Perón ("with 10 attendants and 100 suitcases"), the deposed King Carol of Romania, who took up residence in the Copa, Ali Khan and many others were among the famous guests. Nat King Cole, Edith Piaf, Tommy Dorsey and many others performed.

And so, in curious ways, did Orson Welles and Jayne Mansfield. Orson Welles was

suite every day," recalls Machado. "Five empty bottles came down every night."

But Welles also worked hard filming slum-dwellers, fishermen and samba schools. "He spent RKO's money with incredible ease, but the film, a documentary entitled *It's All True*, was never finished," says Machado.

The story of Welles throwing furniture out of the window of his Copa suite is also true, according to Machado. But there are two versions of why it happened.

According to a retired Copa doorman, Manoel Oliveira, Welles became angry when he heard from actress Dolores del Rio that their on-again, off-again affair was off again,

only 27 at the time of his famous stay in the Copa in 1942.

Says a former show promoter, Carlos Machado: "Everything they say about Welles in Rio really happened. It's all true."

The director arrived with dozens of technicians, hundreds of pounds worth of expensive equipment and at least $100,000 in cash. He flew in on a two-day flight from Washington.

It took days just for the entourage to install itself comfortably in the hotel. And there were a lot of parties at the beginning. "Five bottles of whisky were sent up to Welles's

this time for good. That's when the furniture started flying. In the Machado version the cause of Welles' romantic frustration was local showgirl Linda Batista. The furniture flew out of the window in both versions of the story. "Of course, Welles wasn't arrested," says Machado. "He was the honored guest of the Brazilian government."

Jayne Mansfield was at the center of an embarrassing incident in the late 1950s. It was at the Copa poolside. Someone pulled on the string of the actress' famously overflowing bikini top. The top fell to the floor provoking a reaction typical of the American actress – her famous "*ooh.*" Her modesty was restored by an admirer who helpfully threw her a towel.

At a Copa Carnival ball in 1959, the same thing happened. This time, Mansfield was dancing with a young reporter named Guimaraes Padilha. A reveller grabbed the neckline of Mansfield's party dress, tearing the material to ribbons and exposing the actress's torso. Newspaper reports the next day said the Copa crowd was "aghast." The actress ran to her suite. It was the last time she was seen at the Copa.

In the early 1960s the Copa began its gradual decline. Competing luxury resorts

torn down and a high-rise hotel-shopping complex being put up in its place.

Bought just a few years ago by the British Orient Express company, the Copa has been refurbished to a very high standard and can once again be ranked among the top hotels of Rio. The renovation work is sensitive though very extensive and modernization has provided the old hotel with the facilities expected of a modern five-star hotel while retaining the old charm and opulence of the original Copa.

The nightclub to know: Just down the Avenida Atlântica from the Copa, at the intersection of Avenida Princesa Isabel, is another corner

went up in Rio and, according to Catena, "the Copa became just another hotel."

In fact, by the mid-1970s the Copa was badly in need of a face-lift. Unfortunately it took 10 more years for the Guinle family, the sole owners of the Copa, to get around to it. And even then it was only a government order, making the Copa a national landmark, that prevented the old building from being

Left, the fabled Quitandinha hotel-turned-condominium in Petrópolis, a relic of a bygone era. **Above**, the ageless elegance of the Copacabana Palace Hotel.

of Copacabana where cars and pollution have crept up on traditional night spots. For decades, *Sacha's* was the nightclub to know in Leme, the elegant beach that stretches from the Meridien Hotel towards Sugarloaf Mountain.

Recalls Machado: "Sacha Rubin was the best musician in the history of *carioca* night life. He used to play all night without a break. Nobody knew how he did it. He would learn the names of the regular customers and play a signature tune for each one."

Other bars: There were also other bars clustered around the corner of Avenida

Princesa Isabel and Avenida Atlântica, where the Meridien Hotel is today. They had names like The Wonder Bar, The Carlton, The Bolero and The Espanhol. According to Machado, things only got hot around 3am most nights. There was even one club, the Night and Day, which prided itself on staying open 24 hours.

Carlos Machado: Those working close to the action soon got to be known. Carlos Machado was pretty hot property himself in those days. Starting in the late 1930s, Machado was known as "The King of Carioca Night Life."

He first earned the title because of his dual role as director of a musical group called The Brazilian Serenaders and promotional manager of the famed **Casino da Urca**, located on narrow Urca Beach in the shadow of Sugarloaf Mountain.

After a decade of bumming around four continents working variously as a dancer, actor and promoter, Machado returned to Brazil in 1939 to produce the Casino da Urca floor show.

Machado's boss was Joaquim Rolla, who took over the Urca in 1937. Rolla was one of the great eccentrics of *carioca* night life. Says Machado, "Rolla was barely literate. He kept saying 'exactly' all the time, especially when he didn't understand what people were saying. Oscar Ornstein [a society photographer and then show promoter] used to act as Rolla's interpreter."

A singer of the period attested to Rolla's lack of savoir-faire: "Once I asked him why he didn't put gondolas in the pond in front of his Quitandinha Casino [in Petrópolis] and he said 'I already tried but they all died.'"

But Rolla understood show business very well and became, in the years just before World War II, Brazil's leading purveyor of night life, using Carlos Machado's talents to the fullest.

As backup for the casino's regular performers, Machado formed his own group, The Brazilian Serenaders. A critic wrote, "Carlos Machado ably directed his Brazilian Serenaders even though he knew absolutely nothing whatsoever about music."

But music was definitely not Machado's gift. Promotion was. Says samba musician

Luciano Peroni, "For Machado everything had to be the best, including the best international entertainers."

As Urca impresario, Machado contracted Maurice Chevalier, the legendary African-American singer Josephine Baker and the Xavier Cugat Orchestra among others. Baker, who had escaped US racism to make her career in Paris in the 1920s and 1930s, fled France when the Nazis invaded in 1940. She spent the war years in Rio.

Machado also made sure there was glittering decor, seductive lighting and lots of dancing girls. He believed in packaging and public relations. He was the first Brazilian

band leader to make his musicians wear the same outfit, to play signature tunes and to change his band's repertoire periodically.

Nor did Machado himself miss out on the good times. Many casino employees participated in an active social and gambling life along with the idle rich. Says Machado, "Casino employees were allowed to gamble and we did gamble. Most of us lived right in Urca. There was so much gambling going on, casino tokens were used as money in Urca and parts of Copacabana."

The decline of gambling: Many observers thought the April 1946 decree prohibiting gambling in Brazil would sound the death knell of casinos and the high life.

The Casino da Urca and other Rolla properties did experience a rapid decline. The casino was sold to the Tupi radio and television network. But when the network failed in the 1970s, the garish old building, featuring an archway over Avenida João Luis at the bottle-neck entrance to Urca, was abandoned.

Today, Casino da Urca has the atmosphere of a haunted castle, dark, dusty and teeming with the ghosts of long-gone nobility. But other gambling establishments merely experienced a change in venue, as

Goulart Brazilian who was to become a president of Brazil.

Now an office building, the monumental Serrador, with its glittering chandelier and red carpets, still presides elegantly over Rio's Cinelandia district.

During much of the 1950s the illegal gaming was tolerated by lax officials. The Monte Carlo even had top performers headlining in the main room and featured a risqué revue to entertain its customers.

Another famous spot was the Casablanca, evocative of the sultry, smoke-filled nightclubs of Hollywood movies. Located on Praia Vermelha next to the Sugarloaf cable

did showmen like Machado and Ornstein.

At the appropriately named Monte Carlo near the Jockey Club in Gavea there was an illegal baccarat game that ran nearly 24 hours a day, while at the Hotel Serrador downtown, officials of the Brazilian Labor Party played poker and drank through the night in a back room. Among the participants in the all-night card games was João

Left, inspiration for lovers, a romantic sunset stroll on Ipanema beach. Above, *Cariocas* have no qualms about public displays of affection at a beachside snack stand.

car platform, the club was designed to look like Rick's Café Americaine, the gin mill owned by Humphrey Bogart in the film *Casablanca*. The long, low building, now owned by the Army, can still be seen.

But the masterpiece of exotic Rio was Joaquim Rolla's ill-fated Quitandinha hotel-casino complex in Petrópolis.

Quitandinha was named after the Petrópolis neighborhood of Quitandinha, a name which means Little Green Grocer. At the time of its construction in the early 1940s, it was said to be the most elaborate resort hotel in South America. Today, the

Quintandinha is a cross between a social club and a condominium.

Quitandinha was built between 1941 and 1946 to rival the Copa. It cost $10 million – a sum that was then unheard of – and at one time it employed 10,000 people. The unfortunate fact, for Rolla and his army of employees, was that Quitandinha probably would have been a success except for the 1946 decree ending gambling in Brazil.

Says Machado, "Joaquim Rolla was born in the wrong country."

Following the decree, which came only 15 months after Quitandinha's opening, occupancy rates plummeted and the hotel began to lose money.

Rolla tried to recoup his losses by selling Quitandinha to the US hotel group, Eppely Hotels, but the Americans backed out at the last minute. Next, the state government tried its hand with a management contract. But the state lost money and handed the complex back to Rolla.

Finally, a private company purchased the property in 1963, turning it into a condominium. Since then it has retained its stately facade but lost most of its former glamor.

Although Quitandinha failed as a business proposition, its architectural splendor lives on. Wooden balconies and shuttered windows still grace its facade. There are great arching doorways and peaked towers, like something out of Camelot.

The massive structure was planned by Brazilian architect Luiz Fossati and built with the aid of German engineers. The style is Normandy and the emphasis is on wide, gleaming corridors, overstuffed furnishings and exaggerated decoration.

Today's Quitandinha, which can be visited with permission from the condominium manager, closely preserves the 1940s feeling with most of the original fixtures and much of the original furniture still in place. A visit to Quitandinha is like a walk into a Fred Astaire movie.

The old Hollywood feeling is especially poignant in Quitandinha's huge Grand Ball-

Left, the motorcycle has become a favorite mode of tranportation for Rio's youth. **Above**, nothing like a cool drink, especially on a very hot day.

room dripping with red curtains and elaborate light fixtures. You can imagine Harry James on stage and the Marx Brothers stumbling around the plush anterooms, knocking over cocktail tables and falling over the pink pin-cushion armchairs. Today the roulette wheels are out of sight but not out of mind. They have been stored away, just in case.

Petrópolis Tennis Club: But Quitandinha was not the only 1940s hot spot in Petrópolis. There was also the elegant and highly selective Petrópolis Tennis Club nearby. The club catered to café society and the nation's political elite. It maintained its own casino (where the members were only obliged to

pay their gaming debts at the end of the summer season) and floor show.

One habitual guest was tough-talking Rio de Janeiro Police Chief, Benjamin Vargas, who also happened to be the brother of Brazilian dictator Getulio Vargas.

Recalls Machado, who often performed at the club, "Benjamin Vargas used to send word from the bar to tone it down during the floor show. He would send somebody in to say 'the chief is treating important matters of state in the bar, so tone it down.'" Says samba musician Peroni, "it was the *belle époque* of Brazilian entertainment."

THE BEACH LIFESTYLE

"The beach is the last backyard left for a carioca *who dwells in a city of highrises and congested traffic. Watching the ships sail on the Atlantic Ocean, he tans his skin and meditates on his good luck in only having to cross a few streets to find this marvelous blend of peace, saltwater, sex and beauty."*
– Rio journalist Joaquim dos Santos.

A good look at the beaches of Rio de Janeiro reveals how this city works. Look beyond the golden-tanned, sunbathed beauties on the sands at this metropolitan sundeck and you'll see the customs, habits and amusements of the *cariocas*.

The beach, or *praia*, is the place to read, gossip, flirt, jog, work out, dream, think and even do business deals. The beach is everything at once: a nursery, schoolyard, reading room, soccer field, volleyball court, singles bar, restaurant, rock concert hall, exercise center and office.

Occasionally, someone will also go into the water but only for a refreshing dip before returning to more important activities. On a glorious weekend day, nearly the whole of Rio spends some time on the beach, which is not to say that they are not there during the week as well.

Sit with your binoculars on the beach sidewalk on a Sunday morning, the best day to observe Rio's "zoological" garden. The first to arrive are the beach "employees" – lifeguards, vendors, gymnastics professors, swimming teachers and the entrepreneurs who earn their keep by setting up volleyball nets, and the chairs and lounges of those fortunate *cariocas* who live in beachfront apartments across the street.

These employees are true beach historians, some of whom have had decades of service on the sands.

Then there are the buxom, coffee-colored sunbathers, strapped into, but just barely, what *cariocas* call the "dental floss" bikini

Left, mother and daughter enjoy a morning on the beach.

and prominently displaying their tight bottoms in worship of the sun. Sitting nearby on one of the world's most democratic stretches of land may be jet-set socialites or slum dwellers who have come from the hillside shantytowns.

Volleyball games: It may be another day of scorching 100°F heat (38°C), but the weekly (daily for some) volleyball games on the scorching sands continue. Those agitated, barefoot, bald and paunchy players may appear to be beach bums but during normal working hours, they are transformed into bankers, stockbrokers and executives of multinational companies. Other entertainment

available at a reasonable price at nearby drinks stands on the sidewalk.

Music lovers will note that each vendor has his own rhythm and melody to contribute to a polyphony of tropical beach sounds. Visually, to counterpoint the agitation on the sands, fishermen stand post at the tip of Copacabana beach and rowboats from deeper waters bring in a net's catch for sale at the marketplace.

Late in the afternoon, lone fishermen try their luck from the sand where multitudes had earlier sunbathed.

Treasure hunters: In the morning, noon and evening, treasure hunters comb the sands in

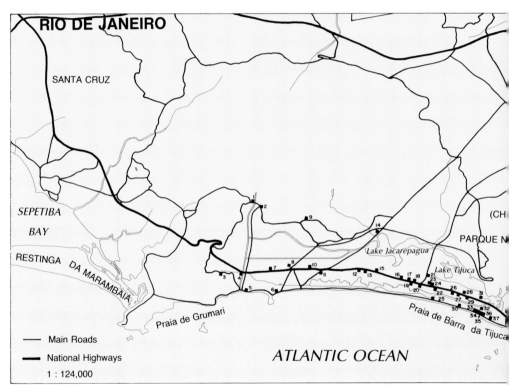

on the city's beaches includes soccer played by the Peles of tomorrow, incessant paddleballing (*"frescobol"*) and samba or *pagode* music-making and dancing.

Cold *chopp* or foaming tap beer sold in paper cups by barefoot hawkers on the sands is another part of the colorful *carioca* beach life. For teetotalers or to quench a thirst, delicious coconut juice drinks are readily

search of valuables left by forgetful bathers: earrings, watches, rings and other items which can include anything from women's panties to leftover chicken wings. Oblivious to the romantic clinches of earnest beach lovers, they are, like many *cariocas*, optimistic that today will bring new rewards.

For the uninitiated, there are surprising and often unforgettable scenes on the beach:

beautiful young women who slip into and out of their bikinis as if they were in the privacy of their homes; the down-and-out entertainer who displays photos of the days he appeared on stage with Frank Sinatra and sings show tunes on the sands for coins; the offerings left by followers of *macumba*, (Brazil's version of voodoo) to the mythical goddess of the sea, Iemanjá; tattoo artists looking for prospective customers; security guards employed by luxury hotels watching over their hotel guests to protect them from petty thieves.

This magical world of Rio beachlife was not always so. At the start of this century, the

to-grave lifestyle. Today, the beach is not part of the life of Rio, it *is* the life. Entire families flock to the beach on weekends, often as part of a neighborhood clique that has a reserved spot on the sand. On the beach, infants nurse, children play and make friends, boy meets girl and the elderly walk hand in hand.

New Year's celebration: On New Year's Eve, the *carioca* beach becomes a giant movie set with *macumba* ceremonies presided over by women smoking hefty cigars to obliterate the evil spirits. Drums beat out a pagan rhythm along the length of Copacabana and Ipanema. In 1999, an aston-

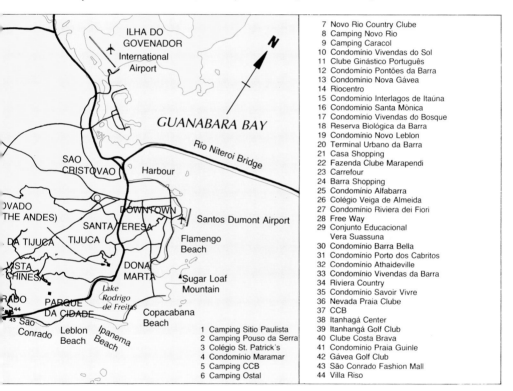

7 Novo Rio Country Clube
8 Camping Novo Rio
9 Camping Caracol
10 Condomínio Vivendas do Sol
11 Clube Ginástico Português
12 Condomínio Pontões da Barra
13 Condomínio Nova Gávea
14 Riocentro
15 Condomínio Interlagos de Itaúna
16 Condomínio Santa Mônica
17 Condomínio Vivendas do Bosque
18 Reserva Biológica da Barra
19 Condomínio Novo Leblon
20 Terminal Urbano da Barra
21 Casa Shopping
22 Fazenda Clube Marapendi
23 Carrefour
24 Barra Shopping
25 Condomínio Alfabarra
26 Colégio Veiga de Almeida
27 Condomínio Riviera dei Fiori
28 Free Way
29 Conjunto Educacional Vera Suassuna
30 Condomínio Barra Bella
31 Condomínio Porto dos Cabritos
32 Condomínio Athaideville
33 Condomínio Vivendas da Barra
34 Riviera Country
35 Condomínio Savoir Vivre
36 Nevada Praia Clube
37 CCB
38 Itanhagá Center
39 Itanhagá Golf Club
40 Clube Costa Brava
41 Condomínio Praia Guinle
42 Gávea Golf Club
43 São Conrado Fashion Mall
44 Villa Riso

1 Camping Sitio Paulista
2 Camping Pouso da Serra
3 Colégio St. Patrick's
4 Condomínio Maramar
5 Camping CCB
6 Camping Ostal

beach scene was confined to the bay, where a more formal and sedate society nibbled at picnic lunches or gently wet their feet and possibly legs in the water.

Liberal ideas, population growth and the opening up via tunnels of Copacabana changed all that. With the passage of time, a day on the beach evolved from tranquil family outings into an all-encompassing cradle-

ishing 3 million cariocas and tourists saw in the new year in Copacabana. Dressed in white in homage to the sea goddess Iemanjá, they mingle with the cult ceremonies that fill the beach with one of the most distinctive and fascinating New Year's Eve celebrations in the world.

Fireworks, pop music shows, free movies and even political campaigns form a part of beachlife. Advertisers know their best public will be on the beach on Sunday. Campaigns to promote films, shows, language schools and new products are often launched in the air by planes carrying streamers.

Even the air force occasionally gets into the act, displaying their best pilots and newest jets. It may seem as if a *coup* is beginning, but during the last coup in 1964, many *cariocas* were sunning themselves on the beach as tanks rolled by.

Legend has it that Rio's beach craze began on an odd note. João VI, king of Portugal, was forced to flee to Brazil in 1808 when Napoleon's forces invaded. Bitten by a tick,

once announced that portable libraries would be set up on the city's sands, as part of a campaign called "Read on the Beach." However, the plan was never implemented.

Popular songs: The beach lifestyle has become an important subject for Brazilian culture, including popular songs like Tom Jobim's "Wave," paintings, plays and literature. The beach is also a favorite subject for Rio's intellectuals, most of whom can be found on or near the beach virtually at any time of the day.

Carioca sociologists claim the beach is Rio's great equalizer as well as its pressure valve. According to this theory, the majority

João was advised by a doctor to bathe in the waters of Rio's Flamengo Beach. Thanks to King João's tick bite, a tradition was born that continues to this day.

That tradition now extends to a time schedule which on weekends and during vacation season is referred to as "before" and "after" the beach. For instance, no local impresario will schedule a musical show or concert on a weekend afternoon at the customary 2 or 3pm but rather at 4.30 or 5pm, long after beachtime.

In acknowledgement of the supremacy of beach culture, a state Secretary of Culture

of the city's residents, the poor inhabitants of its mountainside *favelas* and northern slums, have equal access to the beach and are therefore satisfied with their lot.

Surprisingly, there is some truth to this romantic notion, although a rising crime rate indicates that not all of the poor are entirely satisfied. And, while democratic and integrated, Rio's beaches are not entirely

Above, each summer begins with a basic concern: getting the perfect tan as soon as possible. **Right**, sunbathers must always keep an eye out for stray volleyballs.

classless. A quick walk along the sands of Copacabana will take you past small "neighborhoods" of bathers, each congregating with its own social type or group.

In Ipanema, near the Country Club, the cream of Rio's high society sunbathe, while the gay community favor areas near Rua Miguel Lemos in Copacabana and in front of the Copacabana Palace Hotel. Celebrities and their friends tend to head for the crystal waters of São Conrado, where at Pepino, fruit salads and cold grapes add a "natural" touch to the usual beer and ice cream bars.

Intellectuals get together at Ipanema in front of Rua Farme de Amoedo.

In Leblon, and especially Pepê at Barra da Tijuca muscle boys and their admirers cavort. The upwardly mobile residents of Ipanema migrate to the Barra da Tijuca. Foreign tourists tend to occupy the sands in front of their hotels in Copacabana, Ipanema, Vidigal and São Conrado.

The next day, you will find the same groups in the same places, a "beach corner society" that has become a permanent characteristic of Rio life.

The waves, which usually overwhelm the foreign tourist with their often frightening power, are objects of play for most of the locals who grew up splashing and diving into them without fear. And whereas in most parts of the world a pregnant woman will either stay away from the beach or stay covered up, locally it is very "in" for the mother-to-be to parade about in her bikini.

Topless bathing: Despite a brief spell in the 1980s, topless bathing has never become popular. Ipanema remains virtually the only city beach where women will sometimes remove the tops of their bikinis, but only when surrounded by friends.

Bars along the beach drive, especially in Copacabana, on hot, sunny weekends tend to be an extension of the beach. It is common to see men in nothing but their swimming trunks and beach things and women with tiny shorts pulled over their bikinis or with a colorful canga tied around their hips enjoying drinks or a meal along Av. Atlântica. There are no formalities to observe here.

Not everyone who lives in Rio is privileged enough to live in close proximity to the beach. An entire north zone of the city exists, far from the waters of the Atlantic and its cooling breezes. The governor of Rio de Janeiro state from 1983 to 1987, Leonel Brizola tried to appease the masses during his term by inaugurating a bus system which shortcut the route from the north to the south of the city.

The reaction of the inhabitants of the city's southern zone was, predictably, outrage. They accused the "northerners" of dirtying their beaches, to no avail. The buses have kept coming, turning parts of Ipanema and Leblon beaches into southern outposts of the north zone dwellers.

Common to all *cariocas* is the question, "Will tomorrow be a good day to go to the beach?" For most of the past 400 years, the answer has been a resounding "yes."

Even if you are by nature a workaholic, the sight of people enjoying sunbathing, swimming, singing, dancing, flirting and drinking beer by the refreshing waters of the Atlantic Ocean on a hot summer day would surely make you stop and wonder for a while whose lifestyle is "correct."

Above, "mate" ice tea vendor takes a break. **Right**, the samba is an integral part of life in Rio, extending to the beach.

More than in any other city, the colors of Brazil are the colors of Rio de Janeiro.

The nation's characteristic racial tricolor – black, brown and white – is displayed on every street corner and, in a form that all male Brazilians find almost irresistibly attractive, along every sandy beach of Brazil's second largest city.

The multi-ethnic mix which makes up the *carioca* is largely held responsible for the intense vitality of the city, which many believe is the envy of the world. In a sad capitulation to racial stereotyping, it is said that to European initiative has been added African rhythm and equanimity and the adaptability and ingeniousness of the native South American Indian.

With the mixing of the races came a language to label people's racial heritage, and words considered insulting in many other parts of the world are still in use in Brazil. The true *mulato*, it is said, carries the genes of all three races and is capable of intense dedication and hard work, faces challenges with originality, and always plays hard. To all this is added a ready smile and a heady passion.

Statistically, Rio comes closer than any other metropolis in reflecting Brazil's overall racial balance. The national population is 55 percent Caucasian, 39 percent *mulato* and 6 percent Afro-Brazilian, whereas Rio's 5.7 million inhabitants are 63 percent white, 27.5 percent brown and 10 percent Afro-Brazilian.

For many people, part of Rio's charm is precisely its racial commingling. This has given rise to the theory of the "*mulato* solution," the notion that Rio, like the rest of Brazil, has resolved racial tension through an increasing mix of black and white, resulting in the "browning" of the population.

In Rio the white-brown-and-black tricolor takes shapes and hues rarely seen even in other multiracial cultures. The white Afro-

Left, few cities in the world have the racial mixes that characterize Rio.

Brazilian, for example: some *cariocas* possess all the marks of the African except skin color. Other *cariocas* are black *only* in color, with Caucasian features, green eyes and perpetual tans.

Indeed, a tropical beach city with nearly six million sun worshippers whose population is more than one-third black and brown to begin with, Rio often seems happily *mulato* in its racial and even cultural identity.

Origin: Much of Rio's racial variety is the result of internal migration. Bantu-origin slaves of colonial Rio mixed with Nagô Nation Africans migrating from Minas Gerais after that state's gold rush petered out by the end of the 18th century. Starting in 1877, when a drought devastated Brazil's Northeast, Iorubá-origin blacks from Bahia poured into Rio.

The mix of colors and cultures is most intriguing when it comes to religion. The beliefs of African *umbanda* and *candomblé* are present among many of Rio's white residents, while European practices, such as faith healing, spiritualism and modern, alternative cults, have penetrated the African religions. And most *cariocas* – embracing spiritism or not – still consider themselves Roman Catholics.

Stereotypical elements of Brazil's African religious heritage – the figure of an elderly, pipe-smoking black woman as medium surrounded by chanting spiritists in flowing gowns and loaded down with charms – were exploited in Marcel Camus' 1959 film, *Orfeu Negro,* set during Rio's Carnival. Camus' black Orpheus speaks with the spirit of his dead Eurydice through the sly intervention of a black medium. The noisy, smoke-filled session is one of the movie's climaxes.

Experienced mediums accept possession from a number of spirits, who settle in like old friends from other centuries to chat with "clients." The clients get advice and prophecies. Sometimes they seek favors – the spirit's intervention in a love affair or help in getting a job.

There are few social distinctions among clients. Machado de Assis opens his turn of the-century novel, *Jacob and Essau* with an *umbanda* session attended by the wife of a wealthy aristocrat. The black medium predicts her pregnant white client will give birth to male twins who will perpetually quarrel over money and women. In the rest of the novel the prophecy comes true. In Rio's suburbs, white working and even middle class couples often marry in two separate ceremonies, first at an interminable *umbanda* ritual and later at a Roman Catholic Mass.

The most colorful showcase for Rio's *mulato* solution, however, is without doubt culture now increasingly defines the parade's main themes.

The female *mulato*: The samba parade also highlights an even more heart-thumping aspect of Rio's *mulato* phenomenon – the *mulata* or female *mulato*.

The very word sends expectant shivers down the spines of almost all hot-blooded Brazilian males. In most cases, foreign males take between 24 hours and, at most, a few days to feel the same symptoms – a weakening of the knees and hot and cold flashes along the backbone.

Mulata is a word that appears in a hundred popular songs and is the theme of a million

the annual Carnival parade. Samba composer, Dorival Nery says "the parade is homogeneous. You see rich and poor, black and white, slum dweller and medical doctor, side by side."

Although originally an all-black affair, the parade has widened its appeal and themes during a half century to become the centerpiece of today's Carnival. The original black element is honored by the mandatory *ala das Baianas*, featuring hundreds of elderly but incredibly agile black women dressed in the flowing gowns of Bahia. However, modern Brazil's materialistic, white-dominated daily commentaries by *carioca* men. Poised nearly naked atop the glittering samba parade floats or developing intricate, suggestive dance routines on the street below, the word becomes flesh and dwells among us, even if only for a few glorious moments.

The *mulata*'s allure is not easy to define. Perhaps it's the caramel skin tones – the image of a shapely woman with a perpetual tan. Others, however, perceive a less esthetic element at work.

Black rights activist Percy da Silva maintains that "fascination with the *mulata* is a manifestation of racism. It is part of the image of blacks as destitute of intelligence and with only a precarious hold on conventional morality. The *mulata* may have an exotic, alluring side but she also suffers from a double stigma – as a negro and as a woman."

In fact, nearly all *carioca* blacks and browns suffer a double burden – poverty and the attitude of *cariocas* to their race.

Says da Silva, "In Rio the black population is segregated in the suburbs and the hillside slums. Foreigners don't see it."

There can be no denying da Silva's point. Rio's population becomes darker as its sprawling suburbs stretch away from the

In economic terms as well, non-white *cariocas* fare worse than their pale-skinned brothers. The proportion of whites in the workforce earning one minimum salary (about $65 a month) or less is less than 12 percent. But 16 percent of the *mulato* workforce and 22 percent of blacks in the workforce earn one minimum salary or less. Prejudice abides and permeates through every level of Brazilian society. Says Maria D'Aparecida, a black *carioca* who left Brazil in 1960 to pursue a successful singing career in the Paris Opera, "the fact is you can't sing the leading roles in the Rio de Janeiro Opera Company if you are black."

famous beach neighborhoods. Copacabana is about 86 percent white. Middle and working class Meier, about 12 miles (20 km) from downtown, is 65 percent white. Another 9 miles (15 km) along Avenida Brasil to Bangu, the white population is a bare majority of 53 percent. Six miles (10 km) beyond Bangu is the distant working class suburb of Santa Cruz, 47 percent white and 53 percent black and brown.

Left and above, the faces of Rio show the city's racial mosaic, a mix of black Africans with European immigrants and the native Indians.

"Brazilian blacks are considered good for samba and soccer," she adds, "but little else. Carnival is the public expression of black culture but when it's over, blacks go back to being low-paid, uneducated workers living in slums. Carnival is a paradox."

In recent years, black leaders have become increasingly vocal in their criticisms of discrimination. For them, the *mulato* solution is a myth that clashes daily with harsh reality and allows the problems of racism to be hidden behind talk of social disadvantage. For many Afro-Brazilians, being poor is synonymous with being black.

Everything in Rio has status of one sort or another. Ideas, people, things, places, from the insignificant to the sublime, nothing escapes the *carioca* passion for cataloguing. What is out is unspeakably out and what is in is marvelously in.

The following is an "in" and "out" guide to the status symbols of Rio.

Cars: In a city of sharp social divisions, a car is a symbol of relative wealth. But while having a car is positive, some cars are obviously better than others: the affluent society own shiny imported cars, while the average *carioca* drives a Brazilian-made model.

Beach homes: *Cariocas* never get tired of the beach. While they live beside the sea, those who can afford it build their weekend retreats on the beaches of nearby towns and cities. Those with real wealth also build mountain homes. The most desirable sites for a beach house are the vacation paradises of Búzios and Angra dos Reis. The absolute status symbol, though, is to own an island, for which permission from the Brazilian navy is required.

Penthouses: For Rio proper, status is living on the beach but the ultimate goal is living in a beachfront penthouse. Virtually any beach will do in Rio although for property values nothing comes close to Ipanema's multi-million dollar penthouses. Wise to the *carioca* penchant for penthouses, developers now design apartment buildings with up to four on top: if you can't have a penthouse, then next best is a duplex or, even better, a triplex – but always with a beach view.

Coming up fast are hillside mansions with a sea view, set in the green of a Tijuca forest behind the Barra, away from the noise and pollution of the seafront.

Neighborhoods: Rio is divided into two parts, the north zone and the south zone. In terms of status, there is only one – the south, where from Copacabana to the Barra da

Tijuca Rio's moneyed classes predominate. **Ipanema** still retains its top ranking, which it wrested from Copacabana in the 1960s, but almost of equivalent status now are **Gávea**, **São Conrado** and **Leblon**, (actually Upper Leblon. This reflects a tendency for old neighborhoods to receive new names as their prestige climbs).

A special case is the Lagoon, which is really an extension of Ipanema and Leblon, but is so strikingly beautiful that it deserves its own name and high status. However, increasing pollution in the water of the lagoon and a dramatic rise in burglaries has held down property values in the area. Neighborhood status follows property values which in turn depend on population density, convenience of living, proximity to the beach and overall physical beauty. Overcrowded Copacabana is now definitely out and Ipanema is quickly filling up, opening the door for **Barra da Tijuca**, whose openness and unspoiled, beautiful beach are now attracting those seeking a Rio status address.

The international lifestyle: Just as Brazilians don't really consider themselves Latin Americans, status conscious *cariocas* don't consider themselves simply Brazilians. Like their city, they are international, sophisticated and worldly. International travel is in, travel inside Brazil is out. Imported goods are in, Brazilian goods are out. Foreign books outsell Brazilian books and for pure status, you can't beat owning a private satellite dish tuned in to American, French and British television, even in some *favelas*.

English: A look around shows that English is spoken here. Fashionable shops, restaurants, boutiques, hairdressers all show a preference for foreign names, with English the obvious winner. In their speech, *cariocas* throw in English words and phrases for which Portuguese equivalents either are nonexistent or considered inferior. "Performance" is a must (as is "must"), bars offer "happy hours," businessmen enter into "joint ventures," the stock markets trade "blue chips," computers are "hardware" and oper-

Left, making it in Rio means flaunting it and there's nothing better than a hillside mansion overlooking the sea.

ate with "software," consumers go to "shopping centers." English is clearly in.

Carnival: Although leaving Rio to spend Carnival at a beach or mountain retreat is considered chic, there are definite rewards for those who stay behind. Watching the samba schools parade from a private box with catered meals is a top-rated status symbol. Also in is to be invited to the Carnival *feijoada* by highly regarded party-giver Ricardo Amaral, who is the owner of the city's most exclusive private club, the Hippopotamus. A special treat awaits those who join up with one of the samba schools to parade down the avenue (members of Rio's

Samba: Just as the Carnival parade has become "in" of late, so also has the samba cult. Once viewed as the domain of the lower class, the samba world has come into fashion as a type of adventurous, bohemian lifestyle – slumming as it were (disco, meanwhile, is out and for sophisticates, jazz is in with the hot spots being **Jazzmania**, the **Rio Jazz Club** and **Mixtura Fina**).

Besides the samba school rehearsals, there are samba clubs downtown, in the Barra da Tijuca and in the northern neighborhoods. In addition, there are *pagodes,* which are casual jam sessions where samba musicians play while the onlookers dance and sing.

foreign community have long been participating in the parade, but now some travel agents are putting together packages for tourists who wish to join the fun). This involves buying a costume and attending one or two rehearsals of the samba schools.

Traditionally, the rehearsals (in reality, an excuse for all-night parties) have been held in the poor neighborhoods where the schools are located but as the parade has gathered status, some schools have begun rehearsing in the south zone of Rio. The increasing inness of the parade is shown by the number of *carioca* socialites who dance with the schools.

First-time visitors to Rio can experience the samba rhythm best by taking some lessons at one of the dance academies, after which you can claim to be one of the newest *passista* (samba dancers) to take a place on the dance floor.

There are regular samba shows held for tourists at the **Scala**. The shows are not very authentic but they are lots of fun and have a friendly atmosphere. For the younger generation the place to head for is the trendsetting **Fundiçâo Progresso**.

Food and drink: For this as with almost everything else, the highest ratings go to imports. With the exception of the excellent Brazilian beers (tap is preferred over bottled and always served bitterly cold), and fruit and *aguardente* concoctions called *batidas* (the favorite is a *caipirinha*), *cariocas* prefer foreign brands. Imported scotch, vodka and gin head the list, while rum is acceptable if nothing else is available. Real snobs may pull out a bottle of Jack Daniels or Southern Comfort, although in reality bourbon has never caught on in Brazil. Tourists should be wary as all imported spirits carry heavy import duties which push bar prices up sharply. Brazilian wines, long considered inferior to imports, are now gaining in status

Casa da Feijoada or **Botequim** could be more interesting places to visit if you want to go to where the Brazilians go to.

New Year's Eve: Parties are always in but few excel those that usher in the new year. An absolute must is the fireworks display on Copacabana beach which accompanies the *macumba* (Brazilian voodoo) ceremonies at the water's edge.

Top honors go to the annual celebration at the Meridien Hotel's chic **Le Saint Honoré** restaurant. Real status belongs to those fortunate souls who get invited aboard a millionaire's yacht to see the spectacle from the water. If they are on the right yacht their

as well as quality. White wine is generally preferred over red.

In addition to the excellent international cuisine, *cariocas* still like to be seen enjoying a *feijoada*, the closest thing to a national Brazilian dish. Devoured over several hours on Saturday afternoons, *feijoada* is as much a social event as a meal and thus requires a proper setting. The in spots for Rio's *feijoadas* are the **Caesar Park Hotel** and the **Sheraton**.

Left, the exclusive and very private Gávea Golf Club. **Above**, the goal of all status-seeking *cariocas*, their very own Mercedes.

names will appear in the column of society scribes Hildegard Angel and Danuza Leão. Millionaire yachts are obvious status symbols but there are few. Rio has only two marinas, the more exclusive being the Rio de Janeiro Yacht Club, which prides itself on having rejected three times an application for membership by Brazil's leading pop singer, Roberto Carlos.

Women: When not talking to them, *carioca* males seem always to be talking about them. Women are a classic status symbol of the macho society. To be just right (for the male, that is), a *carioca* woman must be young, alluring, sensual, fashionable and unquestionably faithful. Intelligence is optional. Among the young, professional set, however, this image is changing.

The burden of maintaining a middle class lifestyle has pushed the wife out of the home into the job market. In turn, the new woman concept (assertive and career oriented) has acquired a certain rebellious status of its own. Among these groups, the macho man image is out.

But even for the more liberal *cariocas*, it is an almost sacred obligation for the woman to maintain her beauty regardless of pregnancies, careers, child rearing, etc. Important

Fitness: Staying in shape is not merely in, it is a total obsession. Body building and shaping and the process of maintaining what has been built and shaped are full-time commitments for *cariocas*. Exercise clubs and personal trainers are in. The teachers and the methods used are the real key to status. Jogging is in, but even better is running in a marathon. Unmatched for status is having taken part in the Boston or New York marathon. At the moment surfing is out but body boarding is in. Hang gliding is also losing its status to ultralights. Playing squash is quietly overtaking tennis in popularity. Activities never stay in or out for long and *cariocas*

and powerful men insist on being accompanied by beautiful women. It's a necessary part of their image.

American feminists have been rejected by *carioca* women, not so much for their ideas but because they are considered physically unattractive. No matter how successful and independent Rio's women may be, there's one requirement: they *must* be beautiful.

To help them out, the city has a host of plastic surgery clinics to put right any imperfections. Status may be claimed by those who have been operated on by the king of plastic surgeons, Ivo Pitanguy.

have fun keeping up with the latest fads.

Beaches: Beach status depends on the quality of sand and water but more importantly on the quality of the bathers. Copacabana is out on all counts. Ipanema has been in for three decades but is beginning to age. New arrivals are **Pepino**, on the southern end of São Conrado beach, **Grumari**, **Prainha** and the **Barra da Tijuca**, where Pepê's beach is situated. Outside the city, **Buzios** and the island beaches of the **Angra dos Reis** area garner all awards for status. Buzios is also the only beach area where topless bathing is in. Although topless bathing is still practiced by a well-endowed minority in Ipanema, it has never really caught on.

Restaurants and bars: Each year sees a life or death struggle by new entrants into the bar and restaurant category to acquire status and thus ensure their survival. Some go to extraordinary means to attract the "right" people who will then spread the word to other "right" people. If successful, all this will culminate with a favorable mention in Hildegard Angel or Danuza Leão's column, the next best thing to immortality. Unfortunately, as each year's bar and restaurant obituaries illustrate, few make it. Even for those who do, the war is not over – a slip in quality, the exit of

fervor of the country's sports fans is concentrated on soccer. In Rio, the city's leading teams are literally worshipped by their fans who cite the liturgy of their heroes' conquests with the same ease with which they repeat prayers in church. The top team in recent years has been Flamengo whose colors of black and red T-shirts are everywhere.

The principal challengers to top-ranked Flamengo are Vasco and Fluminense, with a fourth club, Botafogo, filling the role of sentimental favorite and perennial doormat. The giant stadium of Maracanã – which can seat 180,000 roaring fans – is the temple of Rio's *futebol* mania. On days of so-called

a prized chef or any other small error can be fatal for the status a restaurant fought so hard to earn.

Soccer: *Futebol*, or soccer, falls in the category of mixed status for *cariocas*. For the lower classes, it is an all-encompassing passion, while for the upper classes it is one of those unfortunate "things" that must be tolerated when living in Brazil. Brazil is essentially a one-sport country, and all of the

Left, good living also means luxury dining. **Above**, keeping up with top fashion is another must for those who want to be "in."

"classic" matches between Flamengo and Fluminense, the stadium is a war zone, with firecrackers exploding and the huge banners and flags of the teams waving madly throughout the grandstand.

Tourists: Popularly known as *gringos*, tourists are, sad to say, devoid of status. Some, however, are less "out" than others. More favored are fellow Latins, the French and Italians. South Americans and Argentines are out. Americans, Canadians, the British, Germans, Swiss, Scandinavians and Asians all occupy the middle ground while Australians and New Zealanders are almost "in."

Along the curving seashore of Rio de Janeiro stands the pride of this city's affluent citizens, a phalanx of luxury highrise apartment buildings attesting to the wealth of those who have. But behind this formidable wall of money and status, visible in brief glimpses down the streets that separate the blocks of wealth, are the homes of those who have not: hillside shantytowns hanging like tarnished ornaments from the forested granite mountains of Rio.

Called *favelas*, they have become a part of the folklore of Rio. Out of the *favelas* come the samba schools that march in splendid costumes down the parade route on the second and third days of Carnival. Out of the *favelas* comes the samba itself, the seductive rhythm that is both song and dance. And out of the *favelas* come the construction workers who built the high rises of the wealthy; the employees of the rich-man's companies and industries; the waiters who serve them in luxury restaurants and private clubs; the chauffeurs who drive their cars, and the maids, cooks and nannies who tend to the needs of their homes and families.

The wealthy: Each morning in Rio, the residents of the city's beachfront apartments open their eyes to the play of sunlight off the South Atlantic. All see the early morning beach life, the joggers, the fishermen, the arrival of the lifeguards. Some see Guanabara Bay and Sugarloaf while others have views of offshore islands and passing ships. A few, a very select few, live in penthouse pleasure domes with a 360-degree view, capturing the mountains behind as well as the beach and ocean in front.

Their apartments are encased in marble, to protect the owners from the stains of tropical mildew, and they often occupy entire floors – duplexes and triplexes are not uncommon. Inside, the furnishings reflect expensive tastes and the means to satisfy them. Marble is popular as are rare woods. High tech has recently won a place, from automated security systems to private satellite dishes. To maintain these apartments and to service the

people who own them there are staffs composed typically of two to three maids (one of whom will be a cook), a chauffeur, possibly a handyman or boy and (if there are young children) a nanny.

These privileged *cariocas* are proud of their status and feel that they are the equal of any American or European millionaire. Their possessions are indeed very impressive and many also own equally luxurious beach and mountain homes outside of Rio. All of this is

part of the reward, obviously substantial, for those who reach the top of the *carioca* pyramid, itself a smaller version of the Brazilian pyramid. What truly adds distinction to the rich people of Rio de Janeiro is the fact that there are so few of them compared to those at the bottom of the pyramid. Even for the middle class, there is a sense of elitism that is born of the distance that separates them from the "others."

In Rio, only seven percent of households have annual incomes above $15,000. There is another 11 percent that earns between $7,500 and $15,000. The remaining 82 percent bring home $7,500 or less. Some 47 percent survive on less than $1,600 a year.

These statistics and those which follow are based on surveys carried out some years ago and figures may have changed somewhat. However, Brazil still has a famously uneven distribution of wealth.

The inequality of income distribution is just one dividing line between the two Rios. The 18 percent of *carioca* households which enjoy a middle class or higher standard of living have access to quality health care, proper nutritional intake, good schooling for their children and adequate housing. Their Rio is a city of modern consumer goods, of

those on top have nearly unchallengeable authority. There are white collar crimes in Brazil but there are no white collar criminals. Rio's business elite, the top layer of the upper crust, does not wash its dirty linen in public nor does it have to. Cases of fraud or corruption are in general handled quietly and if possible behind closed doors. The elite is careful to protect its members.

The daily expression of this power, however, involves far more mundane subjects. The elite resolves its daily problems through the use of influence. Friendships at the top and family ties through the extended Brazilian family usually are sufficient to handle

shopping centers and fashionable boutiques, highrise apartment buildings, medical clinics, chic restaurants, late model cars, private schools and university education.

What distinguishes Rio's wealthy from their counterparts in other countries, though, is not their means but their power. The elite-driven nature of Brazilian society means

normal difficulties of day to day living. The middle class also avails itself of this system. When facing a financial or professional crisis, the middle class looks to its more successful friends and relatives to provide a helping hand. Usually they do.

The poor: Each morning, the *favelados*, the dwellers of the hillside shantytowns, awake to a view that is not unlike that of the wealthy along the beach. For many of them, it is actually better, encompassing mountains as well as the sea. Their homes, though, have none of the opulence of the apartments of the rich nor even the practical convenience of the middle class. They are, however, better than they once were. The tumble-down shacks hammered together out of scrap pieces of wood that first characterized the *favelas* are now being replaced by more durable dwellings. While shacks still exist, their place is increasingly being taken over by structures of brick and concrete. Most of the homes have electricity and some, a minority, have water. But there is rarely any garbage collection or sewerage system.

For those living on the hillsides, the day begins with a walk down steep, often precarious staircases. When it rains heavily, as it does each summer, the paths down the

is through a precarious public health system. Housing conditions are deplorable and malnutrition is widespread. There is also no influence, other than at election time, when politicians routinely rediscover the *favelas* and their inhabitants only to forget them again as soon as the votes have been counted.

The *favelas* have been part of the Rio scene since the start of the century when federal troops, after putting down a rebellion in the northeast, were discharged and came to the city, setting up shacks on a hillside near downtown. At first confined to the downtown area, the *favelas* began to expand with the expansion of the city. They sprouted

hillside become torrents of water. Mudslides are common and almost every year disaster strikes at least one of Rio's *favelas*.

There are, according to the government, 480 *favelas* in Rio with a population estimated at 1 million out of the city's total population of 5.7 million. They are growing at the rate of five percent a year, double the growth rate of the city.

For these *cariocas*, there are none of the advantages of those who live on the seashore. For them, education, when available, is through the underfinanced and overcrowded public school system. Health care

on the mountains behind Copacabana when that neighborhood underwent its boom years through the 1950s, moving on next to Ipanema and most recently to the Barra da Tijuca and São Conrado, always following the steady southward movement of construction sites and jobs.

Attractive mosaic: While those on the mountainsides are the most prominent, with the colors of their shacks creating an oddly attractive mosaic in the midst of the gray rock and green forest, the *favelas* have also spread in recent years to the flatlands of the northern and southern suburbs of Rio.

Their existence is graphic evidence of the pressures of population growth on a city whose topography drastically limits its physical expansion. Since colonial times, Rio's residents have chosen to live close to the sea with the mountains to their backs, an esthetically correct choice that has made Rio a city with clear boundaries between social classes as well as a nightmare for city planners. Land values have constantly risen for the downtown area and on to the southern beaches, making the south zone, as it is called, the home of the middle class and the wealthy.

At the other extreme, the north zone and the northern suburbs, far from the beaches, east and the underdeveloped interior of the state of Rio make demands for housing and public services which the government cannot meet. It is estimated that there is a housing shortage of 60,000 units for Rio's middle class and 440,000 for the poor.

Northern flatlands: This situation has led to a population explosion in the northern flatlands, an area called the Baixada Fluminense. It is home to 2.6 million people, most living in abject poverty. Here, the incidence of infectious diseases and infant mortality rate are close to those of the Northeast of Brazil, the poorest area of the country, and far from the levels of the neighboring city of

are the working class sector, a constantly growing maze of slums, housing projects and outright *favelas*, with pockets of middle class housing. Even here, land values, pushed up by a chronic housing shortage, are steadily forcing the poor further north and further away from the sites of their jobs, the majority of which are downtown or in the south zone.

At the same time, new waves of immigrants from the backward states of the north-

Left, living in a *favela* means a daily struggle to satisfy common necessities. **Above**, black is the predominant color of the *favelados*.

Rio. In the Baixada, 150 out of every 1,000 infants die before reaching the age of one, while in the city of Rio the rate is 35 for every 1,000. In Rio there is a doctor for every 250 inhabitants but in the Baixada, one hour away from downtown Rio, the figure is one doctor for every 3,500 inhabitants. Lacking sanitation and clean water and awash in garbage, the Baixada is a public health disaster where meningitis, typhoid and tetanus are rife, along with intestinal infections, especially among the children.

Compared to an existence such as this, a hillside *favela* in Ipanema or Copacabana is

a veritable paradise. While the residents of the Baixada each morning face a two-hour bus ride to reach their jobs, for the south zone *favelados*, work is often only a few minutes away. In addition they have spectacular views and immediate access to the beach. These factors have now made the south zone *favelas* the status address for Rio's poorer-class majority. For most, however, even this progress is out of reach. Ever-increasing demand and the improved housing within these *favelas* have produced an inevitable by-product – rising rents.

When they first appeared, the principal attraction of the *favelas* was their proximity

Rio's larger *favelas* were removed by the city government and their inhabitants were forcibly uprooted and relocated into distant housing projects.

Rocinha, however, escaped this fate. Since the 1970s, the *favela* has undergone its own population explosion, first following a construction boom in the nearby Barra da Tijuca neighborhood. More recently, when it received immigrants from the Baixada who wanted to move closer to their work, together with the overflow from other, more crowded south zone *favelas*. Sprawling across a mountainside, Rocinha today is a city within a city, looking down at five-star

to jobs and the fact that they were rent free. Today, the proximity remains but inhabitants of the south zone *favelas* now pay rents, increasingly to absentee landlords, so very little of the rent benefits the community.

Rocinha: Nowhere is this process more evident than in the *favela* of Rocinha, Rio's largest and possibly the largest *favela* in South America. Rocinha began in the 1940s when a group of squatters took over vacant land on a south zone hillside. By the 1960s, the Rocinha *favela* had become a permanent feature of Rio, although its size was still restricted. During these years, several of

hotels, luxury condominiums and a golf course. It also overlooks its unwilling neighbors in São Conrado, a popular, upper income beach area where hang gliders float serenely overhead.

The most urbanized of Rio's *favelas*, Rocinha has a thriving commerce of its own – clothing shops, grocery stores, bars, lunch counters, drugstores, butcher shops, bakeries and bank branches, all of them providing jobs to the *favelados*.

Squatter's rights give ownership after five years but in reality few of the properties in Rocinha have been legalized. However, the size of the shantytown makes removal unthinkable. In addition, Rocinha supplies the doormen, maintenance crews and other auxiliary help for the hotels and condominiums of São Conrado as well as providing cheap labor for Ipanema and other nearby south zone neighborhoods.

It is also the main source of illicit drugs, especially cocaine and marijuana, for the area's high rollers, a fact that has transformed Rocinha into a highly profitable center for Rio's drug trade.

Drug trafficking has also spread to other *favelas* where, as in Rocinha, the economic power of the traffickers has made them the

Autonomy: In the process, the *favelas* have also gained a certain autonomy. Fear and bribes keep away the police and efforts to resettle the *favelados* have been abandoned. But despite endless promises by politicians to complete the urbanization of Rocinha and other major slums, little has been done. Nevertheless, *favelas* like Rocinha are climbing the social ladder, and nowadays there are residents with lower-middle class occupations such as clerical and secretarial work.

The residents of the *favelas* continue to face serious difficulties with water supply. Health conditions are, for the most part, deplorable. Rocinha, with a population that

dominant force. Gangs of drug dealers now control the majority of the large south zone *favelas*, including Rocinha. In return for the support of the *favelados*, they offer protection from petty criminals who inhabit the shantytowns, and they also distribute some of their profits from the drug trade among the local population. These cocaine Robin Hoods have been elevated to the status of folk heroes for the slum dwellers.

Left, middle-class apartment buildings in the Barra da Tijuca. **Above**, pleasure domes along the water.

would not shame a city, has only one poorly-equipped health clinic and there are few schools in the slums. There is the constant danger of landslides and even the protectors of the *favelados*, their Robin Hoods, are unreliable – gunfights between rival gangs often claim innocent victims.

It remains a precarious life on the hillsides of Rio but still, the *favelados* are close to work, they have their view and the nearby ocean and bad as things may be, they are seldom as bad as they are in the flatlands of the northern suburbs. For the hillside-dweller, this is the bottom line.

SENSUAL RIO

Rio de Janeiro is a sensuous city, a feminine personality in a macho society. The sensuality of Rio is expressed not only by its people and their nature but also in the geography of the city. The shore line bends and curves in expressive sensual lines that sometimes make it difficult to understand exactly where you are.

The city is divided into two zones, the north and the south, but for tourists there is only the south, home to Rio's scenic wonders – Sugarloaf, Corcovado, the Tijuca Forest, the lagoon, as well as the famed beaches of Copacabana, Ipanema and the newer beaches of São Conrado, the Barra da Tijuca and Grumari. Life for the residents of Rio and the tourists revolves around the beach, which is the starting and ending point of any weekend day. Fortunately Rio has enough beaches to go around, each with its own personality, its distinctive quality and, as always, its status.

But Rio is more than the sum of its beaches and mountains. As befits a city with a 400-year history, there is also a historical side to Rio, concentrated in its downtown area, the storied hillsides of Santa Teresa and the vast Guanabara Bay, all of which merit a long, reflective look.

Rio also is the capital of the state of Rio de Janeiro, replete with attractions of its own. Day trips from the city take visitors into the nearby mountains, to the refreshing coolness of the resort cities of Teresópolis and the former summer residence of Brazil's emperors, Petrópolis.

The coastline of the state of Rio contains formidable rivals to the city's beaches. For many *cariocas*, the beach resort of Buzios is unmatched anywhere in Brazil, while others insist that the archipelago of Angra dos Reis, with its 365 tropical islands, is number one. Both are within a few hours of Rio.

At night, Rio comes alive a second time. With beach lounging or sightseeing now past, natives and tourists flock to Rio's world-class bars and restaurants, many of which are blessed with spectacular and romantic views of Rio just outside the window.

Preceding pages: landscaped parks of downtown Rio with Sugarloaf in the background; catching up with the news *carioca*-style; jumping in at an isolated beach near Buzios; the Gloria Church, an exquisite relic of colonial days. Left, diving off a schooner.

DOWNTOWN RIO

Every old city has a story to tell. Rio de Janeiro's downtown tells its own colorful story, and much of Brazil's, like an illuminated manuscript.

Museums and landmarks: The tale begins at **The Museum of the Republic**, former residence of Brazil's presidents, in the Catete District. Purchased by the federal government in 1896, the palace served as a presidential residence until 1960. It was closed when the president of the time Getúlio Vargas committed suicide in an upper chamber of the palace but it reopened in 1960 as a museum.

The museum highlights presidential memorabilia of every period from the 1889 proclamation of the Republic to the military regime that ended in 1985. But its atmosphere is the main attraction. A first floor meeting room displays the cabinet table used by Deodoro da Fonseca, Brazil's first president. Each place is marked with the dispatch book of one of Fonseca's ministers.

The second floor features an elegant diplomatic reception room where Brazil's presidents received newly appointed ambassadors. On the third floor were the private quarters of Brazil's presidents. It was in the Vargas Bedroom that the ex-dictator shot himself in the heart on August 24, 1954. The room is preserved exactly as it was that day.

One subway station north of Catete, on a hill overlooking Guanabara Bay, is picturesque **Nossa Senhora da Glória do Outeiro Chapel**. Designed in 1720, the multisided church, with its curved ceiling and gleaming white walls, is Brazil's first important example of baroque architecture. Blue-and-white tiles highlight the interior.

One more subway stop brings visitors to bustling **Cinelândia**. Emerging in **Praça Floriano**, visitors are surrounded

<u>Left:</u> the Santa Teresa trolley running atop the Lapa aqueduct.

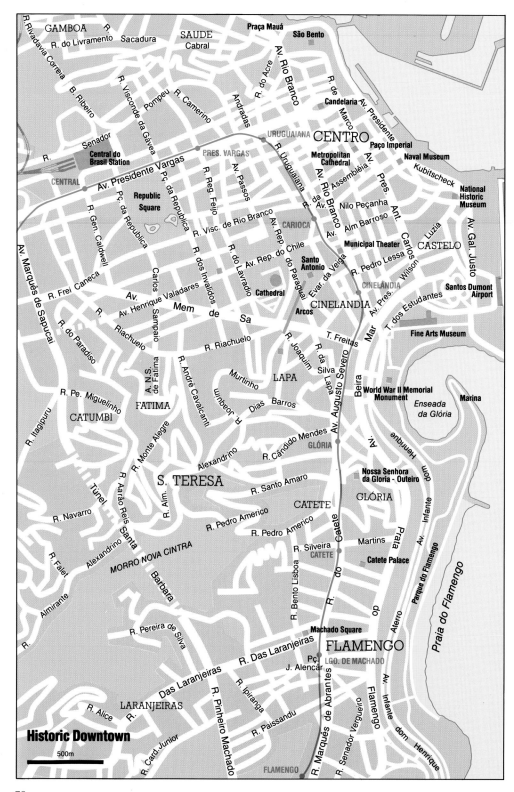

Historic Downtown

500m

by public buildings and spacious movie houses. Just across broad Avenida Rio Branco is Brazil's **National Library**, a gaudy Victorian structure completed in 1910 and recently renovated. The library is the proud possessor of a Latin Bible that was printed in 1492.

Fronting Praça Floriano is the august **Municipal Theater**, a two-thirds replica of the Paris Opera inaugurated in 1909. Nijinsky danced here in 1913, Pavlova four years later. Maria Callas slapped Director-General Barreto Pinto in the face one night in 1952 when he told the great diva she "stank" in *Norma*. Across Avenida Rio Branco from the Municipal Theater is Rio's French neoclassical **Museum of Fine Arts**, completed in 1908.

Brazilian artists: The museum's most popular display is **Pedro Américo's** overblown *Batalha do Avaí*, an immense panorama depicting a forgotten, and forgettable, engagement of the 19th-century war against Paraguay. Américo was Brazil's most popular painter in the last century. His lush landscapes and pompous court portraits had a reverse influence on colleagues, who felt they could learn how *not* to paint by studying the work of Américo.

One such artist was **Victor Meirelles**. Once a student under Américo, the work of Meirelles featured realistic figures and a sharp appreciation for character. His painting *A Primeira Missa no Brazil* (The First Mass in Brazil) is almost as large as Américo's battle scenes, but displays a more subtle touch for both anatomy and color.

Twentieth-century Brazilian art also enjoys a place of distinction in the Fine Arts collection. **Agostinho da Mota's** still lifes, perfectly wrought compositions noted for expert coloring and detail, represent a step away from overblown patriotism toward artistic unity.

Rodolfo Amoedo, took the lessons he learned from Mota's still lifes and applied them to portrait painting. His sensuous *Marabá*, depicting a half-caste Indian girl, combines deft anatomical

rendering with sympathetic treatment of character. Such painters were the precursors for Brazil's most important artistic phase since the 18th-century baroque – the new wave of modern Brazilian art. **Cândido Portinari**, probably Brazil's greatest artist, is represented by two major works: *Retrato de Maria* (1932) and *Café* (1934).

The Portrait of Maria seems conventional at first glance. But a closer look reveals the unreal patterns of shadows, a studied expression and eyes out of proportion to the thin face of the subject. *Cafe* is Portinari at his best, imposing a dominant color scheme – browns and tans – with exaggerated, rounded figures in the foreground. Such works make the Fine Arts archive one of Brazil's most important. The museum also has a permanent exhibition of Brazilian contemporary art including artists of international repute such as Daniel Senise, Tunga, Tomie Otake and Manfredo de Souzaneto.

Religious buildings: Just behind the Municipal Theater is sprawling **Largo da Carioca**, with its numerous bustling peddlers, graffiti-daubed subway station walls and aged **Santo Antônio Monastery** atop a low hill. The monastery complex was completed in 1780 but surviving portions of previous building date from as early as 1608 and are Rio's oldest examples of religious architecture. The main church's interior is typically baroque. Left of the nave is a curved, windowless vault.

Next to the main church is **São Francisco da Penitência Chapel**, dating from 1739. Its gold-leaf interior and stark wood carvings make it even more darkly stylized than its neighbor. Art critics consider it a precursor of Brazil's 18th-century baroque artistic explosion.

Just north of Largo da Carioca is bleak **Praça Tiradentes**. A center of bohemian night life in the 19th century, the plaza today is a concrete wasteland. Its only saving graces are sparkling **João Caetano Theater,** dating from 1810 and, on Avenida Passos, snug

Nossa Senhora da Lampadosa Chapel, built by slaves in 1748. Revolutionary Tiradentes heard Mass there two hours before he was hanged in 1793 on the square which now bears his name.

Nestled just behind Praça Tiradentes is another square mixing gray decay with signs of renovation – the **Largo de São Francisco**. A staging area for buses on one side of the square brings noise, pollution and litter. However, the magnificent **Igreja São Francisco de Paula** that fronts the square's south side is still impressive behind its manicured shrubbery and the rococo facade that was begun in 1756.

São Francisco's striking **Vitória Chapel** displays intriguing religious paintings by baroque artist **Mestre Valentim da Fonseca e Silva**. The portraits on the church's east corridor are a gallery of 19th-century Brazilian notables. A web of shop-filled pedestrian streets stretches from São Francisco back to Avenida Rio Branco and hides some of Rio's oldest churches.

Nossa Senhora da Conceição a Boa Morte, completed in 1735, is one, located on Rua Miguel Couto at an odd angle to Avenida Rio Branco. The church's ornate, rounded windows, like a ship's portholes, are distinctive. The sacristy houses a collection of tropical birds, which sometimes disrupt Mass with their exotic, ear-splitting calls.

One of downtown's busiest churches is Rua da Alfândega's **Santa Efigênia e Santo Elesbão**, site of the 1817 marriage of Dom Pedro I and the Empress Leopoldina. Work on the structure was completed by black slaves in 1754.

Along the southern margin of downtown, on Avenida Chile near the gaudy **Petrobras Building**, is Rio's new **Roman Catholic Cathedral**. A huge, cone-shaped structure, the cathedral is meant to demonstrate the channeling of human energies to the heavens. It reminds some visitors of the first manned space capsules, which were making news when its cornerstone was laid in 1964 (the cathedral was inaugurated in

The magnificent movie and municipal theaters.

1978). Four enormous stained glass windows put rainbows of light into the towering interior.

Just behind Praça Tiradentes, at Rua Luís de Camões, you will find one of Rio's most interesting cultural centers: **Centro Cultural Hélio Oiticica**. Oiticica is considered to be one of Brazil's most important painters. The center has a permanent exhibition of his work and temporary exhibitions of Brazilian and international works of art.

Another major cultural landmark in downtown Rio is **Rua do Lavradio** which dates back to the turn of the century. This is one of Rio's earliest residential areas but today the district is known for its trade in antiques. On the first Saturday of every month the shopkeepers organize a fair along the entire length of the street.

Eating places: Some of Rio's best lunchtime havens are located near Largo da Carioca. For a boisterous atmosphere and generous German cuisine there is **Bar Luiz** on Rua da Carioca. A popular downtown fixture since 1887, the spot is famous for its polished wood furnishings, *apfelstrudel* and draft beer. The **Café do Teatro**, in the basement of the Municipal Theater has dazzling decor, featuring massive pillars and colorful mosaics depicting scenes from life in ancient Assyria.

Rua Gonçalves Dias, near Largo de São Francisco, is home of one of Rio's most traditional restaurants – **Colombo**. A tearoom with turn-of-the-century furnishings dominates the first floor. Tall, jacarandá-wood cabinets display colorfully wrapped delicacies like a 19th-century emporium. Upstairs is the main dining room, featuring a wrap-around balcony with a splendid view of the tea room below, reflected in wall-length Belgian crystal mirrors with rosewood frames installed in 1913. Founded in 1894, Colombo moved to its present location 20 years later.

Restored buildings: On the other side of Avenida Rio Branco, about three long blocks from Largo da Carioca, is

The imposing Candelária Church.

an area that is full of restored buildings and pedestrianised streets rich in history.

Praça XV de Novembro honors the date (November 15, 1889) Brazil's Republic was founded. After years of decline it was recently restored and now it is one of the most interesting points in the center of Rio. One of Rio's most historic structures, the **Paço Imperial**, dominates the plaza's south side. Its straight rows of windows give it marked architectural unity while its iron and woodwork make it pleasingly archaic.

Work on the building was completed in 1743 and, for 63 years, it served as headquarters for Brazil's royally appointed viceroys. King João VI made it his palace in 1808 when he arrived in Brazil, accompanied by the entire Portuguese court, as a refugee from Napoleon. In 1822, Brazil's youthful regent, Pedro I, declared from a palace window that he would remain on Brazilian soil, thus defying Portuguese orders to return home and setting the stage for Brazilian independence.

The former palace now serves as a cultural center. The main attraction is the exhibition of contemporary Brazilian and international art. You can also find one of Rio's best CD shops here, a perfect place to buy Brazilian music. The center also has several other interesting shops and an excellent restaurant, the **Atrium**. Around the square there are restaurants serving *carioca* food.

Two churches on nearby Rua Primeiro de Março are no less historic than the palace. The larger edifice, **Nossa Senhora do Carmo**, was Rio's Metropolitan Cathedral until 1978. Completed in 1761, its now graying façade was once considered Rio's most architecturally harmonious. The blue-tiled bell towers were added in 1850. Carmo's interior includes rococo carvings by Valentim. South America's first Roman Catholic Cardinal, **Joaquim Arcoverde**, governed his archdiocese from the cathedral between 1905 and 1930 and is buried in its crypt. Next to the archbishop are the supposed remains of **Pedro Alvares Cabral**, the Portuguese discoverer of Brazil. Cabral's bones were brought from Portugal in 1913.

Nossa Senhora do Monte do Carmo, dating from 1770, is separated from its larger neighbor by a narrow passageway. The church is noted for its baroque façade with neo-classical touches added in the 19th century. A half block down Primeiro de Março toward Avenida Presidente Vargas is the imposing **Igreja de Santa Cruz dos Militares** completed in 1811. Much of its rococo decor was executed by Mestre Valentim.

But of all the downtown churches, tiny **Nossa Senhora da Lapa dos Mercadores** may possess the most beguiling interior. Located on Rua do Ouvidor near Cruz dos Militares, Mercadores seats only a dozen worshippers at a time. Its tiny dome allows a soft penumbra of light to suffuse the nave, which is crammed with wood carvings. A passageway under the pulpit leads to a miniscule sacristy. The chapel, financed by donations from itinerant merchants, was completed in 1750.

The network of narrow streets and arcades surrounding Praça XV de Novembro forms one of Rio's most fascinating districts, hiding quaint restaurants and high-ceilinged storefronts. Many of the offices on the **Beco do Comércio** are restored 18th-century homes. Most noted is the long, low **Edifício Telles de Menezes**, famous for its archway to the plaza. Nearby **Rua do Ouvidor** was once Rio's newspaper street. With its open-sided bars it became, in the 19th century, one of the city's most colorful meeting places.

Museums and culture: The best way to get to know a bit of ancient Rio de Janeiro is to enter **Arco do Telles** next to Praça XV. Here there are narrow streets without traffic and old, colorful buildings. On Friday night, *cariocas* working in the center gather here to eat and drink before going home. These streets are also known as the city's 'cultural corridor' because of the

Right, downtown Rio, with the Praça Paris parkway in the foreground.

concentration of galleries and cultural centers. Among them is **LGC Arte Hoje**, specializing in modern pottery, crystal and photography located on Rua do Rosário. Just around the corner is **Galeria Paulo Fernandes** which deals in contemporary art. At **Espaco Centro Cultural dos Correios** you will see young, relatively unknown Brazilian painters. Nearby **Casa França-Brasil** exhibits famous artists from Brazil and France. **Centro Cultural Banco do Brasil** has exhibitions, a coffee shop, restaurant, book shop, theater and cinema.

A few blocks south of Praça XV is one of Rio's most important landmarks, the **National Historical Museum**. The museum is a rambling structure reflecting different architectural styles and historical epochs. Its wooden balconies, colorful masonry and glinting red-tile roofs create an irresistible effect of ice-cream cake. Among the items on display are murals depicting the death of Tiradentes (next to a macabre exhibit including chunks of wood from the gallows where he was hanged) and the Proclamation of Independence. Archive materials include the 1888 document freeing Brazil's slaves.

The museum building itself is of indeterminate age. Wings and improvements have been added and subtracted since 1603 when a small fortress was begun at the site. In 1922 the whole of the 17th-, 18th- and 19th-century sections were remodeled to accommodate portions of the fair to celebrate the independence centennial.

About one long block north of the sprawling historical archive is Brazil's attractive **Naval and Oceanographic Museum**. To protect the wooden floors, visitors must don felt slippers before exploring the two-story museum, constructed in 1899. World War II torpedoes and mines make up one part of the display. Other galleries feature maps and paintings of Brazilian naval engagements. But the highlight of the museum for most visitors is its detailed ship models, some over a meter long.

The spectacular and slightly bizarre Assyrian decor of the Café do Teatro restaurant in the Teatro Municipal.

A 15-minute drive from downtown is the **National Museum**, the residence of the imperial family in the 19th century. The impressive palace, next to Rio's zoo, houses natural history, archeological and mineral exhibits. It is located at Quinta da Boa Vista.

Four short blocks west of Praça XV, on Avenida Presidente Vargas, is the impressive **Igreja da Candelária**. Dedicated by King João VI in 1811, Candelária is one of Rio's most striking monuments. Its façade was begun in 1775, following frank baroque lines. But construction took so long the interior decor already intruded on the emerging neo-classical style, explaining the towering columns of multicolored marble. The dome was finished in 1877 and the bronze doors attached in 1901.

Five blocks east, down Avenida Rio Branco toward **Praça Mauá**, is one of Rio's oldest churches – the **Monastery of São Bento**, commanding a magnificent view of Guanabara Bay. Every Sunday at 10am mass is held accompanied by Gregorian chants. Work on the Benedictine monastery began in 1617 and continued for a century. Its façade shares the flat, thick mannerist style prominent in 17th-century Brazilian religious architecture. São Bento is noted for the opulence of its interior, highlighted by the familiar gold leaf and an explosion of baroque wood carving. The hill on which the monastery stands is one of the few that survive in downtown Rio. The others, which existed during the colonial period, have fallen victim to *carioca* progress, a penchant for removing hills to fill in the bay.

The Candelária church, which once stood close to the water, is now far removed, thanks to land fills using dirt from the fallen hills. The most tragic case of this came in 1921–22 when the downtown hill of Castelo was carted off, together with most of Rio's remaining 16th- and 17th-century structures.

Praça Mauá itself, located in Rio's port area, is a contrast of the sacred and the profane. Dominated on one side by the monastery, the plaza's southern wing is a row of rowdy strip joints. The clubs feature relatively tame sex shows attracting sailors and cruise ship passengers. The area also has one of Rio's most popular nightclubs, **Kalesa**, offering beer, cheap food, shows and dancing.

Another downtown area with striptease action is the famed **Lapa District**, which acted as a magnet for bohemians in the 1920s and 1930s. Lapa began losing its allure when Rio's nightlife moved to Copacabana in the 1940s. Today, the strip bars on **Avenida Mem de Sá** are considered seedier than their Praça Mauá rivals and the avenue at night is home to Rio's aggressive transvestites. However, there have been efforts to recapture Lapa's charm with the opening of classy clubs at its downtown end. The best known is the **Asa Branca**, a vast dance hall featuring top pop performers and samba tunes but attracting few tourists. The **Assyrius** and the **Café Nice**, on nearby Avenida Rio Branco, offer elegant decor and dancing.

A crowded pedestrian mall.

SANTA TERESA

Old-fashioned gables and trolley cars, decades of green growth, pastel-shaded masonry and zig-zagging staircases make Rio's downtown **Santa Teresa District** a magic mountain.

Santa Teresa is accessible by car or bus from most points in the downtown area. But the best way to visit the picturesque district is by trolley car.

The trolley system: The trolley ride, which starts at the downtown **Petrobras Building Plaza**, the headquarters of Brazil's state oil company, crosses one of Rio's most notable engineering feats, the 18th-century **Carioca Aqueduct** (also called the **Arcos da Lapa**). The aqueduct once brought water from Rio's central spine of mountains to city dwellers. The structure served its original purpose for a century but was then abandoned until the Ferro Carril Carioca Traction Company obtained its right of way in 1896.

Since then, the massive arches have conducted trolley traffic from downtown into a complex network of tracks that run throughout Santa Teresa – one of the most interesting day trips. (The trollies of late have become targets of petty thieves and pickpockets. Make sure you hold on to your purses, cameras and wallets.)

In 1988, the state government still possessed 19 of the yellow, open-sided trolley cars. However, parts shortages kept many of them out of service. At one point, only two cars were running, with microbuses substituting on the Santa Teresa trolley lines. The state governor promised a complete renovation of the US-built cars (the newest dates from 1950).

Santa Teresa's residents: According to legend, black slaves used Santa Teresa's mountain trails to escape from their owners during the 18th century when Rio was Brazil's leading slave port. Santa Teresa began to receive more permanent residents when a yellow fever epidemic forced the city's population to flee to the hills to escape from the mosquitoes carrying the disease. The 1896 introduction of the trolleys (or *bondes*, so-called because the system was financed by foreign bonds) opened an era of opulence for hilly Santa Teresa, which, by the early 20th century, had become a center for artistic and literary activities. Writers, artists and musicians built lodgings along its winding streets. Bankers and businessmen followed, constructing elaborate masonry staircases to reach their homes, often built at fantastic angles against the slopes.

Architectural styles: Opulent European ironwork, exaggerated statuary and other adornments were added to the staircases. Much of what Santa Teresa was at the turn of the century is today retained in its elegant old mansions.

Santa Teresa is characterized by an odd variety of architectural styles. Among its distinct features are a gabled castle, an onion-domed Orthodox Church, at least one Alpine lodge and rows and rows of 19th-century houses notable for their complex patterns of stained glass and wrought iron.

The district offers unexpected views. From the second trolley station, visitors glimpse the vast blue expanse of **Guanabara Bay**. From many of its cobbled streets, public staircases wind in stages to the neighborhoods of **Glória** and **Flamengo**, hundreds of feet below. The 80- and 100-year-old store-fronts display their merchandise in polished wooden cabinets.

Santa Teresa is also rich in neighborhood pride. Virtually all of its public buildings, including the 1750 **Convento de Santa Teresa**, located near the first trolley station, are well preserved. Most residents have added something to their Victorian-era homes without detracting from the district's charm. Flower gardens are everywhere – many seem to pour over the chipped retaining walls. There are few abandoned structures in Santa Teresa.

Left, ageing villas spilling down the hillside of Santa Teresa.

Brazil's best art museum: One of the most surprising highlights of a district noted for surprises is the **Chácara do Céu** (Little House in the Sky) modern art museum. The museum, at **Rua Murtinho Nobre 93**, was once the residence of Brazilian collector, Raymundo Ottoni de Castro Maya.

The Castro Maya house is probably the best little art museum in Brazil. Its collection includes samples of the finest in modern Brazilian art, including works by Antônio Bandeira, Iberê Camargo, Volpi, Di Cavalcanti and Cândido Portinari, one of Brazil's greatest artists of all time.

But that's not all. Chácara's breezy, sun-bright galleries include works by modern European masters – Braque, Dali, Degas, Matisse, Modigliani, Monet and Picasso.

All its corridors and anterooms are jammed with objects rarely appreciated in Brazil, such as 17th-century Persian rugs, Indian and Chinese ivory and a white, smooth torso carved by a Greek sculptor more than 2,400 years ago. The house itself is an ideal setting for an art museum.

One side of the topaz facade is substantially hidden by trees; the other faces a pleasant lawn with a few stone benches, fountains and grassy recesses at its margin. The view from the grounds is spectacular. On one side is the panorama of downtown Rio; quaint trolley cars cross the aqueduct, looking like toy trains in a plaster and plastic artificial city. On the other side is a classic view of Guanabara Bay.

The emphasis of Castro Maya's magnificent collection is on modern Brazilian art, with special attention to works by the collector's life-long friend, Portinari.

Portinari's collection includes a portrait of Castro Maya, and two canvasses completed in 1941: *A Barca* (The Boat) and *O Sapateiro de Brodowski* (The Shoemaker of Brodowski), featuring the large rounded figures characteristic of much of his work.

The fight to get a seat on the Santa Teresa trolley.

Also noteworthy is the collection of 36 Portinari color drawings depicting scenes from *Don Quixote*.

Among other Brazilian artists represented are Antônio Bandeira, whose *A Grande Cidade* (The Big City) recalls the splashes and splotches of Jackson Pollock and Emiliano Di Cavalcanti, whose works are crowded with playful human figures against a typical Brazilian cityscape.

Among Brazilian sculptures is the huge, dark as death *Asas* (Wings) by Cesar Baldaccini, dated 1921. The iron figure dominates the entire second floor gallery. Modern French painting is represented better, perhaps, than at any other museum in Brazil.

Modigliani's *Portrait of a Young Widow* is displayed in the room which was once Castro Maya's office. In the same room is Salvador Dali's small but suitably surreal *Two Balconies*. The work, with its bizarre formations – a rock with a human ear and man's head that seems to melt into the ground – is as representative a work of Dali's as you could wish to find. A Matisse – *The Luxembourg Garden* – with its pastel colors and tranquility, is also specially displayed.

The collection includes a Picasso, displayed on the ground floor. *La Dance*, dated 1956, is a few brush strokes and some color background and looks like it was scrawled by the artist in his sleep.

What is perhaps most interesting about the Castro Maya collection is the presence of art objects from distant times and cultures. A pair of Chinese cast-iron birds, in excellent condition and fantastically detailed, are more than a thousand years old. A tiny female bust is 7th-century Cambodian.

There is no article of decor or furnishing which is not a precious object of art. The museum represents a lifetime of careful selection by one of Brazil's most astute and public-spirited collectors. Castro Maya, said architect Lúcio Costa, was "a public man in the highest and best sense of the term."

Bus stop with 1986 World Cup soccer mural.

THE BAY

Like a big buttonhole cut out of the Atlantic coast, the 147-sq. mile (380-sq. km) **Bay of Guanabara** is a living map of Rio's maritime past. Its narrow entrance is guarded by two historic forts, the 17th-century **Santa Cruz** which is situated on the eastern bank, today's Niterói, and the 19th-century **São João** on the western, Rio de Janeiro side. Their walls were constructed from solid granite blocks, cemented together with whale oil.

The surviving forts lie on much older foundations dating back to 1555, when the Portuguese realized that they would have to fortify the bay if they were not to lose it to the French. For 50 years after its discovery in 1502, the bay attracted many freewheeling Portuguese and French adventurers. Ships returned to Europe loaded with rare birds, parrots, monkeys, Indian slaves and Brazil wood – the heavy red hardwood from which the dye was extracted that gave Brazil its name. The Portuguese made their base on the Rio side of the bay, the French on the eastern shore, clashing frequently in sea skirmishes.

French effort: In 1555, the French launched a definitive effort to conquer *Rivière Guenère*, as they called the bay. A fleet sent by King Henri II took possession of a region on the Rio side, building Fort Coligny on the isle **Ilha Villegagnon**. But "Antarctic France," as they called their new territory, was short-lived. Within five years they were driven off the island by the Portuguese, the survivors taking refuge with the Tamoio Indian tribe in Niterói.

When surveying the bay today, it is a sobering thought that nothing remains of what the French and the Portuguese fought over – no Indians, no Brazil wood trees, no parrots. ➡ 94

Left, the gentle bay, thought at first by the Portuguese to be a river.

SUGARLOAF

Sugarloaf mountain is undoubtedly Rio's and Brazil's best-known landmark. Today a symbol of the city, it was at its feet that the original city of São Sebastião do Rio de Janeiro was founded in 1565. The Indians had a name for this singularly shaped granite monolith that stood guarding the entrance to Rio's Guanabara Bay. They called it *Pau-nd-Acuqua*, meaning high, pointed, isolated peak.

To the Portuguese, this name sounded like *pão de açucar* (sugarloaf) and the shape of the peak reminded them of the clay molds used to cast refined sugar into a conical lump called a sugarloaf. Still popular with rock climbers, the 1,300-foot (400-meter) summit's first known conqueror was Englishwoman, Henrietta Carstairs, who in 1817 placed a British flag at the top. This was soon replaced with a Portuguese flag by a patriotic soldier.

In the first decade of the 20th century, Brazilian engineer Augusto Ferreira Ramos envisioned an aerial link that would make the view from the mountaintop accessible to all. Despite general skepticism, in 1909 he obtained authorization from the mayor for his project, and the first stage of the cable car line to 705-foot (220-meter) Morro da Urca, the low mountain in front of Sugarloaf, was inaugurated in 1912. The final stage from Morro da Urca to Sugarloaf was completed in 1913. The original 24-passenger cable cars were imported from Germany, and they remained in use for 60 years before being replaced in 1972 by larger cars able to handle the increased demand for their services.

Now visitors are whisked up in Italian-made bubble-shaped cars that hold up to 75 passengers and offer a 360-degree view. Each stage takes just 3 minutes, with cars starting out from the top and the bottom simultaneously, zipping past each other in the middle of the ride.

A cable car ride to the top of Sugarloaf.

Departures from the station at Praia Vermelha where you get your tickets are every half hour from 8am to 10pm.

From both the Morro da Urca and Sugarloaf itself, you have spectacular views on all sides, and there are paths leading to viewpoints. To the west lie the beaches of Leme, Copacabana, Ipanema and Leblon and the mountains beyond. At your feet are Botafogo and Flamengo leading to downtown, with Corcovado peak and its Christ statue behind. Most visitors feel the view from taller Corcovado is more spectacular than that from Sugarloaf, but one of the main reasons for this is that Corcovado also offers the best view of Sugarloaf itself.

To the north, the high bridge across the bay connects Rio de Janeiro and Niterói, and you can see Niterói's beaches stretching away towards the east. It helps if you bring a map out with you to the top to help you get your bearings.

If you go up Sugarloaf late in the afternoon, you can see the city in the daylight, watch the sunset and the first lights coming on and see the city at night. Alternatively, you can have a leisurely lunch at the Pão de Açucar restaurant on Morro da Urca which is open for lunch only.

The Brazil Experience, a 45-minute, 2,500-slide audiovisual presentation is shown hourly from 9am to 8pm on Morro da Urca, with the soundtrack available in English, French, Spanish and Portuguese. While acquainting viewers with Brazil's sights, the show also explains their historic and cultural significance. By outlining the country's evolution from a New World colony to the modern nation it is today, the program offers the foreign visitor a rare and delightful insight into Brazil and its people.

Every now and then there are shows given at the amphitheater atop Morro da Urca. Samba schools and popular singers and bands are scheduled periodically, often with dancing.

Ask for program details and tickets from your hotel. ∎

Corcovado as seen from Sugarloaf.

Looking upwards towards the granite hills, one could easily believe that the surrounds of Rio must be much the same as they were at the time of discovery. But the lower one drops one's glance, from the highrises along the Rio and Niterói shoreline, the industries and oil refineries, to the silted-up mud flats (where lush mangrove swamps once sheltered exotic fauna) and the murky water itself, the more one is aware of the toll that predatory development has taken on one of the world's most beautiful natural wonders. A recent *New York Times* article on the bay was aptly headlined, "The Bay's a Thing of Beauty; Pity It's a Cesspool."

An estimated 1.5 million tons of refuse and sewage find their way into the bay every day, from 10 million inhabitants along the bay's banks, from Rio proper to the sprawling **Baixada Fluminense**, a slum region that spreads mushroom-like around the shoreline. Residents and ecologists alike sigh in despair over the limited prospects of seeing the bay cleaned up. They have seen too many successive electoral promises evaporate in practice.

Center of recreation: Until the 1930s, when *cariocas* started moving to the ocean beaches, the bay was the main center of recreation for the city. People had picnics on its shores and fished and swam in its waters.

The well-heeled *cariocas* built holiday homes on **Paquetá**, the largest of the bay's 84 islands. A ferryboat trip to Paquetá's beaches, lapped by the gentle waters of the bay, so different from the crashing waves of the Atlantic, was a welcome treat.

These days, Paquetá's beaches are fit only for sunbathing, but a boat trip to the island is still a must. There are two ways of getting there: by ferry, leaving from **Praça Quinze**, which costs a few cents and takes 90 minutes or by hydrofoil, *aerobarco*, a swift 15 minutes.

From half a mile out to sea, the buildings of Rio de Janeiro look like small, neat false teeth, dwarfed by the back-

A trip across the bay – a popular activity.

drop of the green and black hills. It is a sight to file away and retrieve on the streets of Copacabana where the buildings seem overpowering.

Bay islands: Turning into the bay, one passes Ilha Villegagnon, the former seat of the ill-fated Antarctic France, which was joined to the mainland by a 1929 landfill during the erection of Brazil's naval academy.

Ilha das Cobras (Snake Island), today a port for naval frigates and Brazil's one aircraft carrier, was, consecutively, an unloading area for slave ships and a monastery. **Ilha Fiscal** is known for its strange spired green palace, which was formerly a barracks for customs officers. It was here that the Imperial Government held its last ball in 1889. Ilha Fiscal is now joined to Ilha das Cobras.

Passing dockland on the left, one goes under the span of the **Rio-Niterói Bridge**. Once the bridge is behind, one is in the bay proper.

A vast panorama of water and islands opens up, although the scene is hardly the tropical paradise portrayed by French engraver Debret in the 19th century. Those that have not been turned into promontories by landfills, such as the 17-sq. mile (44-sq. km) **Ilha de Governador**, which houses Rio's international airport, have been given over to oil tanks and armament depots.

Further into the bay, however, some islands retain a thick crop of wild tropical greenery. One of these is **Ilha de Sol** (Sun Island), where the 1950s cabaret star and striptease artist, Luz del Fuego, set up Brazil's first nudist colony.

She hosted parties which attracted guests from Europe but she met a mysterious end. Whether she was murdered by her politician lover or by a jealous fisherman, or whether she merely drowned, has never been solved.

Paquetá: The island of Paquetá has survived the passage of time well. This feeling is captured by the island's one-story houses that are surrounded by flowers and the fact that private cars are not allowed. Transport is by bicycle

<u>Below</u>, step back in time for a horse and buggy ride on Paquetá Island. <u>Right</u>, view of Rio from Niterói.

(rentals available) or by a horse-drawn buggy which does a trip round the island at 19th-century pace for US$5. There are three small hotels, four seafood restaurants, a string of beachside bars and a small but pleasant park-cum-nature reserve taking up one end of the island. In splendid isolation, on the adjoining island of **Brocoio**, stands one of the official weekend homes of the Rio State Governor.

Niterói: *Cariocas* generally thumb their noses at Niterói, claiming that it is a second-class version of their own city. Its only claim to fame, they sniff, is that it offers an excellent view of Rio proper.

In fact, Niterói's charms are quieter and on a lesser scale than those of Rio. But it is because of this parochial calm that people choose to live there. For exploring **Niterói**, there are ferries and *aerobarcos* leaving Praça Quinze every few minutes.

One of the most interesting attractions in Niterói is the recently opened **Museu de Arte Contemorânea de Niterói**. Besides the collection of art the building itself is worth a visit. This is the famous architect Oscar de Niemayer's last creation, located on the seashore and built in the shape of a spaceship. His concept for the new building was to connect water, earth and air in one expression.

Many of the town's best features lie off the beaten track, such as **Parque da Cidade**, 890 feet (270 meters) above sea level, via a winding road through an unspoilt nature reserve. It offers stunning views over the bay and back over the lush hills of the mainland, plus two takeoff platforms for hang gliders.

Many historical monuments, such as the **Rio Branco-Imbui-São Luis** complex of forts high up on a rough unpaved road, overlooking Jurujuba beach, require permission and private transport to visit.

The climb is worth it, not only for yet another stunning view, but for the sense of timelessness given by the old forts nestled in the green hillside. São Luis is

Ferries and hydrofoils make the passage across the bay.

in ruins; only its splendid portico has been preserved.

Indian chieftain: Of Niterói's many notable churches, the one with the most vivid story to tell is the simple **São Lourenço dos Indios**, where the South-American Indian chieftain Arariboia is believed to be buried. Arariboia, or São Lourenço (an honorary sainthood endowed upon him by the Jesuits), was chief of the Temimino tribe from the other side of the bay. Allying himself with the Portuguese, he led a victorious campaign against the French and the Tamoio Indians in Niterói in the 1550s and 1560s.

The Portuguese first gave him deeds to the region where Rio's port lies today but later transferred him to the Niterói side, where he took possession on November 22, 1573.

This date is celebrated today as the founding of the city. Within a century, however, the Portuguese had forgotten their debt to Arariboia and ousted his descendants from Niterói .

The further away you get from the Niterói city center, the prettier and more unspoilt the beaches: **Samanguaiá** with its yacht club, **Jurujuba** with its seafood restaurants and, last of the bayside beaches, the small twin coves of **Adão e Eva** (Adam and Eve).

Santa Cruz fort: Yet it is on the tip of the promontory that Niterói's *pièce de résistance* lies – the **fort of Santa Cruz**.

Well preserved, the fort is a magnificent compendium of three centuries of military architecture. The oldest parts, such as the rough-hewn stone **Santa Barbara** chapel and the torture chamber, date back to the 16th century.

Garibaldi, the hero of Italian liberation and José Bonifacio de Andrade, Brazil's "patriarch of independence" were imprisoned here. It takes at least three hours to go around the fort's myriad chambers, galleries, dungeons and courtyards. It is still used as a military prison with weekend prison visits, so it is best to see it during the week, by prior arrangement (telephone 711-0462.)

The massive span of the Rio–Niterói Bridge.

COPACABANA

Most educated travelers know of Copacabana but few can actually pinpoint where it is or what it is. Many, quite correctly, think that Copacabana is a beach. Others, quite wrongly, (thanks to a misleading popular song), think it is a nightclub.

Copacabana is one of the world's great beaches. Together with the now demolished church of the Virgin of Copacabana, it has given its name to one of Rio de Janeiro's most populous suburbs, although "suburb" is hardly a just description today.

With a population exceeding 300,000 spread throughout 109 streets, Copacabana can be viewed as a city within a city, rather than a suburb. Its population is a melting pot of class and color living and working side by side, making Copacabana a classless neighborhood, unlike its wealthy neighbor, Ipanema.

Relative newcomer: Measured in historical terms, Copacabana is a relative newcomer to the *carioca* scene. It is a republican suburb, if you like, because its birth and subsequent growth at the end of the 19th century coincided with the end of the Brazilian monarchy in 1889. Its best days were already over by the time Brazil's capital was changed from Rio de Janeiro to Brasília on April 21, 1960.

Except for the transatlantic telegraph that linked *Posto 6* (close to the Rio Palace Hotel) with London, Copacabana was basically untouched and uninhabited at the turn of the 20th century.

Copacabana owes its development and growth to the Rio Tramway, Light & Power Company of Canada, or "Light" as it is called by the *cariocas,* the same company that was responsible for the railway which scales Corcovado. It was

Preceding pages: The famed crescent curve of Copacabana; burst of colorful bird kites; the big bikini market. <u>Left</u>, topless bathing is still an infrequent sight.

Light that invested in the linking of Copacabana with the rest of Rio, a city which was by then nearly 400 years old. The linkage came by blasting through the rock to make tunnels, thus giving trams the easy access they could not find over the mountains. Then, as now, new areas often received transport, light and gas before receiving a resident population.

The first "breakthrough" was the opening, in 1892, of **Tunel Alaor Prata** (*Tunel Velho),* which links the middle of **Botafogo**, on the downtown side of the mountains, with the heart of Copacabana at **Rua Figuereido Magalhães** and **Rua Siqueira Campos**.

A second tunnel, **Tunel Engenheiro Marques Porto** (*Tunel Novo),* was added in 1904 to link Copacabana and its extension, **Leme**, via **Avenida Princesa Isabel**, to the end of Botafogo Beach, where the city's showpiece drive, **Avenida Beira Mar**, had just been completed. With these tunnels Rio de Janeiro's Atlantic Ocean suburbs of Copacabana and Leme, and later Ipanema and Leblon, were born.

Center of activities: After 1910, the urbanization of Copacabana gathered pace as houses were built amongst the dunes. The **Copacabana Palace Hotel**, inaugurated in 1923, quickly became the center of activities in Copacabana. For several decades, it was widely considered to be one of the world's great hotels. Now that it was blessed with roads, tunnels, gas, electricity and fresh water, and with the help of hotels like the Copacabana Palace, casinos and nightclubs, Copacabana started to attract the world's rich and famous, who flocked there in ever increasing numbers in the 1930s and 1940s.

Copacabana's popularity, however, fell abruptly on April 30, 1946, when gambling was outlawed and the country's 69 casinos were closed. But while Copacabana settled back into a less extravagant existence, the war years had seen rapid growth in the district. Houses and apartment blocks sprang up to claim every square inch of building land available, and Copacabana became Rio's most

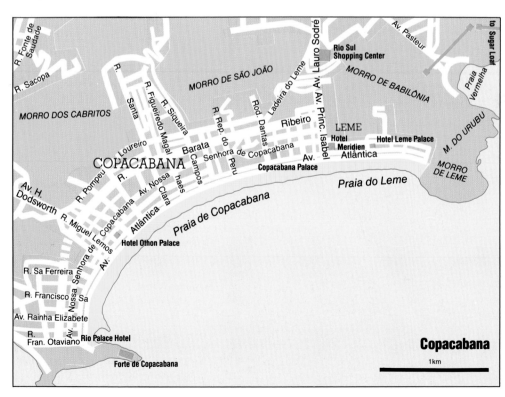

sought-after commercial and residential center. All the city's best hotels, restaurants and nightclubs were to be found along its streets. Many of the hotels and restaurants of this period have survived the passage of time, although their surroundings have changed dramatically.

The original **Bife de Ouro** restaurant in the Copacabana Palace dates from 1938, while other beachfront eateries include **Lucas**, dating from 1941, on the corner of **Rua Souza Lima**, and **Bolero**, one of the most famous and traditional of Copacabana's 35 beachfront bars. Lucas has been operating in the same location since 1945. **Le Bec Fin** is another survivor from the 1940s and remains one of the city's best restaurants.

As early as the 1960s, Copacabana had reached maximum capacity at ground level. Unable to grow out, the answer was to grow up, and every year the apartment blocks climbed higher and higher. The beachfront highrises, however, cast long shadows, leaving much of the beach in shade from mid-afternoon. To resolve this and traffic problems, the beach was widened through landfill. The former two-lane **Avenida Atlântica** became six lanes, lined by wide, sweeping sidewalks with their famous mosaic designs.

In the 1970s the skyline of newly widened Copacabana was radically altered – several large hotels were constructed in a bid to cope with the city's growing tourism and the demand of the international business community.

Hotel landmarks: The two most obvious landmarks on Copacabana today are the **Meridien Hotel**, which towers 37 floors up at the exact spot where Copacabana becomes Leme, and the 27-story **Othon Palace**, which stands further along the beach to the west, on the corner of Avenida Atlântica and **Xavier da Silveira**.

Copacabana came close to getting a third highrise constructed at its most westerly end, but building restrictions led to the luxury **Sofitel Rio Palace Hotel** being built much lower than the original plans had called for.

A new beginning: sunrise on the beach on New Year's Day.

These new hotels have brought back a great deal of life to Copacabana and this is particularly true of the Meridien and Sofitel Rio Palace hotels.

The Meridien is a gourmet's paradise and is topped off, literally, with Paul Bocuse's **Le Saint Honoré**, a restaurant that is considered to be among the best in the world, with a view which is hard to beat anywhere. The hotel also has a jazz bar, and two other restaurants, including the **Café de la Paix**, a French *brasserie* which is open round the clock.

At the other end of the beach, the luxury Sofitel Rio Palace has helped bring the glamor back to Posto 6 and the area of the old Atlântico casino. Since its opening, in 1979, the hotel has offered shows by personalities like Frank Sinatra, Julio Iglesias and Bobby Short and has, in one of Brazil's top French restaurants, **Le Pré Catelan**, a menu orchestrated by Gaston Lenotre.

Copacabana and its residents are different from any others in Rio. They are more traditional. They are also resigned to the parking problems endemic to Copacabana and are therefore likely to walk and shop locally. Corner stores thrive, as do the beachfront bars which in Copacabana fill the role of the traditional British pub. In Copacabana bars, a faithful clientele will return night after night or lunch after lunch. As an additional extra, the owner's takings are boosted by the tourist or visitor who finds his or her way to the bar.

Street markets: Despite the overcrowding, Copacabana has managed to retain its street markets, which bring chaos to their immediate area each week. No visit to Rio would be complete without some time spent examining the exotic fruits and vegetables and the tropical flowers on display in these markets.

The more traditional street markets are those on **Rua Gustavo Sampaio** (Monday), **Rua Domingos Ferreira** (Wednesday), **Rua Belford Roxo** and **Rua Ronald de Carvalho** (Thursday) and the **Rua Decio Vilares** (Sunday).

Flirting with the girls.

Recent years have seen Brazil's better fashion stores setting up branches in Copacabana, sited on seven blocks around **Rua Santa Clara** and **N.S. de Copacabana**. The souvenir trade has also moved back to Copacabana to dominate the roads between **Rua Paula Freitas** and **Praça Bernardeli**, behind the Copacabana Palace Hotel.

The early 1980s saw the establishment of a number of large fashion malls in Rio, one of which, **Rio Sul**, is located just past *Tunel Novo* from Copacabana in Botafogo. The only modern mall located within Copacabana is the **Cassino Atlântico**, below the Sofitel Rio Palace Hotel, which has a predominance of art and antique stores as well as a good selection of souvenir stores.

For visitors interested in antiques a visit to **Shopping Cassino Atlântico** on Nossa Senhora de Copacabana is a must. On four floors over 20 shops sell furniture, art, antiques and bric-a-brac.

Beach life: The beach at Copacabana remains one of Rio de Janeiro's most popular, attracting not only its 300,000 residents but also *cariocas* from all over the metropolis who arrive at weekends on packed buses or by car to park along the beach's crowded 2.4 miles (4 km).

The beach has a life of its own, separate from the rest of Copacabana, and only darkness slows the hectic pace. Even at night, joggers are to be found and games of beach soccer continue under floodlights.

In 1948, three Argentine girls caused a storm on the beach by sunbathing in front of the Copacabana Palace Hotel in two-piece swimsuits, the forerunner of the bikini. From then on, Rio de Janeiro, first through Copacabana and later through Ipanema, would lead the world as far as summer fashion, especially swimwear, was concerned.

By the start of the 1960s, it had become clear that Rio's traffic was outgrowing the available road space. Work started on the filling-in of the bay along the beachfront in Flamengo to create Flamengo Park, while in Copacabana,

A tight fit in one of Rio's ubiquitous beach snack trailers.

work began in 1969 to widen the beachfront street, Avenida Atlântica. Beach lovers, at the time, may have worried about what would become of the beach but as it turned out, they needn't have, since with the new alignment it was made much wider than anyone could have imagined.

Copacabana Beach is so wide that it is more a sandy park than a beach. To get to the water's edge, swimmers must cross an expanse that houses full-size soccer fields and volleyball courts. In summer, the sand is so hot that it is impossible to cross its expanse without shoes. Watching the *cariocas* at play on the beach gives outsiders an idea why Brazil has been a dominant force in soccer and volleyball, both of which are national passions.

Sitting on a beach in Rio, particularly in Copacabana, is never dull. Live theater surrounds you as the beach becomes a stage for the body beautiful and the unforgettable *carioca* girls in their equally unforgettable bikinis. Young-

sters happily share the beach with families and the tourists, whose pale white skin marks them out as non *cariocas*.

The beach is unfortunately also the stage for most of Rio's petty crime. The problem arises when visitors leave their possessions unattended as they stroll along the beach or take to the waters of the Southern Atlantic. Rio's sharp-eyed petty thieves are quick to pounce on cameras, personal stereos and wallets which are left sitting at risk on top of beach towels.

The safest beach locations for visitors are the beaches in front of the big hotels as most of these employ their own minders to ensure that their guests go undisturbed.

Strong currents: As the beach of Copacabana is open to the elements of the South Atlantic, it is affected by strong currents which can be very dangerous for inexperienced swimmers. For most of the year, the waters of Copacabana look rougher than they actually are. As the sea breaks over a sandbank further

Left, paddle ball, another *carioca* passion and below, beach beauty with a tattoo – the latest fad.

out, it is possible to swim through the waves and stand up. The key here is to observe what the *cariocas* are doing, especially the surfers, who have the most experience with local conditions.

Accidents usually occur when the victim panics. In Copacabana, there is little need to panic as it has an excellent lifeguard system which places guards in patrol boats and in helicopters.

The surfers also take it upon themselves to keep an eye out for inexperienced swimmers, taking them beyond the breaking waves, on their boards, to the calmer, deeper water.

A visiting swimmer should remember that the current off Copacabana takes you down the beach and not away from the shore. The current can cause interesting problems for the near-sighted swimmer when he emerges from the sea, far from his towel and friends.

Copacabana's lifeguard stations, the *postos*, were for many years a method of orienting and directing people around the area. *Posto* 1 covered Leme and *Postos* 2, 3, 4, 5 and 6, covered Copacabana. Nowadays, only *Posto* 6 is officially referred to and covers the area from Rua Sá Ferreira to the Sofitel Rio Palace.

The *postos* were knocked down when the beach was widened and new lifeguard stations constructed in the early 1980s. But Copacabana's residents continue to refer to locations on the beach in terms of where the old *postos* stood.

Rio de Janeiro, Brazil and Copacabana are virtually synonymous. What happens to Brazil or Rio is reflected in the streets of Copacabana, especially Rua Miguel Lemos, which closes for a party at the slightest excuse. The soccer World Cup is a month-long excuse, win or lose, but if it is a win, there is no more exhilarating place to be than Miguel Lemos and the streets of Copacabana.

Carnival on Copacabana: Carnival is another excuse to party and despite being some distance from the main Carnival parade grounds, at Marques de Sapucai and Avenida Rio Branco, Copa-

There is logic to sidewalk mosaics but very little to traffic.

cabana is one of the liveliest places in the city during the revelries.

Street bands are one of Rio's most traditional Carnival items and Copacabana has some of the very best, including *Banda do Leme, Banda da Sá Ferreira, Banda da Miguel Lemos, Banda da Vergonha do Posto 6* and the *Banda do Arroxo*. These bands snake their way through the streets of Copacabana, followed by thousands of revelers. The bands normally go out at around 4pm and continue for as long as they have a following, which can be into the early hours of the next morning.

Copacabana's Carnival balls cover the whole spectrum in terms of style, price and content, and range from the exclusive hotel balls to much simpler parties in the smaller bars and clubs in the back streets.

Copacabana also holds what is probably the world's largest party. It takes place every New Year's Eve when more than 2 million people, most dressed in white, crowd onto Copacabana Beach, the beachfront bars and the luxury hotels to welcome in the New Year.

The celebration also has a religious significance for the followers of *macumba*, Brazil's voodoo. For them, December 31 is the feast of Iemanjá, the Goddess of the Sea. Offerings to the goddess are launched into the sea throughout the night, but the activity culminates in a mass offering at midnight, when the faithful hope that the third wave after midnight will take their offerings out to sea. Thousands crowd the beach for this mystical ceremony enhanced by drum beats in the night.

The New Year's celebration in Copacabana is an event that is unequaled anywhere in the world, surprising many visitors who consider it more spectacular than Carnival. A massive fireworks display at midnight coordinated by the big hotels lights up the Southern Atlantic, which comes alive with bobbing pleasure craft out to enjoy the spectacle from the water.

Left, in Copa, every Sunday is Carnival.

NIGHTLIFE IN COPA

While in most cities nightlife begins after dark, on Copacabana the preliminaries start during daylight hours, with the beach serving as a vast singles bar. From the beach it is just a quick hop across Avenida Atlântica to one of the beachfront's numerous sidewalk cafés for a pre-dinner drink.

The options for the dinner itself are wide and appealing, ranging from an informal meal at a *carioca* steakhouse to the heights of sophisticated dining at one of the neighborhood's several exquisite centers of gourmet cuisine. Afterwards, the best option is to simply mingle with the crowd. At night, Copacabana jumps with a special nervous energy.

Throngs gather in front of discos, tourists browse through the wares of street vendors, couples walk slowly along the beachfront and prostitutes, male, female and indeterminate, prowl the edges of this moving mass.

Historically, since the 1930s, Copacabana has been the center of Rio's nightlife having taken over this mantle from the downtown area around the Teatro Municipal, where, at the time, the city's best movie houses, theaters, bars and restaurants were located, right next to **Lapa**, the bohemian district of its day.

Center of entertainment: Copacabana's Golden Age as the center for Rio's entertainment was unquestionably from the early 1930s until the start of the 1950s, during which time the **Copacabana Palace Hotel** and the **Cassino Atlântico** attracted the rich and famous from all over the world to Rio to gamble and enjoy the nightclubs and restaurants which had sprung up around them. The Copacabana Palace Hotel still thrives today, a regal landmark of Copacabana's seafront drive, **Avenida Atlântica**.

Best restaurants: Copacabana's Golden Age was responsible for many of the area's better restaurants, many of which still survive to quench the appetite of the *cariocas*. The Copacabana Palace's **Pérgula**, despite several reforms, dates back to 1938, while close by, in Praça da Lido, is **Le Bec Fin**, which has consistently served some of Rio's best food since its opening in 1948.

The small restaurant of the elegant **Ouro Verde Hotel** is another restaurant with an historic past and has been under the command of the same Swiss chef since 1958.

The opening of the luxurious Meridien and Sofitel Rio Palace hotels in the 1970s gave Copacabana's gastronomic pretensions a further shot in the arm as each hotel inaugurated restaurants which would be the pride of any city in the world, including Paris.

The restaurants in question are the **Saint Honoré**, under the direction of Paul Bocuse, in the Meridien, and the **Pré Catelan**, under the direction of Gaston Lenotre, in the Sofitel Rio Palace. Bocuse and Lenotre are both living legends within French culinary circles.

Copacabana does not, however, only cater to the top end of the market, although it is fair to note that the vast majority of Copacabana restaurants are of excellent quality, and three restaurants at the **Leme** end of the beach deserve a special mention.

Mariu's, at Avenida Atlântica 290, is one of the city's most popular restaurants and is generally agreed to be Rio's best *churrascaria rodizio*.

A *churrascaria rodizio* is a barbecue house with a difference. The difference is that the waiters bring to the table every imaginable type of barbecued meat, set off by a vast array of accompaniments, many of which are peculiar to Brazil. And the waiters keep bringing the meat until the diner screams for mercy. Eating without thinking, they say. *Rodizios* offer extraordinary value for your money and are therefore popular with residents and visitors alike. Wherever a line of people is seen wait-

Left, **Copacabana's** **sidewalk** **cafés are an** **attraction at** **all hours of** **the day and** **night.**

ing to get into a restaurant the chances are that the restaurant is a *rodizio*. Other *rodizios* in Copacabana include **Carretão** and the **Palace**.

Located along the beach from Mariu's is **Le Fiorentina**, which although not as in vogue as a decade ago, is still a popular bohemian watering hole where a table of artists and actors is likely to be found at any time of the day or night.

On the road behind is another bohemian haunt, though bohemian is hardly an accurate description of the clientele of this hole-in-the-wall entery called **Shirley**. Shirley's cuisine, a mix of Spanish and seafood, has been well considered for decades and the clientele invariably includes a number of ex-cabinet ministers and a *carioca* socialite or two.

Many of the restaurants and bars of Copacabana are the equivalent of the British pub in that they cater to their faithful clients who return again and again, the majority of whom live within a short walk of the restaurant.

Most *cariocas* eat late, 9pm still being considered early, and because of this, many of them choose to catch a movie before eating. After dinner, many *cariocas* will go on to the shows and nightclubs, which only start to warm up later in the evening. Because of the very nature of the residents of Copacabana, there is not one set area for entertainment, the restaurants, theaters and nightclubs being split democratically throughout the area's 109 streets.

Movies and theater shows: Copacabana has nine movie houses, most of which show first-run movies that retain their original soundtracks, with Portuguese subtitles added. Copacabana's mainstream cinemas include the **Roxy** and **Copacabana** while the best place to see arthouse movies is considered to be **Estaçâo Cinema 1**.

Live theater is also popular in Rio and Copacabana offers one of the city's best selections of live drama, the standard of which is extremely high. Virtually all the plays are in Portuguese and the vast

Strippers liven up the night.

majority feature Brazil's top actors and actresses, many of whom are known internationally for their work in Brazilian films. It comes as no surprise that Brazil often features in the prizewinning titles at international film festivals, from Cannes to Berlin.

Copacabana used to be the site of the majority of the traditional "tourist" shows, but since the beginning of the 1980s these have moved on to **Leblon**. Today Copacabana theater concentrates on live shows which appeal to the local residents and those visitors who want to discover the real Brazil.

In Botafogo through the Tunel Novo you will find **Terraço Rio Sul**, located inside the Rio Sul shopping mall. This is the best place to see Brazil's stars of tomorrow. Nearby **Canecâo** is one of Rio's most important showhouses offering the best of national and international attractions.

Artists who play Canecão can last for one show or six months, although in recent years Canecão has even managed to stage three different shows in one night, the first show starting at seven in the evening, the next at nine-thirty, and the final attraction going on stage around midnight.

In Rio, Canecâo's only real competitor is **Metropolitan** in Barra de Tijuca. In Copacabana there is competition from the **Golden Room** and **Rio Jazz Club** where the atmosphere is more intimate but the shows less spectacular.

More intimate shows are the domain of the hotels, with the **Rond Point** jazz bar in the Meridien and the **Horse's Neck** of the Sofitel Rio Palace dominating. The hotels also dominate Copacabana's nightclub and discotheque scene, including **Studio C** of the Othon Palace and the **Meridien**'s private club.

Copacabana's most famous discotheque, one of the largest and most modern in Latin America, is **Help**, a landmark in its own right in the center of the beachfront which also holds its own lively Carnival ball. Quite ➡ *120*,

A NIGHT ON THE TOWN

As the sun begins to set behind the buildings of Copacabana, the thoughts of visitors and residents alike start to turn to the evening, an evening which can be well spent in Copacabana without one's ever having to move to another neighborhood in Rio.

But even as the sun sets, a visitor should be on the move if he wants to fit a full program of events together.

For the first-time visitor to Rio, a few basic tips: dress comfortably and casually; *cariocas* are avowed enemies of formal wear, even at their most chic restaurants and bars. So, if you're not relaxed – chill out. Copacabana at night is a fascinating mix of cultures and types; don't be concerned with the wayward figures along the sidewalks – the beggars, street vendors and prostitutes – they are all part of the show.

Pre-dinner drinks can be taken at many varying locations. For the sheer splendor of its views across the open bay to the far coast at Niterói, a table by the swimming pool of the **Sofitel Rio Palace** hotel is an excellent choice. In the early evening, visitors can have a drink and watch the sun at play on the far-off islands and coastline.

The bar at the top of the **Othon Palace** is another popular choice and gives a full panorama of Copacabana's famous mosaic pavements. From the top of the Othon Palace, it becomes clear that there is some sanity in the madness of the patterns below.

At ground level, any **beachfront bar** is an equally suitable choice. They all offer the opportunity to observe the resident Copacabana population at play, as many of the residents stay on at the beachfront bars for dinner. Among the best bars on the beachfront are **Cabral**, **Lucas**, **La Fiorentina**, and the fish restaurants of **Principe** and **Real**, at the Leme end of the beach. The swimming pool area of the **Copacabana Palace** is also a delightful place at street level to sip *caipirinhas*, Brazil's national drink, as day turns to night and a cloak of darkness envelops Copacabana.

For dinner there is a wealth of options available – but not before 8pm at the earliest, please, as most *cariocas* traditionally eat late. The most popular time for dinner is 10pm.

At the top end of the market are **Le Bec Fin** (traditional), **Le Pré Catelan** in the Sofitel Rio Palace, and **Le Saint Honoré** (cuisine with a view) in the Meridien, all of which are outstanding French restaurants. The restaurant of the **Ouro Verde Hotel** is more international in its tastes and offers a *crêpes suzette* that has survived the test of time, whilst **Enotria** serves gourmet Italian.

For serious carnivores, Copacabana offers **Pérgula** in the Copacabana Palace and **Café de la Paix**, the pavement *brasserie* of the Meridien, as well as three barbecue houses that keep bringing the barbecue cuts until the diner

Convivial piano bars, a mainstay of Copacabana nightlife.

begs for mercy. No visit to Rio would be complete without a meal at **Mariu's**, **Carretão** or the **Palace**.

Moenda in the **Trocadero Hotel** is a good choice, while for seafood, Copacabana and Leme offer **Shirley's**, **Principe**, **Real** and the **Marisqueira**. The best choice, however, is **Grottammare**, which sits between Copacabana and Ipanema.

After dinner, it may be just the time to catch that movie or play or return to the beachfront bars as the more raunchy aspects of Copacabana and Rio's nightlife start to emerge.

The girls at play can be observed at the bars which stretch from **Bolero** up to the Meridien, with the popular and lively favorite being **Mabs**, located on the corner of Av. Prado Junior and Av. Atlântica.

For the boys, there is a wealth of choice available between the bars around the **Alaska Gallery** located at the other end of the beach. Erotic nightclubs start to fill around midnight and carry on through daybreak or at least until enough

The night, for cariocas, starts late and runs until morning.

customers have been catered for. Rio also has a lively gay scene. One of its long-standing bars is **Le Ball**, at the Ipanema end of Copacabana, on Travessa Cristiano Lacorte.

For the more up-market, catch some jazz or Brazilian music in the **Round Point** of the Meridien or **Horse's Neck** of the Sofitel Rio Palace. Both hotels, along with the Othon Palace, have their own chic private nightclubs.

Copacabana's bars, beachfront or otherwise, stay open very late, most until 3am or later, with some like **Bolero** staying open for that final late night *chopp* (beer) until 6am. Rio is truly a city that never sleeps.

If the night has gone particularly well, you may still be around to see the sun rise. If this is the case, the direction to head for is any of the major hotels which offer the delights of the tropical fruits at their breakfast table. The best suggestions are the Meridien's **Café de la Paix** or the pool areas of the Copacabana Palace and Sofitel Rio Palace Hotel. ■

recently Help has begun to attract some of Copacabana's abundant crop of young and very beautiful prostitutes. Tourists should be aware that not all of the disco's attractive habituées are there just to enjoy dancing.

Under the same roof as Help is **Sobre As Ondas**, which offers music and dancing at a more sedate pace, a formula which is followed at **Vinicius**, located above the Churrascaria Copacabana.

At the other end of the scale is the slightly insalubrious **Crepusculo de Cubatão**. Partly owned by British train robber Ronald Biggs – Brazil's most famous refugee – Crepusculo plays live rock music and stays open and active from late evening to early morning all through the week.

There are three other discos worth a visit in Copacabana. **Noise/After** draws a rock and rap crowd while **Mariuzinn** attracts fans of seventies and eighties hits. **Fun Club** inside Rio Sul in Botafogo is a good alternative if you want an evening with food and dance among the beautiful and successful. The hottest bar is the **Blue Angel**, a second home for intellectuals, radicals and gays. If you want to make friends with *cariocas* this is the place for you.

Rio's best red light district: Copacabana would not be Copacabana, however, without its red light district, the best in Rio, if not Brazil, which has gained international fame without the notoriety of Bangkok. The red light district splits its activity with geographical precision between the heterosexual to the east of the beach and gay to the west.

The heterosexual bars and clubs spread through the back roads of Copacabana, stretching from behind the Hotel Lancaster up to the Meridien. As Brazil is the world's largest Catholic country, the "shop fronts" remain discreet, only the names giving any hint of what lies behind.

The **Pussy Cat**, **Erotika**, **Swing**, **Don Juan**, **New Munich** and **Frank's Bar** are all to be found in the area and all offer some version of an erotic show and, for the clients, what are generally

accepted to be some of the most beautiful prostitutes in the world.

The gay community has three meeting points in Copacabana. One is based around the bars and clubs of **Galeria Alaska**. Another is one of the small bars along the beach, the one in front of Copacabana Hotel called **Arco-Iris** (rainbow). **Le Boy** is the most popular gay disco in the city.

Copacabana offers entertainment and relaxation that appeal to every taste and budget and offers it seven nights a week, 52 weeks of the year. The streets, bars and restaurants come alive around 9pm and carry on through until the early morning hours. Most restaurants take orders as late as 2am, a time when the bars and clubs are just starting to warm up. The majority of the clientele are the residents of Rio de Janeiro and most of them will have to get up early the next morning and go into the office, where they start to plan the night ahead.

Life is too short for *cariocas* to have only one Saturday night a week.

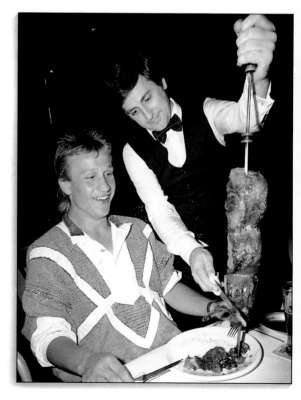

Left, meat is sliced from the skewer right onto your plate at a *churrascaria*. **Right**, samba dancer in a Rio nightclub.

Rio de Janeiro has been taking visitors' breaths away since Portuguese explorer, André Gonçalves 'discovered' it in 1502. Charles Darwin wrote during a visit in 1823, "Guanabara Bay exceeds in its magnificence everything the European has seen in his native land."

Rio's landscape has changed considerably since, yet much of the magnificence which impressed Darwin remains and can be spied from strategic points scattered around the city.

Rio's views can be classified into three categories: classic, out of the way and *very* out of the way (vistas for adventurers with time on their hands).

Classic views: Among classic views, there is nothing quite like the panorama from the top of **Sugarloaf Mountain**. It's all there – the vast curve of **Copacabana Beach**, the perfect curl of **Botafogo**, the **Rio-Niterói Bridge**, and, on clear days, the jagged **Serra Fluminense** mountain peaks more than an hour's drive away.

As with many of Rio's classic sights, getting there is half the fun. But getting to the top of Sugarloaf may be carrying things too far. Visitors should be prepared for a heart-stopping, six-minute glide in swaying, glassed-in cable cars.

Rio's other "best view" is obtained from the commanding height of 2,340-foot (710-meter) Corcovado. Meaning "hunchback," Corcovado is the mountain pedestal of Rio's famed **"Christ the Redeemer" Statue**.

The best way to reach the summit is on the 2.3-mile (3.7-km) Corcovado Railroad, with trains leaving every 30 minutes from a quaint station in **Cosme Velho**. Tunnels of lush foliage and splendid views make the comfortable ride in modern coaches more scenic than a car trip.

Left, sunset behind the mountains of Rio's romantic lagoon.

The railway was originally carved out of Rio's mountainsides by engineer Pereira Passos in 1884. The first trains to chug up the mountain track were foreign-built steam engines. It was a dangerous, smelly and time-consuming trip. Then, in 1912, the Rio de Janeiro Tramway, Light and Power Company electrified the route and it became much more popular.

At the summit, visitors are greeted by a dizzying view which includes Sugarloaf, the southern beaches, swank residential districts and shimmering **Rodrigo de Freitas Lagoon**.

The Christ Statue presiding over the scene is 99 feet (30 meters) tall. The work of a team of artisans headed by French sculptor Paul Landowsky, it was completed in 1931. Behind is a network of sub-tropical jungle known as **Tijuca Forest**. It includes 60 miles (100 km) of narrow, two-lane roads featuring a number of spectacular look-out points.

Without doubt the best one is **Paineiras** just below the Christ statue. During the weekend the road that runs to Barra da Tijuca is closed to traffic and transforms into a big leisure area. The *cariocas* come here to jog, walk, meet friends and enjoy the extraordinary view and cool climate.

The **Mesa do Imperador** offers a high view of Rio framed by exuberant foliage. Visitors gaze straight down the spine of mountains leading to the poking head of Sugarloaf. Below is the sparkling Rodrigo de Freitas lagoon.

Another lookout point, **Vista Chinesa**, gives a low view of Rio – less breathtaking than Mesa do Imperador.

A third classic view on the Corcovado-Tijuca circuit is the **Dona Marta Belvedere**, on the road to the Corcovado summit. From an attractive patio, you can enjoy a wrap-around look at city, beaches and mountains. Straight ahead is a full view of Sugarloaf, surrounded by the blue basin of Botafogo.

Rio also offers classic views from less dramatic elevations (including sea level). Alfred Hitchcock, in his 1946

classic, *Notorious*, exploited Rio's romantic allure by having Cary Grant and Ingrid Bergman dine at twilight on a terrace in Copacabana. Roughly the same view can be obtained today standing at the corner of **avenidas Atlântica** and **Princesa Isabel**. Its counterpart – the south-to-north view of Copacabana with the nub of Sugarloaf rising in the background – is seen from the **Posto Seis** end of the beach. Pleasant bay cruises offer their own intriguing views. Cruise boats go as far as the **Cagarras Islands** for a front view of Rio's ocean beaches, with the city and hills floating majestically in the background.

In many cases, Rio's views are two-way. The view of the lagoon from Corcovado is spectacular but then so too is the view of Corcovado from the lagoon. In fact, the lagoon, a refreshing open space amidst the high rise apartments of Rio's south side, is one of Rio's best sites for extraordinary views.

From the avenue that surrounds the lagoon, you can see Corcovado, the Tijuca Forest, the **Dois Irmãos** Mountain at the end of Leblon beach and the distinctive flat top of Gávea Mountain. If this is not enough, there is always the lagoon, which day or night is a sight that never disappoints.

Directly inland from the lagoon is the **Jardim Botânico** neighborhood, whose streets offer the best vantage point for a head-on view of the sheer granite cliff of Corcovado.

Another haven for photographers and sightseers is the **São Conrado** neighborhood, home to Gavea Mountain. The drive along **Avenida Niemeyer** from Leblon to São Conrado clings to the cliffside, offering a unique view of Ipanema. The best, though, is saved for last when the road descends to São Conrado, and the neighborhood's beach with towering Gavea in the background comes into view. If this doesn't take your breath away, nothing will.

Rio's out-of-the-way views: Visitors seeking out-of-the-way views should head for the **Santa Teresa** trolley lines,

Left, the beach of São Conrado with the imposing Gávea Mountain in the back.

with cars leaving every few minutes from the **Petrobras Plaza**. The second trolley station offers a striking glimpse of **Guanabara Bay**, framed by quaint houses and rambling gardens. (Beware of camera thieves in the trolley cars.)

But the best Santa Teresa view is from the **Chácara do Céu** art museum on **Rua Martinho Nobre**. The expansive lawn behind the museum is a restful setting of fountains, flower beds and benches. At the edge of the lawn, visitors can peek through a frame of hedges and fluttering tree limbs to see the entire panorama of downtown Rio.

One of Rio's most interesting day trips is following the rugged coast road through the city's outer beaches, starting with **Recreio dos Bandeirantes**. The surf is stronger in Recreio than in Copacabana and sometimes shoves a shifting white fog of spray across the road. Between the mountains and the sea are shimmering, tree-lined lagoons.

From Recreio, the road climbs abruptly, revealing a series of spectacular seascapes as it curls around rocky ledges, descending first to **Prainha** and then to **Grumari**, a pair of tiny beaches nestled beneath verdant escarpments.

From Grumari an even older, more pock-marked road lumbers toward **Barra de Guaratiba**. Glimpses of Grumari down below reveal a Gauguin-like vision of virgin beach, the horseshoe of sand set off tantalizingly by green-clad hills. At the top of the rise, visitors are rewarded with another breathtaking view – the vast expanse of the Guaratiba flatlands and a limitless string of beach that is called **Restinga de Marambaia**.

An entirely different set of views awaits visitors to **Niterói**, the city across the bay from Rio. It starts with the ferry ride from Rio's **Praça XV**. The whole panorama of urban Rio, with its backdrop of green mountains, takes shape as the ferry leaves the pier.

Once in Niterói, the most noted views are from the city's bayside beaches,

Right: Vista Chinesa, another lookout point.

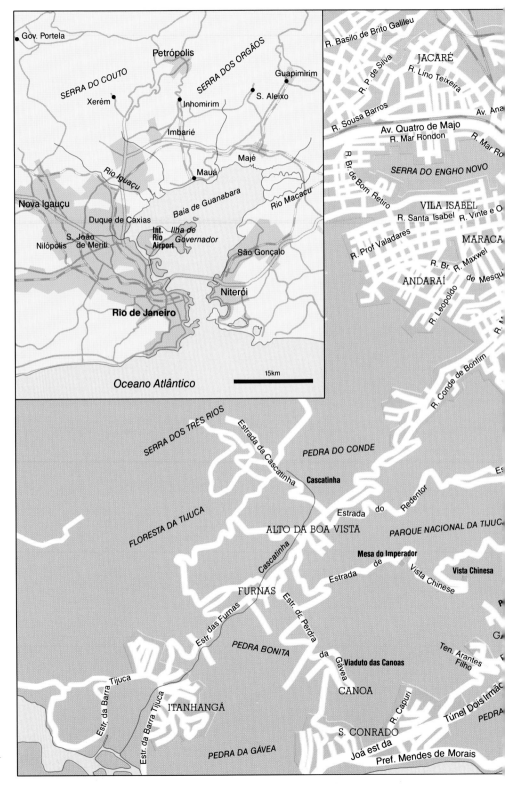

Gov. Portela

Petrópolis

SERRA DO COUTO

SERRA DOS ORGÃOS

Guapimirim

Xerém

Inhomirim

S. Aleixo

Imbarié

Majé

Rio Iguaçu

Mauá

Baia de Guanabara

Rio Macacu

Nova Igaçu

Duque de Cáxias

S. João de Meriti

Nilópolis

Int. Rio Airport

Ilha de Governador

São Gonçalo

Niterói

Rio de Janeiro

Oceano Atlântico

15km

R. Basilo de Brito Galileu

JACARÉ

R. P. de Silva

R. Lino Teixeira

Av. Ana

R. Sousa Barros

Av. Quatro de Majo

R. Mar Rondon

R. Mar Ro

R. Br. de Bom Retiro

SERRA DO ENGHO NOVO

VILA ISABEL

R. Santa Isabel

R. Vinte e O

R. Prof Valadares

MARACA

R. Br. Maxwel

ANDARAÍ

R. Br. de Mesqu

R. Leopoldo

R. Conde de Bonfim

SERRA DOS TRÊS RIOS

Estrada da Cascatinha

PEDRA DO CONDE

Cascatinha

Es

FLORESTA DA TIJUCA

Estrada do Redentor

ALTO DA BOA VISTA

PARQUE NACIONAL DA TIJUC

Cascatinha

Mesa do Imperador

Estrada de Vista Chinesa

Vista Chinesa

FURNAS

Estr. das Furnas

Estr. de Pedra da Gávea

PEDRA BONITA

Viaduto das Canoas

Ten. Arantes Filho

G

Estr. da Barra Tijuca

CANOA

ITANHANGÁ

R. Capuri

Túnel Dois Irmã

PEDRA

Estr. da Barra Tijuca

S. CONRADO

PEDRA DA GÁVEA

Joá est da

Pref. Mendes de Morais

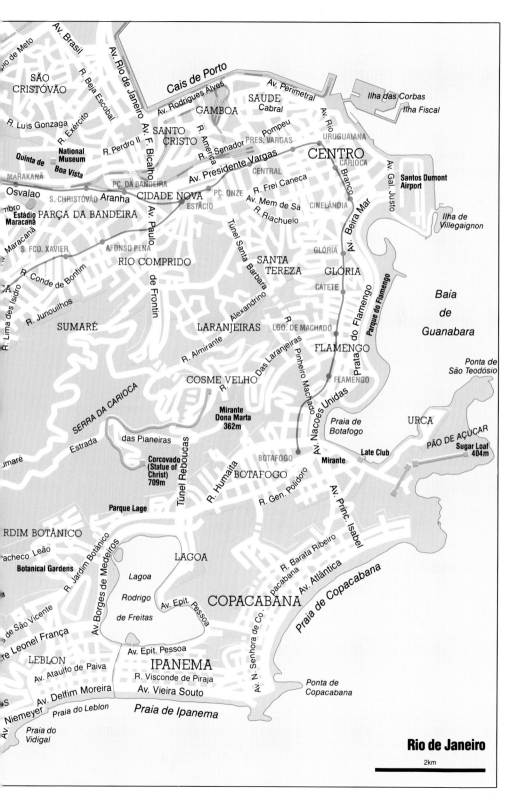

Rio de Janeiro

2km

beginning with narrow **Gragoatá**, about a mile from downtown. The same expansive front view of Rio can also be obtained from **Icarai** and **São Francisco**. Apartment buildings, traffic and numerous bars and restaurants make Icarai the mirror image of Copacabana.

Very out-of-the-way views: Visitors seeking Rio's *really* unusual views have plenty of options too, but should be prepared to expend their blood, sweat, toil and time. The **Niterói side of Guanabara Bay**, for example, includes a number of sweeping, rarely appreciated views. Continuing along the coast road beyond São Francisco, visitors reach Niterói's ocean-side beaches.

The well-known **Itaipu** is a long, low curve of sand separating the Atlantic from a pair of attractive lagoons. The best thing about Itaipu is the panorama of Rio across Guanabara Bay. The view embraces the entire city, from the flat top of **Pedra da Gávea** to the 3,370-foot (1,030-meter) height of **Pico da Tijuca**. An odd juxtaposition, with the southern part of Rio seeming to curve off to the west instead of the south. The effect is startling and majestic.

Backtracking a few miles along the main road leads to the turn-off for **Itaipu-açu**. Steep, winding **Estrada de Itaipu-açu** climbs through tropical forest until the summit is suddenly attained. This offers the same panoramic view of Rio as Itaipu , but is framed by the forest. Continuing on to the other side of the mountain, visitors encounter another view – the long, only partially developed beach of **Itaipu-açu** stretching toward the horizon.

Also on the Niterói side, near Gragoatá, intriguing **Boa Viagem** beach hides one of Guanabara Bay's finest "secret" views. Boa Viagem's tiny curve of sand is naturally decorated by outcroppings that look like meteorites. At the west end of the beach, across a

Right, the Dona Marta viewpoint, encompassing Botafogo, Sugarloaf, the Bay and Niterói.

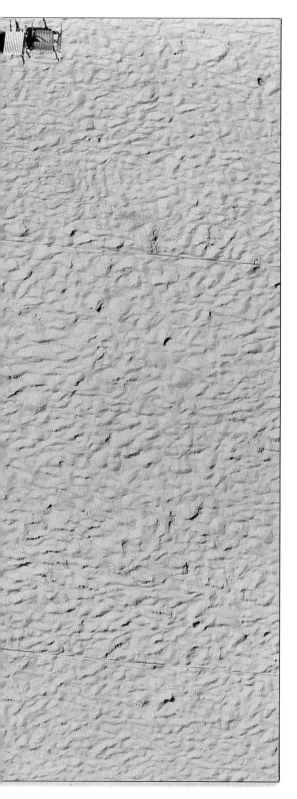

narrow footbridge, is the lush island of Boa Viagem, with its charming **Nossa Senhora dos Navegantes chapel**, dating from 1734. The iron gate at the footbridge is usually locked, so visiting Boa Viagem is risky. Visitors lucky enough to find a caretaker can hike up about 100 chipped, sloping steps to a small plaza gracing the rear of the church. The bright white walls of the chapel are striking and the view of Rio from the esplanade is spectacular.

For one of the most startling views of Rio you have to drive more than an hour on the **Rio-Teresópolis Highway**. A wide lookout point has been landscaped into the roadside near the turnoff for Teresópolis. On clear days it affords an awesome view of Guanabara Bay, embracing the entire watery basin from behind. The shiny surface seems to belly into a vast white puddle then funnel toward the narrow gates of the bay, guarded by Morro do Cão on the Niterói side, and Sugarloaf in Rio. The whole mountainous profile of Rio itself strikes off to the right, including Corcovado, Pedra da Gávea and Tijuca Peak.

Visitors may wish to sample one of Rio's most spectacular, but challenging views – the towering summit of **Tijuca Mountain**. The peak is located deep within the Tijuca Forest Reserve. Cars penetrate only to the **Bom Retiro** picnic ground. Then it's a two-mile hike along often poorly-marked trails to the mountain top. Average climbing time is about an hour and a quarter. The last few yards of the ascent follow a rocky path to Tijuca's round-head summit. Arriving at the peak is vertiginous. The tiny plateau towers above everything, even treetops of the forest below. Many climbers feel compelled to cling to the ground as soon as they attain the peak. But the view is well worth it, encompassing the city and its surroundings, dwarfing even Corcovado – the last, and best, view of one of the world's most beautiful cities.

<u>Left</u>, aerial view of a volleyball game.

IPANEMA

Ipanema is Rio's poshest, most cosmopolitan neighborhood, where international is "in" and Brazilian is "out." It is the gathering place of Rio's "beautiful people," of artists and intellectuals, the locale of chic discotheques, nightclubs, elegant and intimate restaurants, luxurious beachfront apartments, exclusive art galleries, fashionable boutiques and top cinemas and theaters.

The neighborhood's 65,000 residents live in an area stretching from the end of Copacabana at **Rua Bulhões de Carvalho** to the Dutch-like canal at **Jardim de Alah** (Allah's Garden), including a nook with strong waves at the Copacabana end called **Arpoador**.

Seen from above, along the scenic road that passes through the Tijuca Forest, Ipanema, its extension Leblon, and the **Rodrigo de Freitas Lagoon**, known to *cariocas* as the *lagoa*, all form a homogeneous unity of apartment buildings, tree-lined streets and wide expanses of water. This is the money belt of Rio, home to a mixture of traditional wealth and Rio's *nouveaux riches*.

Land development: Ipanema (a South-American Indian name meaning dangerous waters) began as an adventurous land development in 1894, marked by dirt tracks running through the sand dunes, with a handful of bungalows along the sides of the roads. Considered a distant outpost on the fringe of civilization, the neighborhood was mostly ignored until the 1950s, when the crush of Copacabana became too much for its well-to-do residents. Following the same path that had taken them from the bay neighborhoods to Copacabana, they carried on moving south, over to the next beach.

As Ipanema became increasingly prosperous and fashionable, its dirt roads gave way to paved streets and avenues, bungalows were replaced by the homes and apartments of the well-to-do and shopping arcades sprang up where sand dunes once sprawled.

From the 1950s to the present day, Ipanema has undergone an extraordinary real estate boom and population explosion. Its early homes were replaced first by four-story apartment buildings, some of which still survive, and since the 1960s, by a surging tide of high rises, gradually turning the Ipanema skyline into an updated version of Copacabana, but with one major difference: Ipanema property values are the highest in Brazil, with beachfront apartments fetching as much as and sometimes more than US$1 million.

For long-time residents of Ipanema, the neighborhood's steadily increasing population and building density are seen as crimes against humanity that they have vowed to fight. Forsaking the normal *carioca* attitude of what will be will be, the neighborhoods of Ipanema, Leblon, the lagoon and nearby Gávea and Jardim Botânico have launched Rio's first determined effort to preserve the city's natural and man-made charms. Such action is greatly welcomed in a city that is showing deep scars along some of its most treasured routes.

Wave of liberalism: That this should happen in Ipanema is not surprising. In the 1960s, the neighborhood was swept by a highly romanticized wave of liberalism that achieved international fame. Rio's bohemians and intellectuals gathered at Ipanema's sidewalk cafés and bars to philosophize over the movements of the decade – the hippies, rock and roll, the Beatles, drugs, long hair and free love.

Like their counterparts in the United States and Europe, Ipanema's long-haired youth were revolting against the values of their time.

Being centered in Ipanema, however, and not San Francisco or London, the movement quickly acquired a romantic strain. A muse was selected. She was Leila Diniz, a free-thinking and free-living actress who scandalized the still-traditional morals of Rio by expressing her independence and doing her own thing. Her own thing included being the first woman in Rio to wear a bikini while pregnant.

Diniz led the march of the Band of Ipanema, a Carnival street band, in celebration of this short but vibrant moment. Humor was present in a monthly satirical newspaper, *Pasquim*, which proudly announced the founding of the Independent Republic of Ipanema. At its highpoint, the citizens of the Republic were capable of such rousingly romantic acts as rising from the tables of a sidewalk café to applaud the setting of the sun.

Meeting places: The "capital" of the Republic was divided amongst three bars, the meeting places for intellectuals and other bohemians: the Zeppelin (home to the Band of Ipanema), Jangadeiros and Veloso, headquarters of a companion movement, Brazil's *bossa nova*. The guiding light of the *bossa nova*, and one of the Republic's favorite sons, was famed composer, Tom Jobim,

who took *The Girl from Ipanema* in song from the district's streets to Carnegie Hall. Looking back today, Jobim recalls this magical period with nostalgia.

"Ipanema used to be a paradise, one of the best places in the world. Against Paris, Rome and New York, I used to prefer Ipanema, always. Not because of man-made things but because of nature and beauty.

"The ocean on one side, the lagoon on the other. It had an abundance of fish, clean water and forest and you could see the mountains. To give you an idea of what Ipanema was, when I first brought my song to the United States of America I had to fight to maintain my title because no one knew where or what Ipanema was.

"One year later came the tourists and the hotels. Because of *The Girl from Ipanema*, I was once stopped on the street by a furious guy who said I was responsible for rents skyrocketing in the neighborhood!"

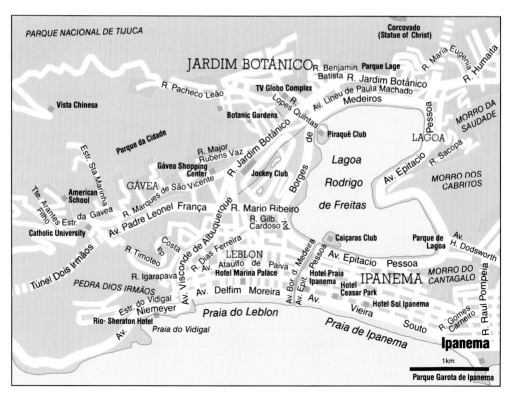

This mystical blend of Camelot and Haight Ashbury received a severe blow with the 1964 military coup and a subsequent crackdown on liberals in 1968. Particularly affected was the nation's most liberal neighborhood and its left-leaning bohemians; many were driven into exile. With this, as writer Heloisa Hollanda remembers, "The neighborhood lost its innocence ... a crisis came and the party ended." The final blow came in 1972, when Leila Diniz, muse of the Republic of Ipanema, died in a plane accident.

Modern spirit: Despite its brevity, this period defined the modern *carioca* spirit – irreverent, independent and decidedly liberal towards matters of the flesh and spirit. It also propelled Ipanema into the vanguard in determining *carioca* style, pushing Copacabana back into a second class status. In a fad-conscious city, the fads of Rio usually begin and end in Ipanema.

Today, Ipanema is the center of chic and sophistication. If it's not "in" in Ipanema then it's simply not "in." Rio's most fashionable boutiques line the streets of Ipanema and Leblon. Separated only by a canal, these two neighborhoods have different names but an increasingly shared identity. The apartments that line beachfront **Avenida Vieira Souto** and its continuation, **Delfim Moreira**, are the most treasured and disputed in Rio.

The beach itself is of similar length to Copacabana, though a bit narrower. At the Copacabana end, **Arpoador** is famed for its surfing and its view. Passionate *cariocas* claim that the best ending to a long night out is to watch the beautiful sunrise from Arpoador, looking out at the crashing waves as early-rising fishermen cast their lines into the sea.

Imposing mountain: At the far end, standing sentinel is the imposing **Dois Irmãos (Two Brothers) Mountain**, which sets off one of Rio's most spectacular natural settings. In the morning, joggers and cyclists fill the side-walk while exercise classes go ➡ *140*

Ipanema's popularity is attested to by the invasion of high-rises in the neighborhood.

THE GIRL FROM IPANEMA

Tall and tan and young and lovely, the girl from Ipanema goes walking, and when she passes, each one she passes goes 'ahhh ... '

In the mid-1960s, that lyric and the mellow, romantic music that carried it exploded on the music scene, immortalized by the tenor sax of Stan Getz and the sultry voice of Brazilian singer Astrud Gilberto. Now a pop classic, *The Girl from Ipanema* was the first big hit to emerge from the *bossa nova* movement of Brazilian singers and composers. The song put Brazilian popular music on the map and brought instant fame to composer Tom Jobim and lyricist/poet Vinicius de Moraes.

But what about the girl, or was there ever a "girl from Ipanema"? There was indeed, and as a matter of fact there still is. The song and lyrics were inspired in 1962 by the beauty of a 14-year-old girl called Heloisa Pinheiro. A schoolgirl,

Helo regularly sauntered past the Veloso Bar sidewalk café on Montenegro Street in Ipanema on her way home from school. Looking on, enchanted, were Jobim and Moraes, two of Rio de Janeiro's more famous bohemians.

After several weeks of religiously following Helo's daily passage, the two felt sufficiently inspired to turn out the song that made them world famous. Today, the street has been renamed after the poet Moraes, and the bar is appropriately called **A Garota de Ipanema** (The Girl from Ipanema).

Looking back with a smile, Helo today is still strikingly beautiful. She attributes her immortalization to "being at the right place at the right time." Other observers, however, most notably Jobim himself, insist that the 14-year old Helo represented *the* image of the stunning Rio beauty. Jobim says of Helo: "She had long golden hair, these bright green eyes that shone at you and a fantastic figure. Let's just say she had everything in the right place."

Composer Tom Jobim with the original girl from Ipanema, Helo (left) and her daughter.

The impact on Helo of the song she inspired the Jobim-Moraes team to write was immediate: "One day a Brazilian journalist told me a song had been inspired by me – I couldn't believe it. Before I knew it, I was being interviewed and appearing in magazines and this is still going on. I was glad to be chosen but I must admit I didn't realize at that time what this meant."

The fame of being the girl from Ipanema eventually lured Helo into a career in modeling and television, where she appeared in Brazilian soap operas and hosted women's programs. Now in her fifties, Helo became a successful businesswoman, owning with her husband a stereo shop called Ipanema Som (Ipanema Sound) and a modeling agency in São Paulo, where this most famous girl from Ipanema now lives.

The mother of a son and three daughters, Helo is proud of the fact that her eldest daughter, Kiki, was also once the Girl from Ipanema, having won the title in a 1986 Rio beauty contest.

By the time of his death in 1994, composer Jobim had become a world-renowned tunesmith. His songs have been recorded by everyone from Frank Sinatra to Sarah Vaughan, and with his own youthful family group he appeared regularly at international stops such as Carnegie Hall.

Moraes, who studied law in Rio and English literature at Oxford, died in 1980. He wrote reams of romantic poems and the lyrics for numerous songs including the score for the film, Black Orpheus (1959). However, none of his subsequent works ever matched the success of The Girl from Ipanema.

And today, when Heloisa Pinheiro passes, do the men still go 'ahhh'?

Helo says: "Sometimes, I'll be walking down the street and somebody will come up behind me and start whistling or singing the song. It's very flattering and I still get a kick out of it, even after all these years. It's a beautiful song from a beautiful era when love was something really romantic." ∎

'ahhh ... ' those beauties from Ipanema.

through their gyrations on the beach. During the day, the golden youth of Rio frequent the beach and waters. Befitting its image of free-spirited youth and daring, Ipanema is virtually the only beach where women go topless, although not many do.

Palm trees add to the special, intimate setting of Ipanema, which faces offshore islands of the Cagarras chain. At sunset, the sidewalk is crowded with lovers of all ages, walking hand in hand through the golden light of day's end, a timeless ebb and flow that continues into the evening's darkness.

Less boisterous and rambunctious than the beachfront of Copacabana, Ipanema preserves the romance of Rio de Janeiro more than any of the city's 23 other beaches.

For more practical pursuits, such as shopping and eating, Ipanema is also in a class of its own. Until shopping centers began to flourish, the neighborhood boutiques and shops were practically the only options for Rio's discriminating shoppers. The high quality of their goods, however, still attracts a significant portion of the city's well-heeled clientele. Ipanema's elegant boutiques also remain the favorite choices of the neighborhood's residents, who are happy to enjoy the ease of shopping close to home.

The Hippie Fair: A modern tradition of Ipanema is the **Hippie Fair**, on Sundays at **Praça General Osório**, from 9am to 6pm. Started in 1975, the fair is now less hippie and more sophisticated. But it is still a pleasant, open-air bazaar of Brazilian handicrafts where natives and tourists mix easily.

As befits the wealth of its residents, Ipanema has also become Rio de Janeiro's jewelry center. The block of **Rua Visconde de Pirajá**, between **Rua Garcia d'Avila** and **Rua Anibal Mendonça**, is one of the world's leading centers of fine jewelry.

Located here are the headquarters of **H. Stern**, Brazil's top-ranked jeweler and one of the most respected in the world. On the same block are branches of **Amsterdam Sauer** and **Roditi**, numbers two and three respectively, plus the stores of four other rivals, making a total of seven jewelers on one block. During the peak summer season, hundreds of foreign tourists are ushered each day to this street in buses chartered by the jewelry chains.

Unlike Copacabana, Ipanema's nightlife is not dominated by beach hotels, of which the neighborhood has only a few. In its entire extension, the Ipanema-Leblon beach has only five hotels and three beachside bars, a far cry from Copacabana. Ipanema, however, does have one of the city's finest hotels, the **Caesar Park**, favored by business travelers.

Famed for its service, the hotel also offers two of Ipanema's better restaurants, the **Mariko**, considered Rio's finest Japanese restaurant, and the **Petronius**, an elegant dining option serving international cuisine. On Saturdays, the Caesar Park puts out what

A family outing in Rio's Botanical Garden.

aficionados consider to be one of the city's top *feijoadas* and on Sundays, the hotel serves unbeatable *cozido*, a traditional Brazilian dish that is a mouth-watering combination of pork tenderloin, sausages and vegetables simmered for hours, to capture each disparate taste and accompanied by a wide variety of delicious sauces.

It is beyond the beach, though, that the art of good eating is most evident in Ipanema. There are fast food outlets for a quick hamburger, croissant, crêpe or pizza, in addition to fruit juice bars and ice-cream parlors.

For meat eaters, the **Porcão**, Rua Barão da Torre 218, is one of Rio's premier steak houses, serving up as much as you can eat via the popular *rodizio* system.

An Ipanema landmark is the **Lord Jim Pub**, Rua Paul Redfern 63, an authentic English pub. The pub is a favorite watering hole for Rio's foreign community and is the only restaurant in town that offers fish and chips and Yorkshire pudding as well as darts. The neighborhood's real fame, though, is as the home of intimate, sophisticated restaurants.

The **Caligula** nightclub at Rua Prudente de Morais 129 is a popular choice among *cariocas* for dining and disco or relaxed conversation around the piano bar. **Satiricon**, Rua Barão da Torre 192: an attractive and reasonably-priced choice for excellent seafood. As Rio's trend setter, Ipanema usually is the site of the city's latest "in" restaurant; one of these is **Sushinaka**, Avenida Epitácio Pessoa 1484, reflecting the current vogue for Japanese food. **Esplanada Grill** on Rua Barão da Torre 600 is another popular place. **Yemanjá**, Rua Visconde de Pirajá 128-A is one of the best restaurants if you want to try Bahia food. Be careful with the "pimenta" pepper. Another excellent restaurant is **L'Arlecchino**, Rua Prudente de Morais 1387, which serves Italian food from Emilia-Romagna, and is favoured by artistic types and advertising executives.

Sipping beer at an outdoor café.

Rive Gauche, Avenida Epitácio Pessoa 1484: one of a select few of Ipanema's restaurants located along the shores of the beautiful Rodrigo de Freitas lagoon. Traditional French cuisine, an intimate setting, live music and a spectacular view. Downstairs is the **Biblos Bar**, one of the few singles bars in Rio.

Antonino, Avenida Epitácio Pessoa 1244: another perfect combination of high quality cuisine (international) with a romantic view.

Several cafés in Ipanema have been a tremendous success among the *cariocas*. **Café Felice** sells outstanding sandwiches and ice-cream. **Le Panetier** is a bakery with a delicatessen and an elegant café. At **Armazén do Café** you will find the best coffee in Rio. **Letras & Expressões** is a book shop and on the second floor you will find the 24-hour **Café Ubaldo**.

Leblon: Neighboring **Leblon** is, like Ipanema, a largely residential neighborhood, with highrise apartment buildings extending up the side of Dois Irmãos

mountain. While it doesn't possess the extensive shopping areas of Ipanema, Leblon is home to the **Rio Design Center** (119 Avenida Afranio de Melo Franco), where the latest in furniture and decorative design is on display.

Traditionally a quiet neighborhood, Leblon has recently begun to kick up its heels. Two of Rio's best nightclubs among tourists, **Scala** and **Plataforma Um**, are now located in Leblon. Both of them offer samba shows by the city's most eye-catching showgirls. Scala (divided into two theater clubs) also offers top Brazilian and international singers and is the venue for some of Rio's liveliest balls during Carnival.

Leblon has also made its contributions to the impressive dining map of Rio. **Florentino** is a restaurant-bar favored by Rio's new money set, and is found at Avenida General San Martin 1227; **Antiquarius**, at Rua Aristides Espinola 19, is an elegant and expensive Portuguese restaurant that specializes in cod (*bacalhau*) dishes.

Left, cold beer on a hot day. <u>Below</u>, an Ipanema artist.

Garcia & Rodrigues has a café, delicatessen, excellent wine cellar, kitchen utensils shop, and also one of the most popular restaurants in Leblon – so it's advisable to reserve in advance. **Carpaccio & Cia** (which now also has a branch in Ipanema) has more then 50 different *carpaccios* to try.

Hangouts for the young: The Dois Irmãos end of Leblon, called **Baixa Leblon**, is a hangout for Rio's restless youth. Their favorite places to pass the night include the **Luna Bar** (Farme De Amoedo 52) and **Alvaro's** (500 Avenida Ataulfo de Paiva, closes at 2am). The area is filled with other small bars and restaurants. On summer nights and weekends its streets and sidewalks overflow with young people who come from throughout Rio for the action.

Another enclave for the young has taken hold at Ipanema's **Praça Nossa Senhora da Paz**. The streets surrounding this public square are packed on weekends by cars, dune buggies and motorcycles as well as with the action-oriented youth of the south zone. If you want to eat cheaply **Pizza Palace** is a wise choice. Besides pizza and pasta it has seafood and traditional Portuguese dishes. **Bofetada UP** has a crowed bar and restaurant and also offers shows.

At **Provisório** you can relax in the bar or have dinner in the restaurant before the disco starts at 10pm. Rio's most private club, **Hippopotamus**, is also at the plaza.

Following the highrises inland, you will uncover another timeless symbol of Rio's romantic side, the **lagoon**. More than any of the city's other beautiful settings, the lagoon has acquired a social function. Thanks to the lagoon's refreshing presence, this one-and-a-half sq mile (2,500 sq meter) space has been saved from the onward march of apartment buildings. This tranquil and open expanse of water provides a vital breathing space for the high-density south beaches of Rio.

A natural lake, originally part of a 16th-century sugar plantation, the la-

A novel approach to tandem sunbathing.

goon has proven to be a dogged survivor. Numerous attempts, some partially successful, have been made to fill it in. The lagoon today is roughly one third its original size, but with the passage of years, **Lagoa Rodrigo de Freitas** has become a sacred appendage of Ipanema and the surrounding neighborhoods. The residents of the beautiful apartments that ring the lake consider it their personal shrine, a sort of *carioca* holy place whose beauty they defend with maximum passion and energy. Their latest victory ended the practice of dumping untreated sewage into the lagoon, thus removing a stench that was at times unbearable, and bringing back the fish. The *lagoa* has generated a lifestyle of its own, dedicated to the outdoors and nature.

Mountain scenery: Around its winding shore, joggers, walkers and cyclists beat a steady path, inspired by the very finest of Rio's mountain scenery – Corcovado and the rich green tapestry of the Tijuca Forest, Dois Irmãos Mountain and the distant flat top of Gávea Mountain.

From sunrise to sunset, the colors of sky, water and mountains shift and change, sometimes forming solid blues, grays and greens, then splitting into rainbow streaks or suddenly breaking into shapes and colors. In the mornings, lines form to play tennis on one of the lagoon's public courts.

In the afternoons, the wealthy and near wealthy gather at the private clubs on the shores of the lagoon. At night, an endless stream of cars forms a ribbon of light around the *lagoa*, home to many of Rio's most famous restaurants and bars such as the **Bar da Lagoa**, known for its insulting waiters (a tradition of the house) and **Chiko's Bar**, an "in" spot for drinks and romance. On weekends, picnickers frequent the lagoon or stroll through the **Catacumba Park** across the street, the former site of one of Rio's largest hillside slums.

Botanical garden: On the Corcovado side of the lagoon, close to the mountain, is Rio's **Botanical Garden**, on Rua Jardim Botanico, an area of 350 acres (140 hectares) containing some 135,000 plants and trees which represent over 5,000 species. Created by Portuguese prince regent Dom João VI in 1808, the garden was used to encourage the introduction into Brazil of varieties of plants and trees from other parts of the world. At its entrance is a double row of 134 royal palms, a soaring, majestic avenue planted in 1842.

Nature is also the theme at the **Parque da Cidade**, 116 acres (47 hectares) of relaxing greenery in neighboring **Gávea**. On its spacious grounds is the **Museu Histórico do Rio De Janeiro** (City Historical Museum) with photographs, maps and exhibitions reviewing the birth and growth of Rio de Janeiro.

Another landmark of Gávea is the city's 19th-century race track, called simply **Jockey** (Praça Santos Dumont 31). Races are held on Saturday and Sunday afternoons and on Monday and Thursday evenings.

Left, afternoon concert in Parque da Catacumba. Right, street sweeper with an ear for music.

SÃO CONRADO AND THE BARRA

South of Ipanema are the outlying beaches, the most isolated and therefore the most unspoiled of Rio. The first, **São Conrado**, rests in an idyllic natural amphitheater, surrounded on three sides by thickly forested mountains and hills including the **Gávea Mountain**, a massive block of granite more impressive in shape and size than Sugarloaf. Closing the circle on this small, enclosed valley is the São Conrado beach which is popular among the affluent youth of Rio.

São Conrado can be reached from Ipanema by a tunnel underneath Dois Irmãos Mountain, but a far more interesting route is **Avenida Niemeyer**, an engineering marvel completed in 1917. The avenue hugs the mountain's cliffs from the end of Leblon to São Conrado. At times you will be looking straight down into the sea, with striking vistas of the ocean and Ipanema if you look back. The best view is saved for the end, where the avenue descends to São Conrado and suddenly, the ocean, beach and the towering presence of Gávea come into view.

Vidigal: On the cliff side of Avenida Niemeyer is the neighborhood of Vidigal, an eclectic mix of rich and poor, where the mountainside homes of the former have been slowly surrounded by the advancing shacks of the Vidigal *favela*, one of Rio's largest shantytowns. On the ocean side of the avenue is the Sheraton Hotel, one of only two resort hotels in Rio. Although access to beaches is guaranteed by law in Rio, the Sheraton's imposing presence, which encompasses the entire width of Vidigal beach, gives it the added distinction of being the city's only hotel with a *de facto* private beach. Unlike the hotels of Copacabana and Ipanema, the Sheraton

<u>Left</u>: soaring over São Conrado.

and its fellow resort hotel, the Inter-Continental located down the road in São Conrado, are blessed with ample space. This has permitted the construction of large swimming pools as well as lighted tennis courts, both of which are rarities at Rio hotels. The two hotels also boast excellent dining and two top-rated nightclubs, making them the center of nightlife for this area of Rio.

São Conrado: Space, and the absence of the crush of Copacabana and Ipanema, are the main factors that separate the outlying beaches from their better-known neighbors. While compact in area, São Conrado has an uncrowded openness guaranteed by the 18-hole Gávea Golf Course which runs through its middle.

A sugar plantation during colonial times, São Conrado remained largely undeveloped until the 1960s, when the construction of the Nacional Hotel on its beach finally brought a spurt of development to the neighborhood. By then, however, the golf course was already in place as were dozens of elegant homes that surrounded the links, thus limiting area available for apartments. Of the original plantation, the main house and its spectacular grounds, known collectively as **Vila Riso**, are still intact and open to visitors.

One of Rio's more exclusive addresses, São Conrado is also a near perfect microcosm of Rio society. On the valley floor live middle and upper middle class *cariocas* in sometimes luxurious apartments, homes and condominium complexes which line the beach front and flank the golf course. The links' privileged location makes it one of the most beautiful in the world and adds to the dominating presence of green in São Conrado.

But as lush as São Conrado is, its beauty is marred by a swath cut out of the hillside vegetation, where **Rocinha**, Brazil's largest *favela* spreads like a blight across the mountain from top to bottom. In this swarming anthill made of narrow alleys and streets, over 80,000

The Barra da Tijuca, Rio's high-growth area.

people live (some estimates are double this), most of them in tumble-down brick houses and shacks, pressed tightly together side-by-side.

Hang gliders: At the end of São Conrado, a highway surges past the massive Gávea, a point where hang gliders soar overhead preparing for their landings on the beach to the left. On the right, another road climbs up the mountainside leading to the takeoff point for the bird men of Rio. This same road leads back to the Tijuca Forest and Corcovado, passing through the thick tropical forest and providing memorable views of the beaches below. For visitors who wish to experience a tandem hang glide, call the Rio Hang Gliders Association at 322-0266 or ask at your hotel.

Barra Da Tijuca: From São Conrado, an elevated roadway continues on to the far southern beaches, twisting along the sharply vertical cliffs where the mansions of the rich hang suspended at precarious angles. Emerging from a tunnel, you suddenly find yourself face to face with the **Barra da Tijuca**, Rio's current high-growth area for the middle class. Low rises and homes fill most of its streets, with a growing army of high rises shooting up along the beachfront. The Barra, as it is called, is where Rio's largest shopping center is located, a phenomenon that has succeeded in capturing the imagination of *carioca* consumers.

The settlement of Barra da Tijuca began officially in 1624, when the area was presented as a land grant to a Portuguese nobleman. At the time composed primarily of marshland (the name Tijuca supposedly means marshy area and was given to the region by African slaves), it was largely ignored by its first and subsequent owners. Its only early claim to fame was the result of an attempt by a French pirate in 1710 to attack Rio by surprise, landing first in the Barra and proceeding overland to strike the city from behind. His scheme, however, failed.

Suburbia, Rio style.

In the 19th century, the Barra was divided into small farms and continued to develop unnoticed by the rest of Rio until the 1960s, when the construction of new roads improved access to the area. Since then, the Barra has enjoyed a rapid if rather disorganized expansion. It is only lately that it has acquired the basic services necessary for its full development.

But despite its growth problems, the Barra is where Rio's most recent large-scale expansion has occurred, for *cariocas* and tourists alike. Mirroring the development of Ipanema and Leblon in the 1970s and 80s, the Barra has seen early low-rise seafront developments swept away by the encroaching army of high-rise developments. It even sports its own shopping center, called **Barra Shopping**, which is the biggest shopping center in South America.

Longest beach: The Barra beach, running for 11 miles (18 km), is Rio's longest and during the week its quietest. On weekends, it fills up with bumper to bumper traffic on the beach drive, Avenida **Sernambetiba**. The beach is now attracting the tourism trade, and several buildings along Sernambetiba have been converted to apart-hotels, one and two-bedroom apartments with kitchens that are rented as rooms. Most are let at rates well below those of comparable hotels in Copacabana, Ipanema and São Conrado. Several of these apart-hotels are part of condominium complexes, providing guests with access to swimming pools, tennis courts, saunas and exercise centers.

The condominiums themselves are proof of the *cariocas'* growing desire to escape the urban crush that has claimed the city's more traditional residential areas. In the Barra, there is room to park your car, take walks, cultivate gardens and engage in a multitude of leisure activities not permitted by the closed-in living conditions in Copacabana and Ipanema. The epitome of what has been dubbed the Barra lifestyle is the condominium, many of them huge complexes

Forested hills surround Grumari Beach.

of highrise apartments and carefully landscaped homes.

What has been missing in the Barra has been an active nightlife but this too, is changing. In recent years, several excellent restaurants have opened up along the beachfront avenue and near the Barra Shopping Center. Highly regarded Barra restaurants include: **Royal Grill**, the Rio branch of one of São Paulo's top steak houses. It is virtually unbeatable for the quality of its charbroiled sizzling steaks, and is located at **Casa Shopping**, an attractive Barra da Tijuca shopping mall that specializes in home furnishings; **Porcão**, a *rodizio* all-you-can-eat steak house, at Avenida Armando Lombardi 591 is very "in"; **Le Petit Paris** is an excellent and unpretentious French restaurant, at Avenida Sernambetiba 6250; **Nino**, part of a chain of businessmen's restaurants serves good food (international cuisine) in a serious, businesslike setting at Avenida Sernambetiba 330; on the same street at No 1596 is **Café do Gol**, owned by the famous football player Romário, a popular soccer-theme restaurant, bar and nightclub specializing in international cuisine. **La Mole**, another chain restaurant that has set up a successful Barra branch, serves Italian food, including pizzas, for a more than reasonable price, at Rua Armando Lombardi 175; another good pizza place is **Gattobarra** in the Via Park shopping center.

Guimas is a very successful restaurant located in the São Conrado Fashion Mall shopping center and famed for excellent international cuisine and, allegedly, the best desserts in Rio. Also located in the Mall is **Sushi Garden**, a good choice for Japanese food. **Alfredo di Roma** is a nice Italian restaurant in the Intercontinental Hotel, open for dinner only.

This area of Rio has also become home to the fast food revolution which established its first foothold in the Barra, led by McDonald's, which is present at the Barra Shopping Center.

Real estate boom in the Barra.

Discotheques, small bars and samba clubs have also invaded the Barra. **Forest Rio Art Club** is the unlikely mixture of a disco, restaurant, cinema, art gallery, whiskey bar, cigar shop and solarium. **Greenwich Village Art Beer** has a disco, shows, sushi bar and a high-class restaurant. **West Side** is a bar and disco where the young and beautiful meet. If you want to dance to Brazilian music or attend shows given by the most popular bands of the moment, **Ilha dos Pescadores** is the best choice.

The **Metropolitan** is a big show house. It is one of the most important places for international and national entertainment events in Rio. Besides popular singers and bands it also has ballet, cabaret, circus and classical concerts. Also recently opened is **Terra Encantada** (Enchanted Land), the first theme park in Rio and expected to be the 'Brazilian Orlando'. The park has taken its inspiration from the three main influences in the creation of the Brazilian nation: African culture; indigenous culture and European culture. The park occupies 75 acres (30 hectares) and has 30 attractions, the best ones taken from the top parks in the world. All rides close at 10pm when the park turns into a great festival with restaurants, bars and shows.

The Barra's trailers: The Barra's answer to Copacabana's sidewalk cafes, nondescript trailers sell cold drinks and hot food during the day to bathers, but on weekend nights they become convivial meeting points for couples and singles. Large crowds gather around the more popular trailers (called *quiosques* or *barracas*), some of which are converted at night into samba centers or *pagodes*. Originally confined to backyards in the city's lower class northern neighborhoods, *pagodes* were no more than samba sing-alongs where musicians, professional and amateur, engaged in midnight jam sessions. In the move to the affluent south zone of Rio, the *pagodes* have maintained their purist samba qualities but have acquired

Roadside vendor offers live crabs.

commercial overtones, becoming in effect open-air samba bars.

Romance and the Barra have a more palpable connection in an area where dozens of motels have sprung up over the years. In Rio, as throughout Brazil, motels are for lovers and rooms are rented out by the hour, replete with such facilities as saunas, whirlpools, and ceiling mirrors. Some of the Barra's love centers outshine Rio's five-star hotels in luxury and sheer indulgence.

Originally aimed at providing young couples with privacy for romantic encounters, as Brazil's youth tend to live with their families until they are married, the motels have retained this function and added another – serving as meeting places for adult love affairs as well. Because of this need for secrecy, the Barra's motels are usually well concealed behind high walls with private garages for each room to protect guests from inquisitive eyes and unfortunate chance encounters with the wrong person.

Recreio Dos Bandeirantes: At the end of the Barra is the **Recreio dos Bandeirantes**, a small beach with a natural breakwater creating the effect of a quiet bay. From Recreio, the road climbs sharply along the mountainside and descends to **Prainha**, a beach popular among surfers, and then to **Grumari**, a marvelously isolated beach where part of the movie *Blame It on Rio* was filmed.

From Grumari, a narrow, pot-holed road climbs seemingly straight up the hill, from the top of which visitors have another of Rio's unforgettable views, the expanse of the **Guaratiba flatlands** and a long sliver of beach stretching off into the distance, the **Restinga de Marambaia**, an army property that is off limits to bathers.

Down the hill is **Pedra da Guaratiba**, a quaint fishing village that beckons with the best seafood restaurants of Rio – **Candido's**, **Tia Palmira** and **Quatro Sete Meia** — perfect places to take a leisurely two-hour lunch to round off an exhilarating day trip.

Seafood repast at Candido's restaurant in Pedra de Guaratiba.

PETRÓPOLIS

Home is where the inheritance is. The pastel hues and green gardens of **Petrópolis** and **Teresópolis** – Rio de Janeiro's mountain retreats – are the nation's 19th-century imperial inheritance, the material traces left by independent Brazil's first rulers, Emperors Pedro I and Pedro II.

Petrópolis: Petrópolis, especially, is like a warm, antique-cluttered, ancestral home. It could be a village of grandmothers. Rio de Janeiro State's leading mountain resort and fourth largest commercial center, Petrópolis is chiefly a monument to Pedro II, emperor of Brazil from 1831 until his exile in 1889 (he died in France two years later). Pedro II's 58-year reign put him in a longevity class with the likes of England's Victoria and France's Louis XIV.

Petrópolis was first envisioned in the 1830s by Emperor Pedro I, who purchased land in the spectacular *Serra Fluminense* for what was to be a summer palace. But it was his son, Pedro II, who actually built the palace and the quaint town surrounding it, starting in the 1840s. The idea was to maintain a refreshing refuge from Rio's wilting summer heat.

Pedro II: Petrópolis, like all good sightseeing experiences, is as much a state of mind as it is a collection of buildings and natural settings. And that state of mind, like nearly everything about its founder, is friendly, human and modest. Pedro II was a rarity in human history – a wise, scholarly and diplomatic king. During his more than half a century on the Bragança throne, Brazil remained comparatively peaceful and prosperous while most of its neighbors seethed with civil strife or settled into austere poverty. During the American Civil War, President Abraham Lincoln told intimates the only man in the world he trusted to arbitrate between North and South was Pedro II of Brazil.

Petrópolis is not as august as its European counterparts. But Brazilians are justifiably proud of the humanity of their kings rather than their grandeur.

Scenic ride from Rio: The city is only 40 miles (65 km) from Rio. The **Rio-Petrópolis Highway** is a marvel of modern engineering. Its concrete bridges soar over the green valleys and the road curves around the mountain walls revealing vistas that seem like aerial photography. From sea level in Rio, the highway reaches 2,750 feet (840 meters) during an approximately hour-and-a-quarter jaunt.

On the way, visitors can still glimpse traces of the old **Petrópolis Highway**, a perilous cobbled affair that once kept royal road workers busy the year round with repairs. The imperial road is still in use today but only for the intrepid. The one-hour climb up the mountains provides a rare sensation of stepping back into history. The road, though, for most of the way is wide enough for only one car at a time.

Streets of Petrópolis: The medium-sized city has a population of 270,000 people, who earn their living mainly as factory workers and shopkeepers. It is centered around two busy streets, **Rua do Imperador** and **Rua 15 de Novembro**, the only part of town with buildings over five stories high. The two thoroughfares are divided by a waterway and aged shady trees that shed their leaves in autumn. Temperatures in Petrópolis are lower than in Rio and the sweater and jacket-clad inhabitants of the city give it an autumnal air during the cool months.

Perpendicular to Rua do Imperador is the city's lush boulevard of kings, **Avenida 7 de Setembro**. The avenue is divided by a slow-moving canal and by shady trees that intertwine with the bushy foliage of the nearby **imperial park**. Its surface is partially cobbled and horse-drawn carriages which are available for rent by the hour form an old-fashioned taxi stand on its sun-dappled stones.

Left, a refreshing bloom of wildflowers on a mountainside near Petrópolis.

The area around the **Summer Palace**, which is now called the **Museu Imperial**, is crowded with tropical and temperate climate trees and shrubs and is criss-crossed by carefully kept pathways. The emperor was fond of Brazil's flora, which are still richly exhibited in the royal gardens.

The rose-colored palace, fronting onto Avenida 7 de Setembro, is modest for a royal dwelling. Everything seems antique. On the topaz esplanade in front of the mansion stands an old-fashioned newsstand. An aged, colorfully uniformed functionary is stationed within. He is selling ... what else could he sell? ... antique news in the form of historical society bulletins with learned articles and quaint photos relating to the royal family.

Imperial museum: The palace was converted into a museum in 1943. (Opening hours are noon to 5pm, Tuesday through Sunday.) Visitors are asked to don felt slippers and must pad gingerly over the gleaming *jacarandá* and brazilwood

floors. The museum's modest furnishings attest to the bourgeois character of its builder, Pedro II, who ordered construction to begin in 1845 (work was completed 10 years later), while its second floor collection of kingly personal artifacts, including a telescope and a telephone, is a reminder of Pedro's scientific dabbling.

The palace's wood-panelled chambers are inviting, the furnishings rich but not extravagant. Among items of interest are the **crown jewels** – a glistening frame of 77 pearls and 639 diamonds – and the colorful robes and cloaks of the emperor's ceremonial wardrobe, including a cape of bright Amazon toucan feathers. Royal photographs on the second floor show, however, that Brazil's second king felt more at home in conservative suits than in flowing robes.

The second floor exhibits also contain a reconstructed throne room. Its uncomfortable royal couch, more like a fixture from a luxurious bathroom than

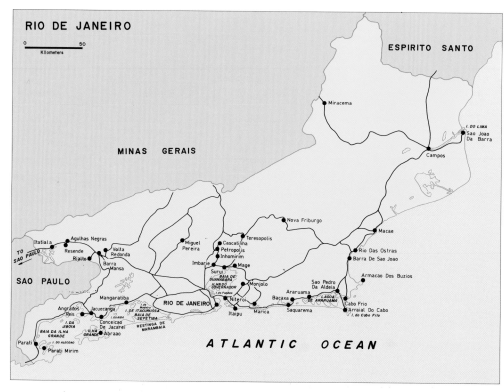

a chair fit for man or beast, is overbearing. Pedro II much preferred the small, intimately furnished office at the rear of the room. Its desk, chairs and gleaming telephone could be the furnishings of a 19th-century telegraph office. It was from this room that Pedro II ruled Brazil six months of the year.

Residence of Dom Pedro's heirs: Across the square from the palace is the former royal guesthouse, now the residence of Dom Pedro's heirs. And the king is in. At least, he is in most of the time. Dom Pedro de Orleans e Bragança, Pedro II's great-grandson, is the home's owner and chief symbol of monarchism in Brazil. Although the house is closed to the public, Dom Pedro himself can sometimes be seen walking in the square chatting with local residents and, occasionally, tourists.

A few blocks up Avenida 7 de Setembro is the French Gothic-style **Catedral de São Pedro de Alcântara**. Begun in 1884, the imposing structure was only finished 55 years later. The bodies of

Pedro II, his wife Tereza, his daughter Isabel and her husband the Count of Eu, were interred in the partially completed cathedral in 1925. The four were principals in Brazil's late 19th-century royal drama. The emperor and his family were expelled from Brazil in 1889 after a military coup. They died in European exile. His daughter and son-in-law survived until the early 1920s but never returned to Brazil. Finally, in 1925, the Brazilian government permitted descendants to bring the bodies back to Petrópolis for burial in the magnificent cathedral which had been built for precisely that purpose.

From the cathedral, a web of tree-shaded, cobbled streets spreads into residential Petrópolis. The city is delightful for its rose-colored homes (including many which were once the dwellings of members of the royal family), its numerous overgrown private gardens and public parks and the simple beauty of its streets, which once brought a royal flush of pride to the city's earnest creator.

Dedo de Deus (Finger of God) mountain as seen from Teresópolis.

A few blocks beyond the cathedral, on **Rua Alfredo Pachá**, is the 1879 **Crystal Palace**, a glass-and-iron frame still used for gardening and art exhibits. The palace was built almost entirely of panels shipped from France. Its style is similar to that of other overly decorated Victorian pavilions that were once popular in Europe, and it is a marvel of solar heating, rainbow colors and acoustics. A pair of fountains in the adjacent garden send spray more than 20 feet (6 meters) into the air.

A few blocks from the Crystal Palace, on the **Catholic University** campus, is the unusual, slightly spooky **Santos Dumont House**.

Santos Dumont: Alberto Santos Dumont, credited by Brazilians and many Europeans as inventor of the airplane, lived in the strange abode, which he himself designed, from 1918 until his death at age 59 in 1932. Scion of wealthy Franco-Brazilian landowners, Santos Dumont moved to Paris at the age of 17 in 1891 to study engineering, and stayed there for 20 years. It was there, in 1906, he made the first fully-documented flight in a heavier-than-air machine. (The Wright Brothers had made an earlier flight – at Kitty Hawk, North Carolina, in 1903 – but they had only produced documentation for the flight in 1908.)

Santos Dumont's home, now a museum, is a reminder of his eccentricity. The house has only one room. Santos Dumont used no tables, only shelves designed for various purposes, no staircases, no bed (he slept on top of a chest of drawers) and no kitchen. His meals were delivered by a local hotel. The house employs built-in, wide-step ladders, one of which leads to a loft where his unique bed is located. But the steps on the ladder entering the house are cut so that one side of each is missing. In this way the ladder obliges users "always to start off on the right hand side," which Santos Dumont regarded as a trick to good luck.

The inventor committed suicide at São Paulo's Santos beach resort after

The Imperial Museum, former residence of the king.

telling friends he was despondent over the use of the airplane in warfare.

Other attractions: Other Petrópolis attractions include the sprawling Normandy-style **Palácio Quitandinha**. Completed in 1945, the luxuriously appointed structure was designed to serve as Brazil's leading hotel-gambling complex. A few months after its inauguration, however, gambling was outlawed in Brazil by the Administration of President Eurico Dutra, and has remained so ever since.

Quitandinha never fully recovered. Today, the still striking complex, on the Rio-Petrópolis Highway 5 miles (8 km) from the main Petrópolis shopping area, is an expensive condominium-cum-social club. (Managers normally set aside a few rooms for hotel guests.)

Quitandinha's lobby, nightclub and ballrooms are vast, gleaming expanses that look like sets from extravagant Hollywood musicals of the 1930s. Like most things in Petrópolis, Quitandinha is a journey through time.

Five miles (8 km) from downtown Petrópolis, on **Rua Maestro Octávio Malul**, is the delightful **Florália nursery**. Pleasantly landscaped rose beds and a quaint tearoom help foster a refreshing away-from-it-all atmosphere. The nursery hosts an annual exposition of rare orchids.

Shopping: In downtown Petrópolis, on long, winding **Rua Tereza**, shoppers will find factory outlets for many of Petrópolis' more than 500 textile mills. Bargain hunters delight in excellent buys for everything from jeans and sweaters to children's clothing.

Other shopping highlights include decoration and hardwood furniture outlets on Avenida 15 de Novembro. Petrópolis is also an antique-hunter's paradise where you can find a dozen or so bric-à-brac-cluttered curiosity shops scattered around the downtown area. The most noted of these, **Solar Imperial** at Rodovia Filúvio Cerqueira Rodrigues 2km n.1945, tel: (024) 222-1537 (Tuesday to Saturday 9.30am–6pm) is so full

Emperor's tomb in the cathedral of Petrópolis.

of objets d'art that it could easily double as a museum.

A string of brightly-painted Italian cantinas, with names like Don Corleone and Falconi's, along the main shopping corridor, are intimate and inexpensive. A soda fountain in a five-and-dime store across the plaza from the Museu Imperial looks like small town USA *circa* 1940.

Teresópolis: The 33-mile (53-km) jaunt from Petrópolis to Teresópolis along steep mountain roads can be made in about one hour. The small towns and valleys of the Serra preserve a sleepy, 19th-century pace (as does the highway maintenance). Antique shops and furniture stores dot the road.

Teresópolis, named after Pedro II's wife the Empress Tereza Cristina, was planned in the 1880s but incorporated only in 1891, two years after the royal couple was exiled.

The picturesque town, 57 miles (92 km) from Rio on the broad Rio–**Teresópolis Highway**, clings to the edge of the *Serra Fluminense* at a bracing 2,960-foot (900-meter) elevation. Population is about 125,000.

Scenic views: Chief among scenic-view attractions are an encompassing, though distant view of Rio's **Guanabara Bay**, complete with the mountainous profile of Rio, and the city's proximity to spectacular **Serra dos Orgãos National Park**. The park, lovingly landscaped with broad lawns and old-fashioned masonry fountains and patios, is dominated by a ridge of sharp peaks, said to resemble organ pipes, from which the park got its name. The highest, **Pedra do Sino**, is 7,410 feet (2,260 meters) above sea level.

But the most striking summit, just below Pedra do Sino, is a rocky spike called **O Dedo de Deus** – The Finger of God (5551ft/1692m). On clear days, the chiseled profile of the Serra dos Orgãos can be seen from Rio itself.

Shopping, restaurants, hotels: Downtown Teresópolis, which occupies a narrow valley in the shadow of the

Banana trees blending in with the scenic rugged mountains of Petrópolis.

160

Serra, offers interesting shopping opportunities in elegant home furnishings, rugs and wall decorations. On Saturdays and Sundays, a handicraft fair is held downtown at the Praça Hygino da Silveina.

For residents of Rio, Teresópolis is a favorite stop for a long, hearty Brazilian lunch in the middle of a day-long drive through the mountains. The city's most famed restaurant is the **Taberna Alpina** at Rua Duque de Caxias 131. The Alpina is a convivial wood-panelled, Alpine-style beer hall serving sausages, sauerkraut and other German specialties, all washed down with cold beer.

Other popular places to eat are: the **Maison Louis**, down the street from the Alpina, which is famed for its fondues and steaks; the **Cantina Riviera Italiana**, at Praça Baltazar da Silveira 112, for traditional pastas and pizza; and the **Don Vito**, at Rua 1 de Agosto 432, another Italian restaurant but with a more exotic menu.

Teresópolis and environs are also home to several excellent resort hotels. The most traditional is the **Pinheiros Hotel**, a romantic, secluded honeymoon hotel (tel: 021-742 3052, fax: 021-742 4188). Located at the end of a bumpy country road, 4 miles (6 km) from downtown, the Pinheiros is noted for its near complete isolation. The grounds blend in with the surrounding forest and the hotel buildings – small, pink-pastel bungalows and mansion houses – are typical of imperial-era Brazilian architecture. The overall impression is one of tranquility and remoteness, as if visitors had stumbled *Through the Looking Glass* – an appropriate metaphor for Teresópolis itself.

Nova Friburgo: Continuing east from Teresópolis one comes to the city of **Nova Friburgo** (population 170,000), a Swiss outpost in the heart of the tropics. The city was founded in 1818, when Portuguese King Dom João VI, then living in exile in Brazil, authorized the immigration of 400 Swiss families from the canton of Freibourg. Upon arrival, the immigrants settled in the mountains and dubbed their new home Nova Friburgo or New Freibourg.

Today the city remembers its founders in the rich green of its flowering parks and the alpine architecture of many of its homes. Walks through the quiet city streets, long hikes through the forest and visits to nearby peaks and rock formations are the favorite pastimes of visitors to Friburgo.

Along the highway between Teresópolis and Nova Friburgo are many of the best hotels of the region. Several are known as *fazenda* hotels, literally farm hotels, a Brazilian phrase used to describe a mountain-style resort hotel with large gardens, trees and ample recreational facilities. The most sophisticated is the **Hotel-Fazenda Rosa dos Ventos**, a European-style hotel with tennis courts, horseback riding, saunas, a private forest reserve and international cuisine, the type of retreat that Pedro II could well have appreciated (tel: 021-742 8833, fax: 021-742 8174).

A long way to go – a salesman with his wares on the highway.

BÚZIOS AND THE SUN COAST

According to history books, Búzios was discovered by the Portuguese at the start of the 16th century. Locals, however, know better. Búzios was actually discovered in 1964, by Brigitte Bardot. Convinced by an Argentine friend to visit this tropical paradise, Brigitte spent two well-documented stays in Búzios, parading her famed bikini-clad torso along its unmatched beaches and in the process, spreading the fame of Búzios across the globe. The memory of Bardot has faded, but the town hasn't been the same since.

Búzios, or more correctly Armação dos Búzios, once was a tranquil fishing village fronting the lapping waters of a bay. After Bardot, however, it became a synonym for all that splendor in the tropics is supposed to be – unspoiled beaches, crystalline water, palm trees and coconuts, beautiful half-naked women and a relaxing, intoxicating lifestyle of careless ease beneath a caressing tropical sun.

What is amazing about Búzios is that all of this is true. It is one of a handful of super-hyped travel destinations that does not delude or disappoint. It is not as good as the posters. It is better.

The Sun Coast: Located 115 miles (190 km) to the east of Rio, along what is known as the Sun Coast (*Costa do Sol*), Búzios has been compared to the fabled island of Ibiza in Spain. It is a sophisticated, international resort that for most of the year manages to retain the air of a quiet fishing village. The exception is the high summer season, just before, during and right after Carnival when tranquil Búzios is overrun by tourists, its population of 10,000 swelling to 50,000.

For the remaining nine months of the year, Búzios is the type of beach town

Left: a fisherman casts his net at dusk.

that most travelers suspect exists only in their dreams. Unlike many of the popular resorts in Brazil, including Rio de Janeiro itself, Búzios has not lost control of its growth. The favorite retreat of Rio's social column set, Búzios has undergone a major real estate boom since the 1970s but fortunately, the city fathers have kept a firm hand on developers. Strict zoning laws limit building heights with the result that Búzios has escaped the highrise invasion that has scarred many Brazilian beaches.

The fashionable homes that dot the Búzios beachscape for the most part blend in with the picturesque fishing village. Many new arrivals have purchased homes from the fishermen. They remodel them completely on the inside while the outer shell looks no different from its neighbors.

The city has also, so far, been spared an onslaught of hotels. Most of the accommodations in Búzios are *pousadas* or inns, quaint and small with no more than a dozen rooms. The largest hotel occupies an island off the coast, the **Ilha Rasa**. The **Hotel nas Rocas** has only 70 rooms and an idyllic resort setting. Most guests are ferried across by boat but the hotel also has its own landing pad, if you prefer to fly in by helicopter. This in turn has helped preserve the relaxed atmosphere of the town and provides visitors with an intimate setting in which to enjoy the sun and beach.

The beaches: There are 23 beaches in the Búzios area, some fronting onto quiet coves and inlets and others, the open sea. The main distinction, though, is accessibility. Beaches close to the town, such as **Ossos**, especially beautiful at sunset, **Geriba** and **Ferradura**, are easily reached by foot or car.

Not surprisingly, the "best" beaches are those that require the most effort to reach; in the case of Búzios, either long hikes, sometimes over rocky ground, or a drive along a pot-holed dirt road. At the end of such efforts are treasures like **Tartaruga**, **Azeda** and **Azedinha**,

Chez Michou, popular Búzios night spot.

164

Brava and **Forno**, famed for their beautiful calm waters and equally beautiful topless bathers. As a general rule of thumb in Búzios, the greater a beach's isolation, the greater the nudity.

Visiting all of the beaches by land is not only tiring but unnecessary. The fishermen of Búzios have become part-time tour operators and tourists can rent boats by the hour or for the day for cruises along the beaches. Sailboats, as well as cars, dune buggies, bicycles, motorcycles and horses may be rented. Diving enthusiasts can also find equipment for rent.

A typical Búzios day begins late (no one wakes up before 11am) with a hearty breakfast, one of the treats of the inns of Búzios. Afterwards, the day centers around beach activities: bathing, long leisurely walks, and exploration of the more distant beaches. All of this is to be interrupted only by occasional breaks for fried shrimp or fresh oysters washed down with cold beer or *caipirinhas* (Brazil's national drink, composed of lime slices, ice and sugar-cane liquor.) For those who want shopping, there are fashionable boutiques along cobble-stoned **Rua José Bento Ribeiro Dantas**, better known as **Rua das Pedras**, or street of the stones, and also on **Rua Manuel Turibe de Farias**.

History: When Brazil was first 'discovered', Búzios, and most of the coastline of the state of Rio, was inhabited by the Tamoio Indians. The Indians later became the allies of French settlers who attempted to establish a colony in what is now the city of Rio de Janeiro. After being driven out, they fell back along the coast. With the help of their Indian allies, the French attacked ships from Rio on their way to Portugal with goods from the colony.

Finally, in 1617, the Portuguese were able to expel the French, and they eventually turned the area surrounding Búzios into a cattle raising region. From then until the second French incursion, the one led by Bardot, Búzios lived in splendid isolation.

Paddling in the sheltered waters of Búzios.

With the passage of years, however, the cattle ranches were replaced by banana plantations, and the banana crops were shipped from Buzios' fishing port to London in the 1930s. It was not until the end of World War II that a road between Rio and Búzios was completed and the *cariocas* were able to discover the beauty of the Búzios coastline.

At night, the bohemian spirit of Búzios takes charge. Though small in size, the city is considered the third best in Brazil for dining out. There are over 20 quality restaurants, some of which are rated among the country's finest. Gourmets have a wide choice, including Brazilian, Italian, French and Portuguese cuisine, as well as seafood and a local favorite – crêpes.

Le Streghe Búzios (Italian), **Au Cheval Blanc** (French) and **La Tropezienne** (French) are considered to be the best of Buzios' excellent restaurants. Other small restaurants are constantly popping up, many of them superb. Among the better ones are **Satiricon**, which specializes in Italian seafood dishes, and **Casa Velha. Don Juan** is a new Argentinian steakhouse with a good wine cellar. **Pátio Havana** is the "in" place for young people, a bar and restaurant with five separate areas – bistro, tobacco shop, whisky bar with billard tables and a patio.

Visitors should also try out the dining options presented by the *pousadas*, in particular the restaurant of the **Auberge l'Hermitage**. A word of caution: the bargain prices of Rio's restaurants are not to be found in Búzios.

After an inspiring meal, the in-crowd of Búzios gravitates to the city's bars, many of which have live entertainment. Bars, like restaurants in Búzios, are as famed for their owners as for what they offer. The town's numerous charms have waylaid dozens of foreign visitors since Bardot's first promenade. Brigitte left, but many others have stayed to open inns, restaurants and bars, providing Búzios with an international air. The Brazilian residents of Búzios have been

A schooner in the placid waters off Azeda Beach in Búzios.

joined by French, Swiss, Scandinavian and American expatriates, all vowing that they will never leave.

Amiable eccentrics: Among Búzios' amiable eccentrics and engaging drop-outs is the Belgian Madame Michou and her daughter Françoise Dominique Nys who together run **Chez Michou,** Buzios' chic *crêperie,* the place where the young crowd gathers at night. Bruce Henry, an American jazz musician, who owns the **Estalagem**, an inn with a popular restaurant and bar; and Matthew, a New Zealand mural painter who lives in a beachside cave. As can easily be surmised, there is no lack of subjects for after dinner conversation in Búzios.

If Búzios has a drawback, it is its distance from Rio and the state of the highway linking the two. However, there are direct buses which ply the route between Rio and Búzios bus station three times a day (tel: 024 623-2050.); the journey takes around 2½ hours.

There is a bus service to the city of Cabo Frio from where you can take a cab for the remaining 30-minute drive to Búzios. If it is by car, it is suggested that all driving be done during daylight hours because of the poor condition of the highway. It takes two and a half hours to drive from Búzios to Rio, but on summer weekends or during the holiday season it can take four hours or more in either direction.

There is, however, hope on the horizon for Búzios' transportation woes. In 1988, the city's small airport was enlarged and weekly service began between Búzios and Rio. The planes, with capacity for 20 passengers, make the trip twice a week, with extra flights on holidays and during peak season. While still not ideal, the air link is a giant step in the right direction. There are charter flights between Rio and Búzios. Contact Aeroporto Humberto Modiano (Búzios Airport), tel: 629-1229.

The individual behind the airport expansion is a Rio businessman who is currently investing in the construction of an ambitious, multi-million dollar

Praia do Forte Beach in Cabo Frio.

marina resort complex for Búzios. The project features man-made canals, a golf course and hotel, plus vacation homes. When it's completed, the marina will be Buzios' first large-scale international resort.

The lake region: Between Rio and Búzios are several beautiful beach areas, starting with what is known as the lake region, a series of lagoons separated from the sea by lengthy sand bars. The sea along this unbroken coastline east of Rio is marked by strong currents and large waves, making it a favorite area for surfers. Major surf competitions are held in **Saquarema**, one of the four beach resorts in the lake region. On the other side of the highway, on state road 106, the lagoons are popular spots for windsurfing.

Near **Maricá**, the first of these cities, is **Ponta Negra** beach, a spectacular, nearly deserted stretch of white sand and wild blue water. After Saquarema, are **Araruama** and **São Pedro d'Aldeia**, popular among *cariocas* during vacation periods

especially during Carnival, when the lake region's hotels and numerous campgrounds are filled till overflowing. Salt flats are also visible off the side of the road along this stretch, culminating in a large area of flats at Cabo Frio, which is officially the end of the lake region and the beginning of the Sun Coast. Located 15 miles (25 km) from Búzios, Cabo Frio is famed for the white, powdery sand of its beaches and its dunes. During vacation season, its population of 40,000 swells with *cariocas* on holiday.

Unlike Búzios, Cabo Frio is an historical city with ruins from the 17th century, including the 1616 **São Mateus Fort**, the 1666 **Nossa Senhora da Assunção Church** and the 1696 **Nossa Senhora dos Anjos Convent**.

Arraial do Cabo: Only 8 miles (14 km) from Cabo Frio is **Arraial do Cabo**, the most beautiful attraction of the Sun Coast next to Búzios. Arraial has yet to be discovered by the tourist trade and has only a handful of small and unimpressive hotels. Thus far, tourists have tended to prefer staying in Búzios and Cabo Frio, and making day trips to Arraial. What the area does have is the clearest water in southern Brazil, making it the preferred site for scuba divers and excellent for spear fishing. The city is located at the tip of a cape with a variety of beaches, some of them with quiet waters and a stunning lush green mountain backdrop, while others, the surfer beaches, are swept by strong winds driving the waves against the sand.

Off the coast is **Ilha do Farol**, site of a lighthouse but more famed for **Gruta Azul**, an underwater grotto with bright blue waters. The island, reached by boat, offers excellent views of the mainland.

Like its neighbor Búzios, Arraial began as a fishing village and is known still for the quality of fresh catches brought in each day. The fishermen of Arraial climb to the top of sand dunes, from where they look into the water below in search of schools of fish, a testimony to the unspoiled clarity of the waters of Arraial do Cabo.

Left, one of Búzios' idyllic *pousada* inns. **Right**, a proud local fisherman with his boat.

THE GREEN COAST

If you wish to get into the *carioca* way of making friends and turning a day at the beach into a festive occasion, stay in Copacabana and Ipanema. But if it's clean beaches with privacy that you're seeking, head south to the yet unspoiled **Costa Verde** (Green Coast).

Named for the dense vegetation that dominates the coastline and descends right down to the sea, the Costa Verde is nature at its best: a unique tropical mix of mountains, rainforest, beaches and islands. The green – in every imaginable shade – is everywhere, invading even the sea with a soft turquoise hue.

Coastal highway: Visiting the area is a must, and is both easy and enjoyable on coastal **Highway BR 101**, known locally as the **Rio-Santos**, for the two port cities it connects. The scenic drive compares with that down Spain's Costa Brava or California's State Road 1. At times, it appears as if you are going to take off, as the road rises high up a mountainside for a wide, unobstructed view, then drops and winds steeply down to the shoreline. The road passes fascinating, contrasting extremes: a national park, the country's only nuclear power plant, tourist resorts, fishing settlements, ocean vessels, tanking stations, cattle ranches, a shipyard, and **Paratí**, a quaint, colonial village.

The most popular attractions are, naturally enough, the beaches. Some are small, encased by rocky cliffs, with clear, tranquil lagoons. Others stretch uninterrupted for miles and are pounded by rough surf. The whole area is a haven for sports enthusiasts, offering everything from tennis, golf and boating to surfing, deep-sea fishing and diving.

So wrapped up are *cariocas* in their own city and Búzios, that it has only been in the past 10 years that they have

Preceding pages: a vacationer framed in a colonial window. **Left**, one of hundreds of secluded coves in Angra dos Reis.

begun to discover the Costa Verde. Now that word of the paradise is out, the area is undergoing rapid transformation. In most cases, too rapid. The Costa Verde is one of the last reserves of the Brazilian Atlantic rainforest. Sadly, only three percent of the forest survives in its original state.

Already, complete hills have been shaven clean, save the thick bush of the fertile valleys on the sides. In the next decade, if this exploitation of natural resources and reckless construction continue unchecked, the Green Coast may become the Bare Coast. But for the time being, the area is still a jewel, a finely polished emerald in the midst of the other sparkling treasures located in and around Rio.

The Costa Verde stretches from Rio southwest 160 miles (260 km) to the São Paulo state border. It is possible to visit the area and return the same day, but to see all the sights, explore the coast and enjoy the beauty, plan on a few days. The area houses some fine hotels and restau-

rants, even on some of the islands. A word of caution: if you're renting a car, don't drive at night. Not only do you miss all the scenery, but in the dark, the highway – with its sharp curves, unmarked shoulders and frequent and poorly-lit construction sites – can be very dangerous.

Schooner trips: After one leaves Rio on **Avenida das Americas** through **Barra** and **Recreio**, the highway turns inland past **Santa Cruz** and returns to the coast some 40 miles (65 km) later at **Itacuruçá** (pop. 3,500), where the Costa Verde really begins. From the town's harbor, schooners which hold up to 40 people leave every morning around 10am on one-day excursions to the nearby tropical islands (36 of them) in the surrounding **Sepetiba Bay**. The trips are good value and include a seafood lunch on one of the islands. Reservations can be made in advance through a local tourist agency.

The schooners stop at several islands such as **Martins**, **Itacuruçá** and **Jaguanum** to give passengers the chance to swim and snorkel. Some of

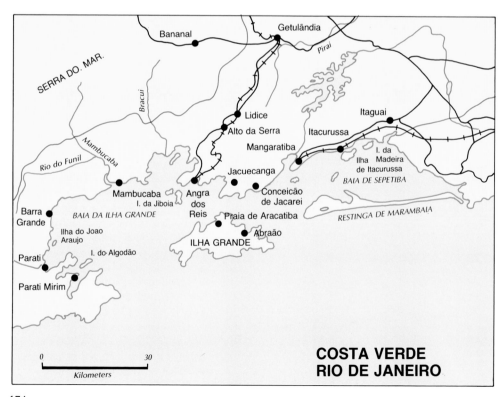

**COSTA VERDE
RIO DE JANEIRO**

the smaller islands (**Pombeba** and **Sororoca** are recommended) can be visited by hiring a boat and guide (usually a local fisherman) at the harbor. If you wish to stay overnight on one of the islands, there are several good hotels, including the **Hotel Ilha de Jaguanum** (235-2893) and the **Hotel do Pierre** (253-4102).

The highway continues past **Muriqui** to **Mangaratiba**, site of a new $40 million, 325-room **Club Méditerranée** (688-5050, toll free: 0800-213782). The scenery improves with each mile as you pass several fishing villages before coming to Verolme, a large shipyard. Here the sea is dotted with tankers waiting for repairs or to load up on oil and minerals from nearby storage plants.

Angra dos Reis: Around the bend from Verolme lies **Angra dos Reis** (King's Cove), the Costa Verde's largest city (population 90,000). The site was discovered only five days after Rio, in 1502, by the Portuguese explorer Andre Gonçalves. But it was only in 1556 that the first white settlers arrived to plant sugar cane. There is nothing beautiful or noteworthy about Angra other than perhaps, its churches, of which the most interesting is the convent of **São Bernardino de Sena** on the **Santo Antonio** hillside. Its original clock, the numerals of which were replaced with the 12 letters of the city's name still works.

People don't come to Angra just to tour the city or its churches. The city lies sprawled over several hills at the beginning of a 60-mile (100-km) long gulf. The Angra Gulf contains 365 islands, 2,000 beaches, seven bays and countless coves. The water is warm, clear and calm, a perfect sanctuary for marine life. Spearfishing along the rocky shores is a popular activity, as is fishing in deeper waters. The tourist information center, across from the bus station near the harbor, can provide you with maps and information on hotels and boat tours.

The best hotels in the area are run by the Frade Hotels Group and include the **Frade Portogalo Hotel** and **Hotel do**

The Santa Rita Church, a classic example of Brazilian baroque architecture.

Frade (369-2244). The hotels have their own bus service from Rio and a 90-foot (30-meter) schooner to visit the nearby islands. The Hotel do Frade also has a scenic 18-hole golf course where international tournaments are held every June and November.

Ilha Grande: Ninety minutes by boat from Angra is the paradise island of **Ilha Grande** (Large Island), a 115-sq. mile (300-sq. km) nature reserve blessed with spectacular fauna and flora and some of the country's most beautiful tropical beaches.

The cheapest way to get to the island is via ferry from Angra or Mangaratiba to **Abraão**, the island's only city. In Abraão you can rent small boats to visit the more distant beaches such as **Lopes Mendes, das Palmas** and **Saco do Ceu**. There are several campsites on the island, but few hotels, with a limited number of rooms. Try **Pousada Mar de Tranquilidade** in Abraão (024-365-3335) or **Pousada Canto Da Praia** (595-0940).

Twenty-five miles (40 km) past Angra and a few bends after the Hotel do Frade lies the country's only nuclear power plant, **Angra I**. Unfortunately, it is a source more of controversy than energy. Once a symbol of pride for the former military government that built it, it now stands as a great embarrassment, having cost six times more than the original $300 million estimate. Of the three planned reactors at Angra, only one has been completed, and it never seems to work. Brazilians have dubbed Angra I *vagalume* (lightning bug) since it has been turned on and off so often for repairs.

Shortly beyond the plant is one of the coast's most picturesque fishing villages, **Mambucaba**. The homes are built right on the beach and a large white church in the town center faces the sea.

As you approach the other end of the Angra Gulf, the mountains gradually recede and are replaced by grassy fields filled with grazing cattle and locals playing *futebol* (soccer).

Paratí: Some 60 miles (100 km) past Angra and a three and a half hours' drive from Rio, is **Paratí**, (pop. 27,000), a charming town of historical importance which in 1966 was named an international monument by UNESCO. Although it is hardly known outside Brazil, this living colonial museum is unique amongst the country's tourist attractions.

Paratí was founded in 1660 and acquired great importance in the 18th century as the port where gold, diamonds and precious stones from the state of Minas Gerais were shipped back to Portugal. Geographically, it served as the link between São Paulo and Rio. All roads between the country's two largest cities crossed at Paratí.

For over a century Paratí flourished and prospered into a city of great wealth with large mansions and estates. But after Brazil gained its independence in 1822, exports of gold and diamonds to the fatherland stopped and a new road was eventually built connecting Rio to

Left, a schooner trip on a tropical islands excursion. **Right**, colonial houses line the narrow streets of Paratí.

São Paulo directly. Paratí lost its strategic position and was forgotten and its colonial heritage was, consequently, preserved.

It is this traditional flavor, combined with the locals' friendliness, which leads visitors to fall in love with Paratí. The city embraces its visitors, seduces them, and if they're not careful, adopts them as well. Tourists come for a few hours and stay a weekend, others come for a short holiday and stay a month, a year, or a lifetime, becoming part of the city as it becomes a part of them.

Unlike Búzios, which has its well-established jet-set character, Paratí is still looking and, one hopes, always will be looking, for an identity. If today it's a fishing town, historical monument, tourist attraction, artist's gallery or hippie hangout, tomorrow it may be something totally different. But it will always be Paratí.

Even in its early days, Paratí was inhabited by diverse groups, as evidenced by the town's many churches, each of which was built for a different race: mulattos, blacks and whites. The first church to be completed, **Santa Rita de Cassia** (1722), is a classic example of Brazilian baroque architecture and also houses the **Museum of Sacred Art**. Next to it, in what was once the town's prison, is the tourist information office.

Colonial area: The best way to get a feel for Paratí is to walk around the colonial area. You don't have to watch out for cars as they are prohibited in this part of town, but be careful not to twist an ankle on the large uneven stones that make up the narrow roads. To test your balance even more thoroughly, the roads slope in towards the center to drain off heavy rains.

Another reason for taking your time is so that you can browse through the many galleries and handicraft stores, and peek politely through the doorways of the *pousadas* (inns) and homes. From the outside, they look like typical whitewashed Mediterranean houses with

Historical charm of Paratí – cobblestone streets and colonial buildings.

heavy wooden doors and shutters painted in bright colored trim. On the inside, however, they open up onto delicately landscaped courtyards decked out with ferns, orchids, rose bushes, violets and begonias. Two of the most beautiful gardens are in the **Pousada do Ouro** (both in the main hotel and across the street) and **Coxixo**. Across from the **Coxixo** is a pleasant and versatile open-air bar and restaurant, which also triples as an antique shop. The Frade Hotels Group runs a friendly *pousada* next door to the **Nossa Senhora dos Remedios Church**.

If you visit Paratí during a full moon, walk down to the port during high tide, but be sure to take your shoes off first as the rising sea floods the area. Locals claim this cleans the streets, but often, the dirt that is washed away is replaced by rotting seaweed.

Although Paratí is not famed for its beaches, schooners such as the 80-foot (24-meter) long Soberano da Costa make day trips to take visitors to the surrounding islands. Reservations can be made through your hotel or at port.

The old gold route: A very different type of excursion can be made by car to **Fazenda Muricana**, 5 minutes from Paratí on the old gold route up the hill to **Cunha**. The 17th-century ranch has something for everybody: a large zoo complete with wild cats, monkeys and rare birds, waterfalls to bathe in, a restaurant specializing in Brazilian country-home cooking, and an ancient but still operating *cachaça* (sugarcane wine) distillery, where you can sample and buy the 10 potent flavors made with different herbs and fruits.

Due south of Paratí is one of the Green Coast's most prized and carefully guarded treasures, the tiny fishing village of **Trindade**. Far from the high-rises of Rio, Trindade and its three spectacular beaches with clear waters and natural pools are an example of the best that the Green Coast has to offer up to visitors – isolation, relaxation and unspoiled tropical beauty.

Sampling the local brew.

Brazil's greatest symbol, appropriately, is not a thing but an event – Carnival. Carnival's sweet song penetrates the Brazilian soul at every level – even those who hate it are influenced by it – and it embraces every social class.

Carnival's influence on literature and art: Novelist Jorge Amado recognized this when he gave Carnival the highest honor by making it the title of one of his books – *País do Carnaval* (The Country of Carnival).

It has been an important theme in Brazilian literature for as long as it has been an important event in Brazilian life. Machado de Assis, founder of the Brazilian Academy of Letters, wrote about it in the 19th century. All the great poets make of it a metaphor for Brazil itself. Vinicius de Moraes placed it at the center of his lyric play *Orfeu Negro, Uma Tragedia Carioca* (Black Orpheus, A Carioca Tragedy), which audiences the world over know as the luminescent 1959 film *Black Orpheus.*

The turn-of-the-century poet, Olavo Bilac described the *carnavalesco,* or Carnival fanatic, eloquently: "He is a different person altogether, from another race. Those who merely love Carnival do not deserve the title, '*carnavalesco.*' The true fanatic is an individual who was born for Carnival and for Carnival alone. He lives for it; he counts the passing years according to the number of Carnivals he has celebrated; when he is about to die, he has only one regret – he will miss next year's Carnival and all the other Carnivals which will mark the life of Rio de Janeiro until the end of time."

A young Frenchman named Edouard Manet was deeply impressed by the many moods and colors of Carnival when he visited Rio in 1875. According to historian João Ribeiro, the French artist later confessed the

Preceding pages: Carnival madness provides stamina to dancers of all ages; green and pink, colors of the Mangueira Samba School; costumes cost anything from $200 up; member of percussion section. **Left,** anything goes!

images he recalled from Carnival influenced the development of Impressionism.

But it is a Brazilian writer, Isis Valeria, who probably captures the essence of Carnival best, in her short story, *Folião*. In her story, a suburban worker who has spent an entire year preparing for Carnival, dies at the moment his name is called out as winner of a costume competition: "He took his first steps, dragging behind him the weight of his costume, almost in a trance. He was in his glory. The crowd in the hall was at his feet. He fell before reaching the other side of the room. His face changed expression with the pain but his dentures, even in death, kept

thought, it comes from the Latin expression Carrum Novalis, a kind of festival float used by the Romans. Another says it comes from the Italian Carne Vale, meaning good-bye to meat, since Carnival marks the last days before the awesome abstinence of Lent. Still others say it means simply Festival de Carne.

Some kind of pre-Lenten observance has existed in Brazil for as long as the Portuguese have been here. But all the way up to the early 20th century that age-old tradition tended to emphasize pranksterism rather than celebration.

This particular aspect of Carnival observance was called *entrudo* and came to Brazil

grinning. He was carried out of the theater. Outside, he was surrounded by enthusiasts who unmindfully congratulated him on his victory." What a way to go.

European in origin: Although modern Rio boasts the most famous Carnival celebration in the world, Carnival's roots are European, going back all the way to Roman times. The ancient Romans had more than 100 festivals during their year, of which the most famous was the week-long Saturnalia, held at the end of December, a Carnival precursor.

Experts disagree over the origin of the word Carnival. According to one school of

directly from Portugal. *Entrudo* featured stink bombs, water balloons, mud balls and even arson as forms of entertainment. At least, it was entertainment for some. The rest of the population saw it as a public nuisance. Interestingly, many of the perpetrators were sons of the rich.

Entrudo got to be so bad that, by the mid-19th century, decent men and women spent the entire time before Lent locked up in their homes. The observance of *entrudo* was outlawed in 1853. But the ban was hard to enforce since the police were often among the most active perpetrators. It wasn't until the early 1900s that a strict enforcement campaign finally put an end to *entrudo*.

Modern Carnival is a class event. As with Roman or Renaissance Carnival, a temporary class inversion takes place. The poor dress up as royalty and strut in front of the rich, who come to the parades dressed in blue jeans. When class lines blur in Brazil, Carnival will begin to die.

Carnival balls for society's upper crust: Still, middle and upper class Brazilians do have their own special Carnival bailiwick – the fancy dress ball. These colorful events, today as in the 19th century, center around loud music and elaborate costumes.

were able to attract an elite crowd and thus charge more for attendance.

The first modern Carnival ball was the High Life, which premiered at a Copacabana hotel in 1908. The extremely formal City Ball was inaugurated in 1932, at the Teatro Municipal.

What Carnival means to the poor and the rich: The Carnival ball's purpose throughout history has been the same. Where the poorer classes seek to forget their poverty during the four days of Carnival, members of the middle and upper classes discard their inhibitions. A secondary purpose – and this one will never die – is to "appear" at the most

Carnival balls hit Rio in 1840 with a chic event at the Hotel Italia, at the site of what is now the São José Theater on Praça Tiradentes. The São Jose is now the site of an annual transvestite Carnival ball. However, the Italia ball lost money and it wasn't until 1846 that a second ball was held, this time in the upper-crust district of São Cristóvão. The São Cristóvão event was honored by the presence of royal guests, so the ball's sponsors

Left, clowns carrying balloons joining in the dazzling parade. **Above**, bare-breasted women are a thing of the past for parade floats.

fashionable balls. There are some socialites who attend so many of these events during the course of a single evening that they spend more time in the limousine going from place to place than on the dance floor.

For Rio's poor, music, dance and drink were, and still are, the main Carnival options. Crude musical instruments, simple but frenetic dance routines and popular music are still the basis of Carnival celebration in most parts of Rio.

How Carnival developed: A Portuguese immigrant named José Nogueira Paredes (dubbed Ze Pereira by revelers) is credited

with inventing the first Carnival club. One of his innovations was to get everybody in the club to play the exact same kind of drum, creating a powerful, unified sound, the basis for the modern samba school *bateria* or the percussion section.

The white working-class clubs were called *blocos* or *ranchos* and played European-origin ballads known as *choros*, many of which are still popular.

The late 19th century also saw the first involvement of blacks in Carnival. This was at least partly due to an 1877 drought in the Northeast which sent many *nordestinos*, including some freed black slaves, to Rio and São Paulo.

The former slaves brought their own brand of musical and dance traditions with them to the city's Carnival celebration. By the 1890s, black groups were marching around different parts of downtown during the four days of Carnival.

The most colorful event: Everyone agrees the most colorful event in Rio's contemporary Carnival is the main Samba School Parade, held on the Sunday and Monday nights of Carnival. Of all the Carnival events, the parade is the most African in its roots, especially when it comes to samba, Brazil's "national music," a composite of European folk influences and African techniques brought by the slaves.

The parade is also Carnival's most obviously class-oriented event. The samba schools, composed overwhelmingly of working and poor people from the city's sprawling suburbs, compete against one another for the most luxurious presentation. The socialites and businessmen who come to watch the parade are dressed in their designer jeans, although increasingly they too are taking part in the parade.

While Carnival is hundreds of years old, the parade is a 20th-century innovation. The very first samba school was called *Deixa Falar* (Let 'Em Talk) and was organized by the mainly black residents of Rio's Estacio district in 1928. (In honor of Estacio's con-

tribution to Carnival, the site of the annual parade was moved there in 1978.)

Deixa Falar paraded for the first time in the Carnival of 1929. Paraders followed no fixed route and weren't well organized. But their very size made them different from ordinary *ranchos* and *blocos*. And, unlike the other parading groups, *Deixa Falar* designed colorful costumes and clever dance routines.

Other black neighborhoods set up rival samba organizations almost immediately. During the 1930 Carnival, there were five such groups and so many spectators that police had to clear a special area around Praça Onze on the day of their parade.

Things became even more sophisticated when the *Mundo Esportivo* newspaper offered a prize to the best samba group in 1932. (By then the black-dominated Praça Onze parade groups had acquired the name "school," probably because local public schools let them practice on school grounds on the weekends before Carnival.) The 1932 prize went to Mangueira, one of the schools which first paraded in 1930.

By 1935, the samba parade had blossomed into one of the major Carnival events. In that year the city government paid a small subsidy to the largest schools and took ➡ 194

Left, massive parade floats tell part of the theme-story of the samba school. **Right**, participant in the Most Elaborate Costume contest.

So what does it actually feel like to samba in a Carnival parade? "It was so emotional," sigh *cariocas*. Which tells one as much about Brazilian values as it does about samba. To say something has the ability to stir emotions is the supreme *carioca* accolade. And nothing stirs a *carioca*'s emotions like the collective catharsis of Rio's Carnival parade.

The anticipation is a significant part of Carnival. It starts almost as soon as one

Inevitably, it has gone over budget, but you have no choice but to cough up or have nothing to wear at the biggest event of the Rio social calendar.

Months earlier, you provided the seamstress with measurements that would have impressed a Saville Row tailor – upper arm circumference, upper thigh and inside leg, calf, ankle, neck, length from top of shoulder to elbow and so on. But, inevitably, something just doesn't fit. You've got someone

Carnival is over, with the first rumors of the samba school's theme for the next. By mid-year the samba has been composed. By October, costume designs are off the drawing boards and the booklets of receipts for the monthly instalments printed. The simplest costume in a major samba school costs from US$200 upwards.

It's one of the golden rules of Carnival that anything and everything possible is left to the last moment. Seamstresses always promise to deliver costumes days in advance, but everyone knows they never do. You get your costume a few hours before the parade.

else's hat. The shoes are two sizes too large. Welcome to the run up to Carnival.

With just a few hours to go, a veil of surrealism descends upon Rio. Twenty thousand dancers dressed in gleaming costumes called *fantasias* – literally fantasies – converge on the *concentracāo*, the meeting point behind the grand parade avenue. Spangled kings squeeze through subway turnstiles, hoop-skirted elderly women in *Baianas* costumes sway on crowded suburban trains, flustered drivers seek parking spaces that simply don't exist, their tassels tangling with their gears, and feathered hats sticking out of their hatch-back. And one of the most magical sights of all – the Cinderellas and princes-for-a-night, picking their way on foot down the stony paths of hillside shantytowns, gilt and sequins glinting ephemerally in the dark of the tropical night.

The veterans come prepared with thermos flasks, piles of sandwiches, and six-packs. For the other inevitable rule of Carnival is that everything runs late – and this means having long hours to while away in the darkness. Heady wafts of marijuana blend with the smoke from improvised charcoal grills. Dancers help each other with eyeliner and dust the shoulders and thighs of strangers with glitter.

As each *escola* ahead of yours in the queue parades away, you move up a place. The wait seems interminable.

Then suddenly you are on. Your samba blasts out. You march forward in formation, turn that special right angle out of the darkness of the *concentracão* into the arc lights of the parade, and wham... your butterflies disappear and the crowd up there is singing along with you.

The stewards of your samba school wield their batons and dispense instructions: "For God's sake, smile," they yell, "Sing up, keep in close." Just in case you had forgotten, there is a competition to be won.

The vainest in the Carnival crowd are the posing, pouting transvestites, their platform soles raising them head and shoulders above the rest. One *baiana* tries in vain to get her costume through a door into a portable WC. She tries squeezing in with the hoop-skirt horizontal. Then she tries with the hoops vertical. Then she gives up and floats gracefully away to some discreet corner.

Left, samba school "officials" overseeing their school's performance. Above, young participant and, right, a not-so-young *baiana* shares the joy of dancing in the parade.

About halfway through the parade, euphoria sets in. Your limbs move automatically, you're bellowing the chorus for the 46th time, as if your life depended upon it, but your voice seems to belong to someone else. You dance past the drummers and feel the rush of air from three hundred pairs of hands beating simultaneously.

In 50 minutes, it's all over. You've got blisters on your feet, bits of your costume were shed on the way down the avenue. The municipal water carts are waiting to hose down dancers prostrate with sweat and exhaustion. And, yes, it was "emotional." ∎

over the parade organization and the awarding of prizes. By 1935, 25 schools were participating.

Samba: What *Deixa Falar* added to the black celebration of Carnival in 1929 was size, costume and organization. But the samba music itself existed long before that. Most experts agree that the distinctively black samba tradition dates from the late 19th century, when the crude music of the former slaves met the stylized European sound of Rio. (The word samba is believed to derive from the Angolese word *semba* describing a rhythmic dance.)

The most famous of the early sambas is *Pelo Telefone* (By Phone), which is about Rio's police chief. *Pelo Telefone* is considered the first samba song to have been recorded for record sales. That was in 1917. The author of the song was Ernesto dos Santos (nicknamed Donga), who was originally from Bahia.

Since the glory days of the 1930s and 1940s, when legendary composers such as Pixinguinha, Noel Rosa, Ari Barroso and Cartola were working, samba has become a national landmark. But it wasn't always so. Samba is a poor people's and principally a black people's music.

In fact, it wasn't until the 1950s that the samba parade became one of the main attractions of Carnival for foreign tourists in Rio. Said Pixinguinha at that time, "Twenty years ago those of us playing samba were getting beaten up by the police. Today, we're the national music."

Today's celebration of Carnival in Rio de Janeiro has three main features: colorful, often frenzied street events, the traditional club balls and, finally, the world-famous samba parade.

Street Carnival: Street Carnival can be described as "the opposite of everything."

men impersonating women ...

children impersonating adults ...

adults acting like children.

It starts on the Friday night of Carnival when Rio's mayor, in a hectic ceremony staged on Avenida Rio Branco downtown, delivers an oversized Key to the City to Rei Momo, the rolly-polly "King" who presides over Rio until Ash Wednesday.

But the best Street Carnival is found in Rio's suburbs – the huge working class districts which sprawl away from downtown.

Street Carnival in **Meier**, **Madureira**, **Bangu**, **Realengo** and other distant neighborhoods draws hundreds of thousands of revelers. Most of these *cariocas* dress, often elaborately, as clowns, transvestites, TV and film personalities or as bats, tigers and other assorted animals.

The most common get-up, however, is men dressing as women. The "Bloco das Piranhas" is an elaborate version of this idea. It usually includes a number of men dressed as high-priced prostitutes.

Another popular presence is the "Bloco dos Sujos." Members smear themselves with cheap but colorful paint and dress up in Indian garb or as vagabonds and parade through the streets.

The "Bloco de Empolgação," however, is the most common of the street Carnival phenomena. These groups stimulate the largest number of people into dancing themselves into the dizziest possible frenzy. They do it in the same way as the big samba schools – with lots of drums and well-known samba tunes.

Although most districts in the northern suburbs have plenty of activity, music and color, the official headquarters of Street Carnival is Avenida Rio Branco.

A number of special events are featured every year. One is the awarding of the annual Street Carnival costume prize. One recent award went to a group of men calling themselves "The Young Widows." They were splendidly dressed as middle-class women and worked out an elaborate dance routine to please the judges.

Another annual affair, the "Bloco dos Intocáveis" (The Untouchables) parade, takes place in Copacabana. This event, like most street Carnival phenomena, is totally disorganized and open to everyone. Says an organizer, "All you need is to be 18 years old so you can drink." And even that rule gets broken most of the time.

An unusual event inaugurated in 1981 is the parade of the "Bloco Scandinavia." The

Right, revelers cut loose at a Carnival ball.

bloco is composed entirely of strippers, who titillate bystanders with an open-air display of their craft. They are assisted by a bevy of bouncers from downtown strip bars, who keep oglers at a "decent" distance.

Street Carnival in Rio's sophisticated Zona Sul is less frenzied than in the working class Zona Norte. However, there are two traditional Zona Sul events marking any year's Carnival Calendar – the famous "Banda de Ipanema," about 15,000 strong, which annually parades through the streets of that famous district, stopping at every bar along the way, and the "Banda da Sá Ferreira," which does the same in Copacabana.

Annual club balls: Carnival nights belong to club balls. Among the annual events which attract both *cariocas* and tourists are nightly bashes at the **Sírio-Libanês**, **Flamengo**, **Fluminense** and **Monte Líbano** clubs.

Monte Libano boasts the "hottest" of the balls, especially its annual "Night in Baghdad" held on Carnival Tuesday. The "Night" is so popular, real live Middle Eastern sheiks have been known to attend. However, Monte Libano also has a reputation for over-selling. The hall becomes unbearably hot. Long lines form in front of the bar and the bathroom.

Some of the more interesting balls include the annual Sugarloaf event. This all-night affair takes place atop Rio's landmark, Sugarloaf Mountain. Promoter Guilherme Araujo annually attracts a long list of local and international celebrities, puts on a tasteful show and usually has one of the most picturesque and luxuriously decorated of all Carnival balls. The show goes on until sunrise and guests are permitted, indeed encouraged, to cart the cardboard and colored-paper decorations away with them when they leave.

Another big event is the annual City Ball, the official entertainment event of the city government. This ball takes place on Saturday night, usually at one of Rio's large nightclubs. The music is of the very best quality and all the celebrities in town show up. A highlight of the ball is the parade of the prize-winning Carnival costumes, which invariably feature outrageous and extravagant creations depicting anything and everything

from medieval troubadours to Roman Catholic archbishops.

The most talked about balls are those promoted by Rio's transsexuals. They take place at the São Jose Theater on Praça Tiradentes, starting on Friday with the "Baile dos Enxutos" and until Tuesday. The most notable thing about these balls is the surprising success these former men have in assuming secondary female sexual characteristics. They usually parade themselves, open-bloused, in front of the São Jose on each of the transsexual ball nights.

Samba parade: But the samba parade, recently divided into two parts, with seven

schools parading on Sunday night and seven on Monday, is the undisputed centerpiece of any Rio de Janeiro Carnival – a veritable compendium of *carioca* and Brazilian culture, the whole history of samba and Carnival in two nights.

Just the names of some of Rio's traditional samba schools – **Mangueira**, the oldest, **Salgueiro**, **Imperio Serrano**, **Beija-Flor** – give most *cariocas* goose bumps.

The parade is witnessed by millions of television viewers and 85,000 ticket-holders in the soaring **Sambódromo**, a $27 million stadium designed especially for the parade by noted Brazilian architect Oscar Niemeyer and inaugurated in 1984.

The parade is most certainly an eyeful. But the interesting thing is that there's more to it than meets the eye. Lavish costumes, soaring floats and the magic of samba form the colorful facade. But to understand what lies behind the parade you need a score card. Because, first and foremost, the samba parade is a competition.

Presentation of the parade: The 14 samba schools parading down Avenida Marques de Sapucaí are judged by a government appointed jury for every aspect of their presentation. The emotions (and controversies)

The theme embraces almost every aspect of the school's effort. The costumes must be in accord with its historical time and place. The samba song must recount or develop it and the huge floats that push ponderously down the avenue must detail it in depth through the media of paper mâché figures and paintings.

Finally, the samba parade is a resurrection of classic samba themes of the past. There are certain things which every school must present even though they do not necessarily combine with the specific theme of the school for that year. In fact, these items are often the most carefully judged and they give a certain

stimulated by this unique contest are every bit as hot as those which surround the year-end play-offs in most sports.

The samba parade is an artistic presentation, and not only in the sense of design and musical arts. There is also a literary dimension to each performance. Each school's effort must be based around a central theme. Sometimes that theme is an historical event or personality. Other times it's a story or legend from Brazilian literature.

Left, some of the faces of Carnival. **Above**, the party continues.

unity to the parade as a whole. Key elements present in each school's presentation include the following:

The *Abre-Alas*, literally, "The Opening Wing." The *Abre-Alas* consists of a group of colorfully costumed *sambistas* (*sambista* is anybody having anything to do with a samba school) marching just in front of or just behind a large float. The float usually depicts something like an open book or an old-fashioned scroll.

Written on this figurative page are the letters GRES (which stand for Gremio Recreativo Escola de Samba – the Samba

School Recreational Guild). This first float is, in effect, the title page of the samba school's theme.

Behind the *Abre-Alas* is a line of formally dressed men, the *Comissão de Frente*, literally "The Board of Directors." These men are usually chosen for their dignified air. Sometimes they are members of the school's actual board of directors, but usually they are simply honored but aging *sambistas*. The real board of directors is working hard along the sidelines to make sure the parade is on time and that all its members are playing their proper roles within the school's complex choreography.

The real event begins when the *Porta Bandeira* (Flag Bearer) and the *Mestre Sala* (Dance Master) appear a few steps behind the *Comissão de Frente*. These two individuals dress in lavish, 18th-century formal wear no matter what the samba school's theme is that year. The *Porta Bandeira* is a woman dancer who holds the school's flag, one side of which bears the school's emblem, and the other the symbol of that year's theme. While carrying the flag, the *Porta Bandeira* performs an elaborate dance with her consort. The pair must develop a devilishly complicated set of steps but without

breaking rhythm, and they have to do it while proceeding at the rate of about one mile per hour, down the avenue.

The weighty part of the samba school follows directly behind the *Porta Bandeira* and the *Mestre Sala*. A number of different components are involved, of which the most important is probably the *bateria*. The *bateria* is nothing less than a small army of percussion enthusiasts. In the larger schools they number up to several hundred. Their job is to maintain a constant rhythm, so the other members of the school can keep up with the tempo of the *samba* song, and to provide an exciting, pulsating undercurrent to the overall enterprise.

All the members of the *bateria,* sometimes called *ritmistas* (meaning anyone in the school providing musical accompaniment), must wear the same uniform, which is usually designed in accord with the school's theme.

The *bateria* stops about half way down the avenue to perform, with deafening power, before the judges' box. Meanwhile, the rest of the school proceeds to the end of the approximately 1,000-yard long (1-km) parade route.

Marching both in front of and behind the *bateria* are the major *alas* of the samba school. These groups of scores or even hundreds of people present different aspects of the school's theme through the medium of costume. Thus, if the school's theme is based on an Amazon myth, then one of its main *alas* might present *sambistas* dressed as Indians; another could have its members dressed in costumes suggesting the animals of the Amazon; a third would represent some of the figures of Amazon Indian mythology, and so forth.

However, there are some *alas* which must be part of every samba school parade no matter what the theme. The chief such *ala* is the *Ala das Baianas*. This group consists of dozens and sometimes hundreds of older women, usually blacks, dressed in the flowing white attire of the northeastern state of

Left, pounding out the samba rhythm for an hour. **Right**, exotic float replete with tropical birds and Amazon "Indians."

Bahia, home to Brazil's African traditions. The presentation of this motif honors the earliest history of samba.

To be chosen for the *Ala das Baianas* is considered a high honor. Says Maria de Lourdes Neves, a long-time member of the Imperio Serrano samba school, "To be a *baiana* you have to be a respected *senhora*, preferably of dignified bearing and advanced age… and you have to be ready to do everything a young person can do."

In between the major *alas* are a number of lavishly costumed individuals depicting the main figures of the motifs of the school's theme. These *sambistas* are called *figuras de*

Just in front of its main parade floats the school places a small, colorfully decorated van with a musical group and a singer on top. The male singer is called the *puxador de samba*. His job is to keep belting out the school's samba song. Everybody in the parade is expected to sing the song all the way to the end of the presentation. Often members of the school distribute copies of the lyrics in the grandstands just before the parade begins.

At the start and the middle but mainly towards the end of the parade, the samba school will bring up its big guns – the giant Carnival floats, which are called *alegorias*.

destaque, literally "prominent figures." They often include local celebrities, with a preference for voluptuous actresses and models.

Also mixed in between the various *alas* and the giant Carnival floats are groups of dancers known as *passistas*. These incredibly agile young men and women stop in the middle of the street to perform complicated dance routines. They often use a tambourine as a prop and perform acrobatic feats as part of their routines. The women *passistas* wear little more than a G-string. The *passistas* are among the most heartily applauded *samba* performers.

These immense papier mâché and styrofoam creations present the major figures and motifs of the school's theme.

Using the Amazon example again, the floats might present papier mâché figures depicting incidents or characters from a mythological Amazon story plus historical characters and lots of appropriate background scenery such as trees and rivers and wild animals. The floats also feature a number of live models, with a strong preference for minimally dressed females.

The whole presentation, of course, is penetrated by the music of the *samba enredo*.

The *bateria* is thumping out its rhythm on the drums, the *puxador de samba* is belting out its lyrics and every last *sambista* is singing as loud as possible. The *samba enredo* is the musical version of the school's theme. The words of the song are supposed to tell the story verbally while the costumes and floats tell it visually.

Financing the Carnival: Members of the big samba schools spend all year preparing for the event. They are mostly poor people. Support for their efforts comes from a small government subsidy, from dues paid by members and from donations made by businesses and individuals in the neighborhoods

time-honored *jogo do bicho*, the illegal numbers game. The numbers chiefs support the parade because it is great public relations. Most of Rio's poor have three passions: soccer, samba and the *jogo do bicho.*

Some critics, however, say the parade has become too extravagant, with major schools spending up to $300,000 each year on preparations. Responsible for the move toward Las Vegas-style opulence was Joaozinho Trinta, artistic director for one of Rio's largest samba schools, Beija-Flor. Trinta defended his insistence on big-budget productions with the classic remark: "Only the rich enjoy poverty. The poor want luxury."

where the schools have their headquarters. In recent years, in addition, the samba schools have become popular entertainment in the off-season. Most of the big-name schools appear at nightclubs or concerts during the year where they earn a percentage of the gate or a flat fee.

In practice, however, most of the school's money comes from donations and most of the donations come from the bosses of Rio's

Left, enthusiastic spectators dance and sing along with samba schools. **Above**, tired paraders make their way home at dawn.

Because of the emotions involved in the samba parade, the announcement of the winning school on the Thursday after the parade is one of the most dramatic events of the year in Rio. The losing schools are rarely, if ever, satisfied with the results and cries of fraud are common.

For the winning school and its fanatic followers, however, there is an instant coronation – the kings of samba – and a celebration that lasts all the way to the following Sunday! Indeed, all the way to the following year, where another Carnival and another samba parade await.

For shoppers, Rio is a tropical bargain basement. In addition to the usual souvenir shops, the city offers some of Latin America's most fashionable boutiques, jewelry stores and leather goods shops. It is a world center for summer fashions, the main outlet for Brazil's sophisticated gemstone business and the T-shirt and bikini capital of the universe.

Since the 1960s when Brazil first began experiencing inflation woes, the country's currency has taken an annual beating in relation to the American dollar and other strong currencies. Coupled with Brazil's cheap manpower, this has meant lower prices for items made in Brazil. The exception to this rule is electronic products. Although Brazil has a thriving high-tech electronics industry, decades of protectionist policies have left it uncompetitive. Because Brazil's currency, the *real*, is pegged to the American dollar, any decline of the dollar means that for European and Japanese tourists, the prices of goods in Rio are even cheaper than for Americans.

The Rio shops are loaded with products which are not only a bargain but are also of excellent quality. In the virtually unbeatable category are summer clothing, especially swimwear, leather goods, with the emphasis on shoes, sandals and handbags, and the ubiquitous gemstones, which appear to adorn store windows in every street of Copacabana and Ipanema.

Shopping centers: Until the start of the 1980s, Rio had no shopping centers, an oversight which was corrected with the opening of the **Rio Sul Shopping Center**. Since then, malls and shopping centers have sprouted at a rapid pace, giving residents and tourists alike a wide range of options. Rio's principal shopping centers are:

Rio Sul – located in the neighborhood of Botafogo, a short distance from Copacabana, Rio's first shopping center remains the most popular amongst residents of these two neigh-

Left and **above**, art and T-shirts for sale on the city's sidewalks.

borhoods and tourists as well. Buses take tourists free of charge from Copacabana's hotels to Rio Sul, where they will find over 400 shops and restaurants plus a supermarket. The latter is a rarity for a Rio shopping center. The mall is open from 10am to 10pm, Monday through Saturday.

Rio Off Price – located just a stone's throw from Rio Sul, Rio off Price shopping center is smaller, has fewer designer labels, and is not as elegant as its neighbor, but is

nevertheless an acceptable alternative for a spot of retail therapy.

Barra Shopping – the largest shopping center in Brazil and (according to its promoters) also the largest in Latin America, Barra Shopping has the look and feel of an American suburban mall. Contributing to this is its location in the heart of the Barra da Tijuca, Rio's suburbia. Barra Shopping offers free transportation from the hotels to the mall and back in air-conditioned buses. Like the city's other shopping centers, Barra offers top boutiques, department stores, a wide selection of restaurants including a McDonalds, several movie theaters, bookstores and jewelry stores. It also has a mini-amusement park for children and bowling alleys. It is open 10am–10pm, Monday through Saturday.

Cassino Atlântico – on Copacabana's beachfront drive, Avenida Atlântica, at the Sofitel Rio Palace Hotel, this mall is excellent in terms of location but falls short of Rio Sul and Barra Shopping in the quality and quantity of its shops. It does, however, have some of Rio's best souvenir shops, in addition to excellent art galleries and antique shops. Open 9am–10pm, Monday through Friday and 9am–8pm on Saturday.

São Conrado Fashion Mall – close to the

ers devoted exclusively to interior decorating and home furnishing. The **Rio Design Center** is located in Leblon at Avenida Ataulfo de Paiva 270 and **Casa Shopping**, behind the Barra Shopping Center.

Boutiques: The fashionable shops are on **Avenida Nossa Senhora de Copacabana**, between Rua Paula Freitas and Rua Constante Ramos, in Copacabana. Souvenir shops run from Avenida Princesa Isabel to Paula Freitas, on Rua Visconde de Pirajá in Ipanema and to a lesser degree along the pedestrian streets downtown, off Avenida Rio Branco.

The trendiest are found in Ipanema, mainly on **Visconde de Pirajá** but also on side

Sheraton and Inter-Continental hotels and a 5-minute drive from Ipanema, this mall is, as its name implies, devoted to fashion – sports and casual wear as well as elegant fashions, for both men and women. Open 10am–10pm, Monday through Saturday.

Shopping Center da Gávea is a small shopping center a few minutes from Ipanema and Leblon. This mall is famed for its art galleries, which are among the best in Rio de Janeiro. It also has several excellent home furnishing stores.

Besides these more traditional shopping malls, Rio also has two other shopping cent-

streets running in both directions. **Rua Garcia d'Avila** is the most popular. Visitors will discover that *cariocas*, men and women, dress as casually and expansively as they behave. The accent is on color and verve, with excellent lightweight summer clothing. Ipanema's shops and boutiques cater to men, women and children, offering leather goods and shoes in addition to clothing and gifts. The recognized bikini king is the **Bum Bum** boutique at Visconde de Pirajá 437. Most of Ipanema's top boutiques are also present at the Rio Sul and Barra Shopping malls. Credit cards are nearly always accepted.

Department stores: The accent on small, intimate shops and boutiques has meant that Rio has not been a boom market for department stores, although the arrival of the shopping center fad has opened up a new outlet for the big stores. The largest Brazilian department store, **Mesbla**, is present at Rio Sul and Barra Shopping and has a downtown store at Rua do Passeio. Rio's other department store chain, **C&A**, has stores at Rio Sul, Barra Shopping and at Avenida Nossa Senhora de Copacabana 749.

Street fairs: For souvenir hunters who are looking for something different, Rio's street fairs are the best bet. The most popular is the along the median strip of Copacabana's beach drive, Avenida Atlântica. The median is a popular selling point, attracting crowds of tourists from the hotels across the street, thus serving as a meeting place as well as a street fair.

Further away, in style as well as distance, is the **Northeastern Fair** (Feira do Nordeste). It takes place on Sunday (from 6am–1pm) in a large public square in the neighborhood of **São Cristóvão**, a half hour journey by car from Copacabana and Ipanema. This fair is not aimed at tourists but caters to the thousands of *cariocas* who have been transplanted from their native northeast, Brazil's

Hippie Fair in Ipanema, at **Praça General Osório**, Sundays 9am–6pm. A leftover from Ipanema's flower children days of the 1960s, the fair has an excellent choice of wood carvings, paintings, hand-tooled leather goods, other assorted handicrafts and multicolored T-shirts.

Despite its origins, there is nothing hippie or amateurish about the fair today. Many of the vendors also sell their wares at night

Left, fresh produce for sale at a street market. **Above**, an artist paints with his toes at a handicraft fair.

most glorified region in national folklore. The dozens of wooden stalls sell regional dishes and beverages of the Northeast plus such exotic ingredients as tripe and dried salted meat. Some of the region's handicrafts are sold at the fair but tourists will find little to buy. The attraction of the fair is its northeastern spirit, offering visitors an opportunity to see the northeast of Brazil without leaving Rio de Janeiro.

Antiques: For antique collectors, **Rua do Lavradio** on the first Saturday of every month from 10am–5pm and **Praça XV** on Sunday from 8am–5pm are places to discover. The **Cassino Atlântico** and the **Rio Design Center** also contain antique shops. Indian crafts are found at **Artindia** (Museu Do Índio), Rue Das Palmgiras 55 (Batafogo). It is run by the government Indian bureau, Funai.

Crafts and native arts: High-quality indigenous handicrafts can be found at **Arteíndia** in Botafogo which sells items such as masks, musical instruments and baskets. **Brumado**, Rue Das Laranjgiras 486/924 offers handicrafts from all over Brazil as well as colonial furniture, paintings and antiques. **Pé de Boi**, on Rua Ipiranga 55, also in Laranjeiras, displays and sells handicrafts

are unpacked from trucks and assembled along the streets. Within two hours, a tranquil residential neighborhood is transformed into a maze of wooden stalls offering everything from bananas to eggplant as well as fish, meat and flowers. The vendors bark out their prices as shoppers stroll by, with prices falling as the noon hour approaches and the fairs close down.

Jewelry stores: At the other end of the sophistication scale are Rio's jewelry stores, some of which have evolved into veritable gemstone empires. Brazil is the world's largest producer of colored gemstones and the effects of this are obvious as soon as a tourist

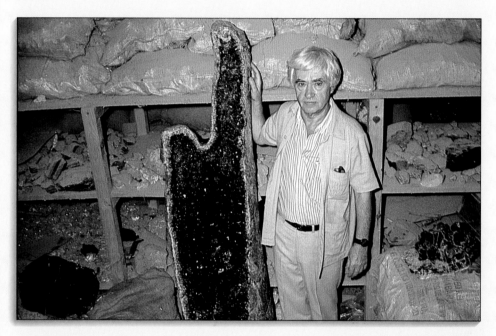

originating from almost all the countries in South America.

Fruit and vegetable markets: A typical *carioca* tradition is the street fruit and vegetable market (*feira* in Portuguese). Although such markets should have been relegated to the history books with the advent of supermarkets, the *cariocas* stubbornly hang on to their habits despite the monumental traffic jams they are capable of causing in Copacabana and Ipanema.

Filling entire streets for blocks, these huge mobile markets arrive at each day's site in the early morning darkness when the stalls

steps off the plane. Gem dealers are literally everywhere in Rio as are their salesmen. In most cases, the gem sales pitch is low key and cultivated. Salesmen and saleswomen tend to be multilingual, cultured and often fascinating in themselves. They exude confidence in their products. Brazil is not only famous for its variety of stones but also for prices which are unbeatable, given the quality of the gems, settings and design. Costs are kept down because the operation is 100 percent domestic, from the mining of the gems to the cutting, crafting and designing of jewelry.

As valuable as it is to be armed with some prior information about gemstones, shoppers should be aware that unless you are an expert, it is always wiser to buy from a reliable jeweler, where you can be sure that you are getting exactly what you are paying for. Rio has several reputable and even world-renowned jewelers. Do watch out for souvenir shops offering cut-rate gemstones – many are no more than colored glass.

Rio's two leading jewelers are Jules Sauer and Hans Stern, owners of Amsterdam Sauer and H. Stern jewelers respectively. Both men and their firms are famed throughout the world, with Sauer receiving top marks

Ipanema at **Rua Visconde de Pirajá 490**. In addition to Rio's poshest souvenir shop on the ground floor, Stern offers, free of charge, a tour showing the process by which a raw stone becomes a polished piece of jewelry. Tourists may arrange for the tour at any Stern outlet in Rio.

Obviously, not all tourists are interested in high quality gemstones. For the more common souvenir stones, mainly agates in a variety of settings or polished stone ash-trays, any of Rio's gift shops will do the trick. Other popular items at these stores include clay figurines and pottery from the Northeast of Brazil, soapstone objects from

for craftsmanship and Stern for marketing. Shoppers looking for quality gemstones in which they can place absolute trust cannot go wrong with either of these two.

The shops of **Amsterdam Sauer** and **H. Stern** are located throughout Rio, at the airports, the main shopping centers and streets and the city's leading hotels. A special treat awaits visitors to Stern's world headquarters, an impressive, modern high-rise in

__Left__, Jules Sauer of Amsterdam Sauer Jewelers with an example of Brazil's wealth in gemstones. __Above__, Rio's colorful T-shirts.

the state of Minas Gerais (where the majority of Brazil's gem mines are located), straw baskets and hats, colorful cotton hammocks and wooden salad bowls and trays. Brazilian primitive paintings are also sought after by foreign visitors.

Art: Contemporary Brazilian art is on display at several galleries in Rio especially in Ipanema. **Galeria Cohn Edelstein** is probably one of the most interesting. If you are in Gávea, **Galeria Anna Maria Niemayer** always has exhibitions of well-known artists. In the center the best gallery is **Galeria Paulo Fernandes**.

CARIOCA MEN AS DRIVERS

"Driving in Rio is more frightening than racing in a Grand Prix," according to Nelson Piquet, Brazil's three-time Formula One world racing champion.

In theory, foreign tourists can drive in Rio. But then in theory, so can the natives. Something strange, however, happens to a male *carioca* when he sits behind a steering wheel. Normally a complacent, easy going and relaxed fellow, he is suddenly transformed into an aggressive, wild, macho man of the roadways in Rio.

Most visitors to Rio come away slightly dazed by the mayhem of the city's streets, avenues and even sidewalks. Pedestrians beware – Rio's drivers see nothing wrong with climbing onto the sidewalks to beat a traffic jam. To the uninitiated the city's thoroughfares resemble a war zone populated by thousands of crazed kamikaze drivers.

Cariocas are acknowledged masters at lane switching, cutting in, tailgating, running red lights, speeding and turning from all lanes, except the ones you would expect them to turn from. The painted lines marking lanes on the streets are considered an affront to a driver's creativity and are therefore ignored. It is not unusual to discover four lines of traffic moving along smartly on a two-lane street.

The real art of Rio's drivers is their ability to switch lanes without warning at 60 miles an hour (100 kph), cutting off the car in the lane next to them, provoking a din of shrieking brakes and blaring horns, before driving on casually, with a smile and a flip of the hand, to the next near disaster.

Not surprisingly, *cariocas* see nothing odd or unusual in their driving habits. They point out that despite the apparent mass confusion of the city's traffic, it does move. In fact, the secret to surviving this madness is to discover exactly *how* it moves. Foreign tourists who decide to brave the traffic and take to the

streets quickly find that the rules of safe driving do not apply here.

Red lights: No self-respecting American driver would run every red light he sees and certainly never with a police car beside him. In Rio, however, such an attitude is pure nonsense and actually dangerous. The unflappable *cariocas* will tell you that stopping for red lights at night is not wise – you'd be a sitting duck for robbers. Should you mention that Rio's drivers also ignore traffic

lights during the day, they will answer that it seems foolish to waste your time at an intersection if there are no cars coming. The point is that imported morality and logic carry no weight on the streets of Rio. Those poor souls who stop at red lights soon learn that the cars behind them don't, an often painful experience. As for the police, well, there is no reason to worry about them, as they too run the traffic lights.

There are approximately 1.2 million vehicles in Rio, counting cars, buses, trucks, motorcycles and scooters, all of them hustling about in a space that by any logic can

Left, a Rio bus driver, one of the demons of the city's streets. **Above**, tunnels have been Rio's solution to the city's mountain barriers.

only handle one-third their number. The result is the usual chaos of the morning rush hour, which often extends well past noon, followed by the chaos of shoppers returning home and mothers picking up school children and ending with the evening rush hour. There is seldom a moment in a normal working day when part of the city is not bogged down in hopeless traffic jams.

The problem is easy to explain – with the ocean on one side and mountains on the other, there is simply no way that six million people and their one million vehicles can fit comfortably in between. The classic example is Copacabana, where 300,000 people are

Copacabana qualifies as the world's worst designed parking lot. Most of its apartment buildings were built at a time when lax building codes and a smaller population permitted developers to get by with a bare minimum of parking spaces in their garages. The result today is that an estimated 60 percent of the neighborhood's automobiles have no place to sleep at night. These homeless cars are stacked up on sidewalks, in public squares, on top of bushes, or packed bumper to bumper on the streets in double or even triple rows. If there were a way to park a car in a tree, the residents of Copacabana would have found it.

squeezed into high rises that fill a mere 109 streets. Each day, the neighborhood is crisscrossed by an estimated 600,000 vehicles or half of all the vehicles in Rio. With only 109 streets to choose from (of which no more than six could possibly be called thoroughfares), as soon as the traffic backs up on one street, it immediately overflows onto dozens of others.

Parking: For those weary residents of Copacabana who manage to fight their way home on a hot summer evening, the struggle has only just begun. They must now find a place to park. With over 250,000 cars of its own,

This problem is not confined to the night. Tourists and pedestrians may think that the exotic mosaics of Copacabana's wide beachfront sidewalks were designed for them, but car owners think otherwise. The daylight hours see a repetition of the unending war for parking spaces – legitimate or otherwise. The referees of this combat are a singular band of entrepreneurs who appear mysteriously at the right moment, pointing out empty spaces and mediating between rival motorists who saw the same space at the same moment – but their services come at a price, of course.

Acutely aware of this problem, city officials routinely launch massive campaigns aimed at ridding the sidewalks of cars. Horrible punishments are threatened and all *cariocas* are urged to defend their city against selfish *motoristas*. For the next month, the sidewalks are amazingly free of cars (where the cars actually go no one has yet been able to discover). All too soon, though, everything returns to normal.

Buses and Taxis: Visitors will quickly discover that Rio's bus drivers belong in a special category – Rio's other drivers will tell you they belong in prison. Underpaid, with working shifts that often reach 12 hours

that on most occasions you will have no trouble finding one – except, naturally, when its raining – the passengers of Rio's cabbies should be prepared for virtually anything. These demons of the streets have nerves of steel which will turn yours to jelly.

The worst mistake you could make is to tell a Rio taxi driver you're in a hurry. The city's cabbies normally exceed the speed limit by a significant margin. Telling them to hurry up only makes it worse. Tourists should also be wary of price gouging, a favorite pastime of the city's taxi drivers. If you don't know your way around or you don't speak the language, it is best to ask your hotel to

straight behind the wheel, the bus drivers are always in a hurry. As a result, they are responsible for a fair share of the city's frequent traffic accidents. The basic rule of Rio's streets is amazingly simple: buses have the right of way, always. It does no good to quarrel over this since the buses have an enormous advantage – they are bigger.

The other scourge of Rio traffic is the city's huge fleet of taxis. While this ensures

Left, waiting for the bus ride home after a day at the beach. Above, traffic jams are a fact of city life.

call a radio cab. Although their rates are higher you have the security of knowing that you won't be cheated, plus their drivers tend to be more courteous and slightly more sane.

The Subway: Rio's subway, which ran out of funds at the start of the 1980s, has now been extended to Copacabana with the opening of Praça Cardeal Arcoverde station.Optimists predicted that this improvement would create an idyllic Copacabana by the end of the 20th century, with traffic flowing normally and ample parking spaces. Unfortunately it looks as if they will have to extend that prediction by another few years.

As with almost everything else in Rio, it undoubtedly began on the beach. When it began, however, nobody knows. But somehow, overnight it seems, there it was: Rio de Janeiro, playground of the beautiful people.

Who *are* the beautiful people? At first, they were imports – movie stars, heiresses, princes and princesses, an occasional dethroned king or queen and of course, the tycoons, all of them dripping with notoriety, glamour and cash. Rio was one of their favorite backdrops: the most eye-catching and unquestionably the most exotic.

With time, however, the beautiful people discovered other favorite backdrops – the Riviera, Acapulco, Tahiti, Cancun. Rio slipped in popularity, lost its status and finally became a stop-over for only second class beautiful people, not the **real** ones.

New concept: But in the 1960s, two *cariocas* wrote a song that turned Rio's entire concept of beautiful upside down. That popular song was called *The Girl from Ipanema* and not only did it become a pop classic but suddenly the focus was inverted; it was realised that the beautiful people were, and still are, the *cariocas* themselves.

As visitors to Rio quickly discover, there is not one girl from Ipanema, but thousands, an eye-popping variety of beautiful, lithe young women whose shapely forms (in particular their rounded bottoms) add a new dimension to the word ecstasy. And while no one has written a song about them, the men of Rio are not bad either.

For both the men and women of Rio, the beach remains the essential ingredient in the *carioca* version of the body cult. It is on the beach that the beautiful people parade their beauty and it is because of the need to be on the beach that often extraordinary efforts are made to obtain and preserve this beauty. It should surprise no-one that Rio de Janeiro is an international center for gymnastics clubs and plastic surgeons.

Left, the body cult is alive and well in Rio, a paradise for joggers.

Color and shape: As soon as the weather warms up each year, *cariocas* begin to concern themselves with two details – their color and their shape. No one would be caught dead looking like a tourist, pale white with a red topping, especially when a trim form is vital in a city where swimwear is designed to reveal, not to cover.

In previous decades, *cariocas* solved their form problems with crash diets at the start of summer. The health and fitness craze of the 1980s, however, changed all that. Today, well before the temperature starts to climb, a master *carioca* is fit and ready to expose his or her torso on the sands of Copacabana or Ipanema. For this, Rio's health nuts turn primarily to the city's hundreds of health clubs and gymnastics centers. People in the trade claim there are 3,000 of these scattered throughout the city, but concentrated in the affluent south zone.

The gymnastics fad has become an all-consuming passion, generating a minor industry of manufacturers of equipment and designers of exercise "fashions," (a **must** in fashion-conscious Brazil) as well as clubs and centers. A walk down Visconde de Pirajá, the commercial center of Ipanema, shows just how extensive this fad has become. In the street's 10 blocks, there are at least 20 gymnastics centers and health clubs. In addition, the city is overflowing with dance academies, karate schools and other centers for the teaching of martial arts.

Gym centers: The most popular are the gym centers, with their club atmosphere, serving at the same time to firm up silhouettes and bring together attractive, energetic singles. Nearly all of them follow a prescribed formula, heavy on aerobic exercises done to a disco beat – a tropical version of the Jane Fonda formula. Weightlifting has also caught on in Rio following the success of the *Rambo* and *Rocky* films and today, Sylvester Stallone clones strut along the beaches of Ipanema, São Conrado and Grumari. And although most Rio women prefer soft, sensual curves over hardened muscles, a growing number of them are also pumping iron, with the top 20 gathering annually for the title of Miss Rio Muscles.

The majority of the adherents to the exercise clubs are young women, many of whom are looking for what has become a legitimate *carioca* status symbol, the Ipanema *bunda* or behind. The exuberant, well-rounded cheeks of this Rio phenomenon is one of Brazil's most sought after treasures and are amply displayed in *carioca* bikinis, most of which would capture international prizes for truth in packaging. Some exercise class professors are known to have the "secret" for developing this classic *bunda* look (others use more practical sales pitches such as offering to improve a woman's sex life by teaching sex exercises).

In fact, the key to most gym centers is the head professor. Each has his own method, some mixing the metaphysical with the physical, producing sometimes exotic theories on "body analysis," an odd blending of Sigmund Freud and Arnold Schwarzenegger. Others stick to the basics – sweat followed by more sweat. Brazil's leading actresses and singers, many of whom live in Rio, routinely announce they have discovered the ultimate professor, the man with the cure-all method for gaining the perfect form.

Currently, the exercise class professor who has the final word is Rio's João Gaspar Mello, a true artist who only accepts new students if they are recommended by old students and who insists that his followers adhere completely to his program, doing no other physical activity ("How else can I evaluate my work?").

Jogging: For those who eschew the social club atmosphere of the exercise centers, there is always the sidewalk and the beach. Jogging came late to Rio but has become a *carioca* passion. Each day starting at dawn, the beach becomes the city's most densely populated gymnastics center. Regular exercise groups gather to do their sit-ups on the sands of Ipanema, while along the sidewalks from the bay to the distant Barra da Tijuca, thousands of joggers do their thing. In addition to the wide sidewalks that flank the beach and bay, the most popular jogging trail is the path that encircles the Rodrigo de Freitas Lagoon, just behind Ipanema. The jogging mania, which encompasses all ages, has also led to more strenuous forms of running, with marathons and more recently triathlons becoming fixtures of the *carioca* fitness scene.

The pain, effort and discipline of the jogger and runner is the same in Rio as anywhere else but nowhere else in the world do the men and women who pound feet against pavement have the scenery of Rio de Janeiro to accompany and inspire them. Joggers who have lived in other countries state that, without a doubt, it is easier to run in the sun and beauty of Rio.

Plastic surgery: Obviously, there are those for whom regular exercise is simply not enough to produce the *carioca* form. To compensate, these individuals have become regular customers of Rio's dozens of plastic surgery clinics. The man who popularized cosmetic surgery in Brazil is Dr Ivo Pitanguy, a legend in his own right. Considered by many as the foremost plastic surgeon in the world for both cosmetic and reconstructive surgery, Pitanguy's sophisticated clinic in the neighborhood of Botafogo is a Rio landmark, frequented not only by Brazilians but by international figures such as Ursula

Andress and Gina Lollobrigida. Pitanguy, however, is not a name dropper and prefers to keep his patients' names to himself. The same is not true of his patients who proudly announce that they bear a Pitanguy nose or a Pitanguy uplift. They are laying claim to one of Rio's premier status symbols.

Urbane and communicative, Pitanguy is a friend of stars and celebrities. He has also published hundreds of internationally respected works on plastic surgery. As well as his high-society work, he also finds time for reconstructive surgery on poor accident victims, which he does for free. His fame has made him Rio de Janeiro's most sought-after

the latest fad, suction lipectomy, or simply, liposuction. Brazil's plastic surgeons, led by Pitanguy and his colleagues in Rio, are at the forefront of international research. Breast operations are still the most common procedure performed in Rio, followed by face and nose work.

Hairdressers: Along with the growth of plastic surgery clinics has been the expansion of Rio's weight loss clinics and skin treatment centers. Health spas are just starting to appear but some of the city's hairdressers come close to being mini spas in their opulence and variety of services. Heading the list is the Jambert Haute Coiffure, a

plastic surgeon, but since he blazed the trail the city has attracted many other excellent surgeons.

Each day, Rio's clinics do battle against wrinkles, blemishes, fatty deposits, cellulite, sagging derrieres, non-aesthetic noses and breasts that need to be reduced or expanded. The struggle to rejuvenate *carioca* matrons or to give the young the perfect body involves all the techniques of the profession, ranging from face lifts and breast implants to

Left, morning scullers. **Above**, *carioca* musclemen on the beach in Copacabana.

beauty salon in Leblon that is a temple to narcissism, serving men as well as women. Run by its founder and owner, Spaniard Miguel Jambert Garcia, the salon is five stories of marble decorated with Persian carpets, oriental statuary and crystal light fixtures. Luxury and the leisure lifestyle ooze from the salon's walls, which house veritable artists in hair styling, facials, massages, manicures, etc.

With so much working in their favor, it is easy to understand why the beautiful people have become endemic to Rio. International celebrities, eat your hearts out.

INSIGHT GUIDES
Travel Tips

Insight Guides portray destinations in depth, providing the complete picture and the top photography

Insight Pocket Guides focus on the best choices for places to see and things to do and include large fold-out maps

Insight Compact Guides' portability makes them the perfect books to carry with you for on-the-spot reference

Three types of guide for all types of travel

INSIGHT GUIDES Different people need different kinds of information. Some want *background information* to help them prepare for the trip. Others seek *personal recommendations* from someone who knows the destination well. And others look for *compactly presented data* for on-the-spot reference. With three carefully designed series, Insight Guides offer readers the perfect choice. Insight Guides will turn your visit into an experience.

The world's largest collection of visual travel guides

CONTENTS

Getting Acquainted

The Place

Area: Brazil has an area of 3,285,632 sq. miles (8,511,965 sq. km). Rio is in the highly populous Southeast Region, and covers an area of 452 sq. miles (1,157 sq. km).
Population: Rio is home to 5.6 million of Brazil's 154 million, with a further 4 million inhabiting the suburbs, which are mainly to the north.
Language: Portuguese.
Religion: 90 percent Catholic, remainder Protestant (Pentecostal, Evangelical, Episcopal, Methodist, Lutheran, Baptist, Mormon). Also Muslim, Jewish and Buddist. *Candomblé* is a derivative of African religions brought over by slaves which many Brazilians follow, usually in addition to Catholicism. The state is secular.
Time zone: GMT minus 3 hours, Eastern Standard Time plus 2 hours.
Currency: the Real, made up of 100 Centavos. For exchange, US$1 is about 1R$ and £1 about 1.5R$. (*See page 221, "Money" for more details.*)
Weights and measures: metric.
Electricity: 110 or 220 volts, 60 hertz; two-pin plugs. Voltage differs throughout Brazil.
International dialing to Rio: +55 21.

Climate

Rio, located just north of the Tropic of Capricorn at a latitude of 22.5° south, is at the southern extreme of the tropic zone. The climate, because of its location on the Atlantic coast, is humid tropical.

The mean temperature in Rio is 73°F (23°C). Temperatures in summer (December–March) are hot, from 84° to 95°F (29°–35°C) on average but can climb up to a sweltering 104°F (40°C). Winter weather (June–August) is a comfortable 68°–70°F (20°–21°C), occasionally dipping down to 65°F (18°C).

Summer and winter are marked by rainfall, with more frequent and heavier rain falling in the hot summer months. Summer rains can be terrific cloudbursts, and because the city is nearly at sea-level and surrounded by mountains down which the rain water streams, streets often become rivers within minutes.

The mountain cities above Rio (such as Nova Friburgo, Petrópolis, Teresópolis) have a high altitude tropical climate, slightly cooler than the low-lying coast. The rainy and dry seasons are more pronounced and temperatures average 64°–73°F (18°–23°C). In winter, although there is no danger of frost, the mountain air is nippy.

The Economy

Brazil's main problem throughout this century has been political instability. The revised Constitution of 1988 is the country's fifth since 1930. During this period, Brazil has suffered frequent intervention by the military, leading to a situation where brief attempts at democratic, civilian rule have been substituted by either increased military influence or a direct military take-over. The last military regime began with a coup in 1964 and extended until 1985 when the presidency was returned to civilian hands.

Despite its political problems, Brazil has enjoyed excellent economic growth rates for most of the past 30 years. Today, the country is the recognized economic leader among Third World nations.

Through loans and direct investments by multinational companies, Brazil in the 1960s and 1970s underwent a rapid phase of industrialization, emerging as the eighth largest economy in the world in terms of gross national product. Brazil is also the leading exporting nation in Latin America: today, 70 percent of its exports comprise manufactured goods.

The Government

Rio de Janeiro is the capital city of the state of Rio de Janeiro, one of 27 states which make up the Federal Republic of Brazil, each with its own state legislature. Since the federal government exercises enormous control over the economy, the political autonomy of the states is restricted. The overwhelming majority of government tax receipts are collected by the federal government and then distributed to the states and cities.

The head of government is the president who has huge power and, in fact, exercises more control over the nation than the American president does over the United States. The legislative branch of the federal government is a Congress divided into a lower house, the Chamber of Deputies, and an upper house, the Senate.

Etiquette

Social customs in Brazil are not vastly different from what you will find in "western" countries, but Brazilians can be both awkwardly formal and disarmingly informal.

Surnames are little used. People start out on a first name basis, but titles of respect – *senhor* for men and most frequently *dona* or *senhora* for women – are used to be polite to strangers but also to show respect to someone of a different age group or social class. In some families children address their parents as *o senhor* and *a senhora* instead of the equivalent of "you", although this is increasingly rare.

While handshaking is a common practice when people are introduced, it is customary to greet not only friends and relatives but also complete strangers to whom you are being introduced with hugs and kisses. The "social" form of

Ten Facts About Rio

•The first telephone line outside of the United States was installed by Emperor Dom Pedro II between Rio and Petrópolis.

•Flamengo Park contains a museum entirely devoted to Carmen Miranda, the flamboyant star who wore fruit for headgear.

•Pão de Açucar derives its name from Indian words meaning 'high, pointed, isolated peak'. The similarity to the Portuguese for Sugarloaf is purely coincidental.

•Maracanã Stadium is the largest in the world, with a capacity of 180,000 people.

•Rio is the world's leading center for cosmetic and plastic surgery.

•Rio was originally colonized by the French in 1555, under the command of Admiral Nicolas Durant de Villegaignon. The French were finally evicted by the Portuguese in 1567.

•Rio's domestic airport is named after Alberto Santos Dumont, who made the first *fully-documented* flight in an aeroplane, in 1906. The Wright brothers flew in 1903 but did not document the flight until 1908.

•Rio was the official seat of government of the Portuguese Empire from 1808, when Emperor Dom João VI fled Portugal and Napoleon, until 1821.

•Rio was the capital of Brazil for almost 200 years, until the realization of President Juscelino Kubitschek's dream to create a new capital city in the center of the country.

•The famed 'Girl from Ipanema' really existed – and still does. Her name is Heloisa Pinheiro, and she is now a successful businesswoman in her fifties, living in São Paulo. Her place in Rio has been taken by a never-ending succession of beautiful young pretenders, as anyone can testify who has sat in the **Garota de Ipanema** bar, where composers Vinicius de Moraes and Tom Jobim first spied Heloisa.

kissing consists usually of a kiss on each cheek. While men and women greet each other with kisses, as do women among themselves, in most circles men do not kiss each other, rather shaking hands while giving a pat on the shoulder with the other hand. If they are more intimate, men will embrace, thumping each other on the back. Although this is the general custom, there are subtleties about who kisses whom that are governed by social position.

Apart from the more formal forms of hugging and kissing, visitors from some cultures remark that Brazilians seem to be quite unabashed about expressing affection in public.

Brazilians are generous hosts, ensuring that guests' glasses, plates or coffee cups are never empty. Besides the genuine pleasure of being a gracious host, there is the question of honor. The pot luck or bring-your-own-bottle party is not popular in Brazil. Even poor people like to give a party.

Although Brazil is definitely a male-dominated society, machismo takes a milder and more subtle form than is generally found in neighboring Hispanic America.

While they are at all other times a polite, decent people, something happens when Brazilians get behind the steering wheel. Be cautious when driving or crossing streets and be prepared to make a dash. Drivers expect pedestrians to watch out for themselves and get out of the way.

Expect schedules to be more flexible than you may be used to. It's not considered rude to show up half an hour to an hour late for a social engagement. Even business appointments are often leisurely when compared with the US or Europe. Don't try to include too many in one day, as you may well find your schedule badly disrupted by unexpected delays.

Planning the Trip

What to Bring

Brazilians are very fashion conscious but are actually quite casual dressers. What you bring along will depend on where you will be visiting and your holiday schedule. São Paulo tends to be more dressy; small inland towns are more conservative. If you are going to a jungle lodge, you will want sturdy clothing and perhaps boots. However, if you come on business, a suit and tie for men, and suits, skirts or dresses for women are the office standard.

Although some restaurants in the downtown business districts of the larger cities require a tie at lunch, other restaurants have no such regulations – although obviously in a posh establishment you are expected to dress appropriately and you will feel better if you blend in. Still, a suit and tie are rarely called for when you go out. Generally speaking, suits and ties are used less the further north you go in Brazil, even by businessmen, and the opposite holds true as you go south. Bring a summer-weight suit for office calls. Linen is smart and cool.

If you do like to dress up, there are plenty of places to go to in the evening in the big cities. Avoid ostentation and using jewelry that will attract more attention to yourself than you may want. There are many desperately poor people in Brazil and foreign tourists make attractive targets for pickpockets and purse-snatchers.

Shorts are acceptable for men and women in most areas, especially near the beach or in resort towns, but they are not usually worn downtown. Bermudas are comfortable in hot weather.

Most churches and some museums do not admit visitors dressed in shorts, and the traditional *gafieira* dance halls will not admit those dressed in shorts, especially men. Jeans are acceptable dress for men and women and are worn a great deal in Brazil – but they can be hot.

Don't forget to pack your swimsuit! Or buy a tiny local version of the string bikini, called a tanga, for yourself or someone back home – there are stores that sell nothing but beachwear. New styles emerge each year, in different fabrics and colors, exposing this part or that. They seem to get smaller every year, but somehow they never disappear completely. The tiniest are called *fio dental*, or dental floss!

Although there have been a few timid – or rather brave – attempts at topless sunbathing on Brazil's beaches, it has never really caught on. Women exposing their breasts on the beach have often been hassled and sometimes even attacked, which is rather ironic because the skimpy bikinis that Brazilians wear are much more provocative than nakedness.

While everyone can walk around practically naked on the beach, decently dressed women get ogled too. Brazilian men don't go in for catcalls, but they draw their breath in sharply between clenched teeth and murmur comments as the women pass by. Brazilian women certainly don't let this cramp their style.

In Rio and São Paulo nothing will be considered too trendy or outlandish. In smaller towns, although the locals may dress more conservatively, they are used to outsiders, including Brazilian tourists from the big cities. Somehow, no matter how foreign tourists are dressed, Brazilians seem able to spot most of them a mile away.

For Carnival, remember that it will be very hot and you will probably be in a crowd and dancing nonstop. Anything colorful is appropriate. If you plan to go to any of the balls, you will find plenty of costumes in the shops – you might want to buy just a feathered hair ornament, flowered lei or sequined accessory to complete your outfit.

Many women wear no more than a bikini and makeup and sometimes less. Most men wear shorts – with or without a shirt – or sometimes a sarong. There are fancy-dress balls with themes like Hawaii or Arabian Nights.

If you are traveling in the south or in the mountains or to São Paulo in winter, it can be quite chilly. Even in the areas where it is hot all year round, you may need a light sweater, jacket or sweatshirt, if not for the cooler evenings, then for the air conditioning in hotels, restaurants and offices!

Rain gear is always handy to have along – Brazilians tend to use umbrellas more than raincoats. Something that folds up small and can be slipped into your bag is best. Sunglasses are another essential item, especially for the beach. Seaside hotels will provide you with sun umbrellas and beach towels.

As on any trip, it is sensible to bring a pair of comfortable walking shoes – there is no better way to explore than on foot. Sandals are comfortable in the heat. Sandals or beach thongs, even if you don't plan to wear them for walking

Photography

Both Kodakcolor and Fujicolor film for color prints, as well as Ektachrome, KodaKchrome and Fujichrome slide film, can be bought and developed in Brazil.

Hotel shops will have film and specialty shops, easily spotted by signs out front advertising the brands of film they sell, carry equipment and accessories and will take your film for processing.

Developing is quick and of good quality, but quite expensive. There is 24-hour finishing and even one-hour service at the Rio-Sul shopping center. Reliable labs include Kodak, Fuji, Multicolor and Curt. Find out from your hotel where you can take your film to be developed. (*Revelar* = to develop; *revelação* = developing; film is *filme*).

Although it is often easier to have your pictures developed when you return from your trip, if you are going to be traveling around a great deal, remember that exposure to heat and multiple X-ray security checks at airports could ruin them.

For tourists entering with photographic equipment that is obviously for vacation picture-taking, there are no customs restrictions. If you are bringing in a lot of professional equipment, it must be registered with customs for temporary entrance and then leave the country with you.

In this case, it would be wise to contact a Brazilian consulate before traveling. Depending on what you bring, you may need written authorization from a diplomatic mission outside Brazil. It's best to check.

Try to avoid taking pictures during the middle of the day when the sun is strongest and tends to wash out colors. Light in the tropics is very white and bright and you may want to bring an appropriate filter along. Mornings from sunrise to 10am and any time between 3pm and sunset, are best for photography.

Don't walk around with your camera around your neck or over your shoulder – it makes you conspicuous and an easy target for a snatcher. Carry it discreetly in a bag slung in front of you. Never leave a camera unattended at the beach. If you have expensive equipment, it's a good idea to have it insured.

around the streets, are very convenient for getting across the hot sand from your hotel to the water's edge. If there's one thing that gives Brazilians the giggles, it's the sight of a "gringo" going to the beach in shoes and socks.

Brazilians often wear high-heeled shoes and show special agility on the sidewalks – which can be veritable obstacle courses of holes, puddles, beggars, vendors, garbage cans and cobblestones and are frequently completely taken over by parked cars. You may want to buy shoes or sandals in Brazil – leather goods are a steal.

A sturdy but unobtrusive shoulder bag carried or tucked securely under your arm (not slung behind you in city streets) is a practical item. Use it to carry your camera discreetly. Better still, copy the Brazilians and wear a small rucksack-type bag, slung in front of you instead of on your back. Toss in a foldable umbrella, guidebook and map and you're ready for a day's outing.

Clothing made of synthetic fibers may be handy – it is easy to wash and doesn't need ironing. But in the tropics these fabrics do not breathe or absorb perspiration as natural fibers do and will make you feel twice as hot. Bring washable clothes instead, or if you have anything that needs special cleaning, have it washed when you return from your trip. While laundry service in the hotels is usually excellent, dry cleaning in Brazil is generally not very reliable.

There is nothing better for the heat than cotton, and since Brazil produces linen and exports cotton you might want to pack the bare essentials and acquire a new wardrobe. When buying clothes, remember that although most material is preshrunk, some natural fabrics will shrink. *Pequeno* = Small; *Médio* = Medium; and *Grande* = Large (often marked "P," "M" and "G"). *Maior* means larger; *menor* means smaller.

Entry Regulations

VISAS AND PASSPORTS

Until just a few years ago, tourist visas were issued routinely to all visitors upon arrival. Brazil has now adopted a reciprocal policy, requiring an entry visa, which must be obtained before arriving in Brazil, for citizens of those countries which also require Brazilians to apply for visas to visit. US citizens are required to arrive with a visa in order to enter the country; Britons and Germans are not. Your airline or travel agent should be able to tell you whether you need to apply for a visa before traveling. Alternatively, contact the nearest Brazilian consulate or embassy.

If your passport was issued by one of the countries whose citizens are not required to arrive with an entry visa, it will be stamped with a tourist visa upon entry that will permit you to remain in the country for 90 consecutive days. If you apply for a visa abroad, it will permit entry into Brazil for 90 days following the issue date. Upon entry, you will receive the same tourist visa, valid for 90 days beginning with the entry date stamped in your passport. If you are traveling to several countries and not straight to Brazil, the entry visa needn't be issued in your home country, but it's a good idea to allow for enough time to make sure you avoid unpleasant surprises and hassles.

Temporary visas are issued to foreigners who will be employed in a specific activity in Brazil, for which they must stay longer than a tourist visa would allow or who will be working or doing business in the country. This is usually the case of a student, journalist or researcher, or someone in the employment of a multi-national company. If this is your case, contact a Brazilian consulate or embassy well before you plan to travel, as it is usually difficult or even impossible to change the status of your visa once you are in the country. If you come with a tourist visa, you will probably have to leave the country to obtain and return on another type of visa.

Permanent visas which allow foreigners to reside and work in Brazil without giving up their own nationality are more difficult to obtain. Once again, it's best to contact a Brazilian consulate or embassy for more specific information applying to your particular situation.

CUSTOMS

You will be given a declaration form to fill in on the airplane before arrival. Once at the airport, customs officials spot check 50 percent of incoming "nothing to declare" travelers. If you are coming as a tourist and bringing articles obviously for your personal use, you will have no problem. As in most countries, food products of animal origin, plants, fruit, and seeds may be confiscated.

You can bring in $500 worth of anything bought at the airport duty-free shop – with no restriction as to quantity, type of goods or age – and $500 worth of anything brought from abroad, except liquor which is limited to one bottle (each) of wine and spirits.

If you are coming on business, it's best to check with the consulate as to what limitations or obligations you are subject to. If you must bring some type of specialized equipment, especially computers, into the country, apply for written authorization through a Brazilian consulate before traveling and then register with customs for temporary entrance – you must bring it along when you leave the country.

Electronic devices worth no more than $300 can be brought in on a tourist visa and need not leave the country with you. Although you are obviously not meant to sell such items while visiting as a tourist, they can be left in the country as gifts. Professional samples may be brought in as long as the quantity does not lead customs inspectors to suspect that they are, in fact, for sale.

Items that may be allowed into the country, although they won't be confiscated, may be detained by the customs service and returned to you as you leave the country. Once again, if in doubt, consult the nearest consulate and bring their written reply with you.

Baggage of outgoing travelers is usually never checked, except for a security check on hand luggage. If you have purchased what could be considered a reasonable amount for a tourist of any item – including semi-precious stones – you have nothing to worry about. Be wary of wild animal skins, including alligator, as hunting of these species is strictly prohibited. It's a good idea to find out first what you can bring back into your own country.

EXTENSION OF STAY

The 90-day tourist visa can be renewed once only for another 90 days, so that you can stay a maximum of 180 days as a tourist in Brazil. To obtain such an extension, you must go to the immigration sector of the federal police located at Av. Venezuela, 2 (downtown, near Praça Mauá), tel: 291-2142 ext. 1136. Opening hours: Monday to Friday 11am–4pm. This can be a bit baffling for someone who has not mastered the language. Contact your country's consulate for help and orientation.

It is important to remember that, due to new legislation, a person with a visa extended to 180 days cannot enter the country again within one year.

Health

Brazil does not normally require any health or inoculation certificates for entry, nor will you be required to have one to enter another country from Brazil. However, if you plan to travel from Rio into areas outside of cities in the Amazon region or in the Pantanal in Mato Grosso, it is recommended that, for your own comfort and safety, you have a yellow fever shot (protects you for 10 years, but is only effective after 10 days, so plan ahead). It is also a good idea to protect yourself against malaria in these jungle areas and although there is no vaccine against malaria, there are drugs that will give you immunity while you are taking them. Consult your local public health service and be sure to get a certificate for any vaccination. You can get a yellow fever shot in Rio at the Health Ministry vaccination post located at Praça Marechal Ancora (near the ferry boat station), tel: 240-8628.

Drinking Water

Don't drink tap water in Brazil. Although water in the cities is treated and is sometimes quite heavily chlorinated, people filter water in their homes. Any hotel or restaurant will have inexpensive bottled mineral water, both carbonated (com gas or "with gas") and uncarbonated (sem gas or "without gas"). If you are out in the sun, make sure you drink extra fluids.

SUNBURN PREVENTIVES

Don't underestimate the tropical sun! Often, there is a pleasant breeze as you loll on the beach and you are not aware of how the sun is baking you, until it's too late. You should be especially careful if you're coming from a cold, northern winter where your skin has not seen the sun for months.

Use an appropriate sunscreen or filtro solar (there are several excellent brands on sale in Brazil), start out with short sessions and avoid the hottest part of the day. It's silly to be too eager and end up with a painful sunburn that will cause peeling. Take care of your skin after being at the beach by using a moisture cream. Remember to drink enough – coconut water, fruit juice or mineral water are excellent.

Money

The plano Real swept away the previous currency, the Cruzeiro. All the old bills were withdrawn, and new bills and coins introduced. The exchange rate is now (more or less) US$ 1.00–R$ 1.85.

The use of commas and decimal points in Portuguese is the opposite of what you are probably used to. In Portuguese, one thousand Reais is written R$ 1.000,00.

You can exchange dollars, yen, pounds and other currencies at accredited banks, hotels and tourist agencies. If you can't find one, just about any travel agency will exchange your currency, although this is, strictly speaking, an illegal transaction. The few hotels that exchange traveler's checks give a poor rate. They cannot change any leftover Reais back into your currency at the end of your stay.

Banks will not exchange Reais or traveler's checks into foreign currency. The only exception is the Banco do Brasil branches located at international airports. As you leave the country, they will exchange back, at the official rate, 30 percent of the currency you exchanged at a similar airport branch bank on your way into Brazil as long as you show the receipt for the initial exchange. You can't get your traveler's checks cashed into dollars anywhere at all.

TRAVELER'S CHECKS/CREDIT CARDS

Most hotels will accept payment in travelers checks or with almost any major credit card. Many restaurants also take credit cards and will usually display those which they accept at the entrance – most frequently Diners Club, American Express, MasterCard and Visa – which all have offices in Brazil. Back home, your bill will be calculated using the tourist exchange rate. The exception to this is for airline tickets purchased on credit in Brazil (including tickets for travel just within Brazil). These will be calculated at the less favorable official rate.

Of course, you could also pay for items with dollars. However, this is not recommended, as it is against Brazilian law.

Public Holidays

National holidays in Brazil are moved to the nearest Monday, with the exception of New Year's Day, Christmas, Easter and Carnival.

January 1: New Year's Day (national holiday)
January 20: Saint Sebastian Day, Rio's patron saint (holiday in Rio only)
Feb/March: Carnival, celebrated all over Brazil on the four (moveable) days leading up to Ash Wednesday
March/April: Easter (Good Friday is a holiday, moveable)
April 21: Tiradentes Day honors martyred hero of Brazil's independence (holiday)
May 1: Labor Day (national holiday)
May/June: Corpus Christi (national holiday, moveable)
June/July: *Festas Juninas*, a series of street festivals take place in June and early July in honor of Saints John, Peter and Anthony and feature music and dancing, bonfires, and mock marriages and special food and drink
September 7: Independence Day (national holiday)
October 12: Nossa Senhora (Our Lady) de Aparecida, Brazil's patron saint (national holiday)
November 2: All Souls' Day (national holiday)
November 15: Proclamation of the Republic (national holiday) also election day in Brazil
December 25: Christmas Day (national holiday)
December 31: Gifts are offered to *Iemanjá*, the African-Brazilian goddess of the sea, on Rio's beaches.

Getting There

BY AIR

A total of 29 airlines offer international services to and from Brazil with a variety of routes, but most incoming flights head for São Paulo. Depending on where you are coming from, there are also direct flights to Rio de Janeiro and Brasília, Salvador and Recife and Manaus on the Amazon River – all of which have air links with Rio. Direct international flights connect Brazil with both the east and west coast of the United States of America, as well as with Canada, major cities in Europe and South America, Japan and several African cities. The flight to Rio from New York is 9 hours, from Miami slightly less, and from Los Angeles 13 hours; flights from Europe average 11–12 hours. Almost all international flights are overnight, so that you arrive in the early morning.

There are a variety of special low-cost package deals, some of them real bargains. A travel agent will be able to find out what is available and make arrangements at no extra cost to you.

Upon arrival, Rio's International Airport has facilities for exchanging currency and information posts to help you find transportation into town.

Varig Brazilian Airlines
Chicago: 35E Monroe Street, IL 60603. Tel: (312) 750 1406.
London: 61 Conduit Street, W1R 0HG. Tel: (0171) 478 2105.
Miami: 200 South Biscayne Blvd. Suite 65-A, FL 33131. Tel: (305) 358 4935.
New York: 630 Fifth Avenue, Suite 1670. Tel: (212) 459 0210.
San Francisco: 124 Geary Street, CA 94108. Tel: (415) 398 0972.

BY SEA

There is no regular ocean passenger service to Brazil, although it is possible to come by boat. Both Oremar and Linea C,

which operate cruises up and down the Atlantic coast of South America during the European winter, will take on transatlantic passengers when the ships come over and return. One of Linea C's cruises out of Rio visits Miami. Several round-the-world cruise ships call at Brazilian ports and it is possible to book for just the trip to Rio. Special cruises are also organized to Rio for Carnival. The Blue Star Line, headquartered in London, carries a limited number of passengers on its cargo boats which cross the Atlantic and call at several Brazilian ports, including Rio. Passenger trips with cargo operators can be booked through Strand Cruise and Travel Centre, London. Tel: 0171-836 6363, fax: 0171-497 0078.

BY ROAD

There are bus services between Rio de Janeiro and major cities in neighboring South American countries, with direct lines to Asuncion (Paraguay), Buenos Aires (Argentina), Montevideo (Uruguay) and Santiago (Chile). While undoubtedly a good way to see the countryside, remember that distances are great and you will be sitting in a bus for several days and nights.

On Departure

You must *always* re-confirm your flights by telephone or at an office of the airline at least 48 hours beforehand. If you don't, you risk being 'bounced' onto a later flight.

Remember to have at least a few *Reais* at the end of your stay to pay the airport tax as you check in for your outbound flight. It is about US$36,00, but can only be paid for in local currency.

Useful Addresses

TOURIST INFORMATION

Brazil's national tourism board, Embratur, headquartered in Rio, will send information abroad.

Embratur, Rua Uruguaiana 174 8th Flr, Rio de Janeiro, tel: (021) 509-6017. Embratur has also re-opened its New York bureau, its only foreign office to-date.

BRAZILIAN EMBASSIES

Australia, 19 Forster Crescent, Yaralumla, Canberra, ACT 2600, tel: (6) 273 2372, fax: (6) 273 2375.
Canada, 450 Wilbrod Street, Ottawa, Ontario, K1N 6M8, tel: (613) 237 1090, fax: (613) 237 6144.
Republic of Ireland, Harcourt Centre, Europa House, Harcourt Street, Dublin 2, tel: (1) 475 6000, fax: (1) 475 1341.
United Kingdom, 32 Green Street, London W1Y 4AT, tel: (0171) 499 0877, fax: (0171) 493 5105.
United States
Washington DC: 3006 Massachusetts Avenue NW, DC 20008, tel: (202) 745 2700, fax: (202) 745 2827.
Houston: 1700 West Loop South 1450A, TX 77027-3006, tel: (713) 961 3063.
Miami: 2601 Bayshore Drive 800, FL 33133-5412, tel: (305) 285 6200.
There are Brazilian consulates in Atlanta, Chicago, Dallas, Dayton, Los Angeles, New Orleans and San Francisco. Besides general information, if you are a US citizen you will have to contact one of these missions to obtain a visa before traveling to Brazil.

Practical Tips

Business Hours

Business hours for most offices are 9am–6pm Monday through Friday. Lunch "hours" may last literally hours.

Banks open at 10am and close at 4.30pm Monday through Friday. The *casas de câmbio* currency exchanges operate usually 9am–5 or 5.30pm.

Stores are mostly open 9am–6.30 or 7pm, but may stay open much later, depending on their location. The shopping centers are open Monday through Saturday 10am–10pm, although not all the shops inside keep the same hours. Large department stores are usually open 9am–10pm Monday through Friday, 9am–6.30pm on Saturdays. Most supermarkets are open 8am–8pm, although some stay open later.

Service station hours vary, but they have the option of staying open 24 hours a day, seven days a week.

Religious Services

Catholicism is the official and dominant religion in Brazil, but many people are followers of religions of African origin. Of these, *Candomblé* is the purer form, with deities (the *orixás*), rituals, music, dance and even the language very similar to what is practised in the parts of Africa from which it was brought. *Umbanda* involves a syncretism with Catholicism, in which each *orixá* corresponds to a Catholic saint.

Spiritualism is widely practised in Brazil, combining African and European influences. Many nominal Catholics attend both Afro-Brazilian or spiritual and Christian rites.

Candomblé is practised mostly in Bahia, and while there are followers in Rio de Janeiro, they keep quite a low profile. *Umbanda* and spiritualism, however, have a large following in Rio and your hotel can assist in arrangements to see a ceremony – visitors are welcome so long as they show respect for other's beliefs. Ask permission before taking any photographs.

If you wish to attend a church service while in Rio, besides numerous Catholic churches, there are several Protestant sects and synagogues. Both Our Lady of Mercy (Catholic) at Rua Visconde de Caravelas, 48, Botafogo, tel: 537-9065, and Christchurch (Anglican) at Rua Real Grandeza, 99, Botafogo, tel: 538-2978, have English-language church services. For information about other denominations and services in other foreign languages, enquire at your hotel or call a consulate.

Media

NEWSPAPERS AND MAGAZINES

The *Miami Herald*, the Latin American edition of the *International Herald Tribune* and the *Wall Street Journal* are available on many newsstands in the big cities, as are news magazines such as *Newsweek*, *Time* and *Business Week*. At larger newsstands and airport bookshops, you can find other foreign newspapers and a good range of international publications, including German, French and English magazines.

Newsstands in Copacabana selling international newspapers are: On Rua Santa Clara, between Nossa Senhora de Copacabana and Domingos Ferreira and corner of Avenida Prado Jr. and Barata Ribeiro. In Ipanema/Leblon: Rua Visconde de Pirajá in front of Praça General Osório and the corner of Avenida Ataulfo de Paiva and Rua Rita Ludolf.

You may want to buy a local paper to find out what's on in town (besides the musical shows, there are many foreign movies showing in the original language with Portuguese subtitles) or to check the exchange rate. You don't need to be proficient in Portuguese to read the entertainment listings under the headings cinema, show, dance, *músic*, *teatro*, *televisão*, *exposições*. *Crianças* means "children," and the exchange rates for foreign currencies are listed under *câmbio*.

If you know some Portuguese and want to read the Rio newspapers, the most authoritative and respected are the *Jornal do Brasil* and *O Globo*. There is no nationwide paper, but these large dailies circulate throughout a good part of the country.

RADIO

There are close to 2,000 radio stations in Brazil – over 100 in the state of Rio de Janeiro – which play international and Brazilian pop hits, as well as a variety of Brazil's rich musical offerings, reflecting regional tastes. A lot of American music, as well as classical music, is played, including Sunday afternoon operas in some areas. The Culture Ministry station often has some very interesting musical programs. All broadcasts are in Portuguese. If you have a radio that picks up short-wave transmissions, the *Voice of America* and the *BBC World Service* broadcast English-language programs to Brazil.

TELEVISION

Brazilian television is very sophisticated – so much so that Brazil successfully exports programs, not just to developing nations, but to Europe as well. There are five national and about 250 local networks, which bring television to nearly all parts of Brazil.

Only one network, the educational channel, is government-controlled. Brazil's giant *TV Globo* is the fourth largest commercial network in the world. With over 40

Tipping

Most restaurants will usually add a 10 percent service charge onto your bill. If you are in doubt as to whether it has been included, it's best to ask (*O serviço está incluido?*). Give the waiter a bigger tip if you feel the service was special. Although many waiters will don a sour face if you don't tip above the 10 percent included in the bill, you have no obligation to do so. Tipping at a lunch counter is optional, but people often leave the change from their bill – even as little as US10¢ is appreciated.

Hotels will also add a 10 percent service charge to your bill, but this doesn't necessarily go to the individuals who were helpful to you. Don't be afraid that you are overtipping – if you tip as much as you would at home, it will be considered very generous indeed. If you tip too little in hotels, however, it could be insulting and it would have been better not to tip at all.

Tipping taxi drivers is optional, most Brazilians don't. Again, if your driver has been especially

helpful or waited for you, reward him appropriately. Drivers should be tipped if they help with the luggage. Tip the airport porter (he may tell you how much it is) and tip the last porter to help you. What you pay goes into a pool.

A 10–20 percent tip is expected in barbershops and beauty salons. Shoeshine boys, gas station attendants, etc. should be paid about a third to half of what you would expect to tip at home. Boys offering to watch your car on the street expect a few coins when you return to collect the car. It's sometimes better to pay in advance if they ask you, especially outside a busy nightclub or theater, or you may find the car scratched when you return.

If you are a house guest, leave a tip for any household help (who cooked or laundered for you while you were there). Ask your hosts how much would be appropriate; you can always tip in dollars if you want to – this will be especially appreciated. A small gift from home may be even better.

stations in a country with a high illiteracy rate, it has great influence over the information many people have access to, so much so that there is considerable controversy over its role in elections, not least the presidential elections.

The Brazilian soap opera or *telenovela* is a unique feature. They're shown on prime time and just about everybody watches, getting so caught up in the continuing drama that they schedule social and even professional activities so as not to clash with the crucial chapters. The well-made soaps both reflect customs and set trends in fashion, speech and social habits. You might find it interesting to watch a few simply because they are considered a true mirror of Brazilian urban middle-class society.

Only about a third of all television programs are imports – mostly from

the United States. Foreign series, specials, sports coverage and movies are dubbed in Portuguese, except for some of the late-night movies and musical shows. Most top hotels have satellite dishes and receive the English-language *Armed Forces Radio and Television Service* with a selection of news and sports from American networks. Cable television is the fastest growing media industry in Brazil.

Postal Services

Post offices are generally open to the public 8am–5pm Monday–Friday, and are closed on Saturday, Sunday and holidays. Some branch offices stay open until much later. The post office in the Rio de Janeiro International Airport is open 24 hours a day. Post offices are usually designated with a yellow sign reading *correiros* or sometimes

"ECT" (for *Empresa de Correios e Telégrafos*, translated – Postal and Telegraph Company).

An airmail letter to or from USA takes about a week. Domestic post is usually delivered a day or two after it is mailed. National and international rapid mail service is available, as well as registered post and parcel service (the post office has parcel boxes available). Stamps for collectors can be purchased at the post office.

Have mail sent to you at your hotel. Some consulates will hold mail for citizens of the country they represent, but tend to discourage this practice.

Telecoms

Pay phones in Brazil use either tokens or phone cards which are sold at newsstands, bars or shops, usually located near the phones. Ask for *fichas de telefone* (the "i" is pronounced like a long "e" and the "ch" has an "sh" sound). Each *ficha* is good for three minutes, after which your call will be cut off. To avoid being cut off in the middle of a call, insert several tokens into the slot – unused tokens will be returned when you hang up. For long-distance calls, you will need the higher-value *fichas de telefone DDD* (pronounced "day day day"), which can only be used in special long-distance phones. The phone card is a *cartão de telefone* and comes in several values. The sidewalk *telefone público* is also called an *orelhão* (big ear) because of the protective shell which takes the place of a booth – yellow for local or collect calls, blue for direct-dial long-distance calls within Brazil. You can also call from a *posto telefônico*, a telephone company station (at most bus stations and airports), where you can either buy tokens, use a phone and pay the cashier afterward, or make a credit card or collect call.

International calls to almost any country can be made from Brazil. Country codes are listed at the front of telephone directories. To place a call:

Direct dialing – **00**+country code +area code+phone number.
000333 – information regarding long distance calls (area codes, directory assistance, complaints).
000111 – international operator. Go through operator to place person-to-person, collect and credit-card calls. Operators and interpreters who speak several languages are available.
000334 – information regarding rates – international rates go down 20 percent 8pm–5am (Brasília time) Monday–Saturday and all day Sunday.
Long Distance Domestic Calls: Area codes within Brazil are listed on the first few pages of directories.
Direct dialing (IDD) – **0**+area code+the phone number.
Direct-dial collect call – **9**+area code+phone number. A recorded message will tell you to identify yourself and the city from which you are calling after the beep. If the party you are calling does not accept your call, they simply hang up.
107 – operator-assisted collect call from pay phone (no token needed). Domestic long-distance rates go down 75 percent every day 11pm–6am and are half price weekdays 6–8am and 8–11pm, Saturday 2–11pm and Sunday and holidays 6am–11pm.
Other service telephone numbers:
101 – domestic long-distance operator
102 – local directory assistance
area code+102 – directory assistance in that area.
108 – information regarding rates
135 – telegrams (local, national and international)
134 – wake-up service
130 – correct time

TELEX

Telex can be sent from certain post offices – the branch at Av. N.S. de Copacabana 540-A is close to most tourist hotels. The post office at the International Airport has telex facilities and most hotels are equipped with this service for their guests.

Tourist Offices

Besides the national tourism board, Embratur, each state has its own tourism board – Rio's is called Turisrio. Rio has a city tourism board as well – Riotur. Tourist facilities at the Rio de Janeiro international airport are available to orient the visitor and help you find transportation and accommodation (if you don't have reservations). If you would like the address for a tourism board in an area not listed here, you can obtain it through the national tourist board, Embratur.
Embratur, Rua Uruguaiana 174, 8th floor. Tel: 509-6017/ 6185/6292.
Riotur, (City of Rio Tourism Authority), Rua da Assembléia 10, 9th floor. Tel: 217-7575, fax: 531-1872, email: http://www.rio.rj.gov.br/riotur Turisrio runs the information counters at the arrival section of the international airport, from 5am–11pm, tel: 398-4073/ 4077. Hotels are always an excellent source of information and can indicate local happenings and tourist offerings such as sightseeing and excursions, entertainment and transportation.
Turisrio, Rua da Assembléia 10, 7th and 8th floor, 20.011 Rio de Janeiro, RJ. Tel: (021) 531-1922, fax: 531-2506, telex: 213 7575 email: http://www.turisrio.com.br Information Centers: International Airport, Bus Station, Corcovado, Sugar Loaf, Cinelândia Subway Station, Marina da Gloria.
International Airport, Blue Area, tel: 398-4077, Red Area, tel: 398-4073, Green Area, tel: 398-3034. Open 6am–midnight.
Tourist Services Center, Avenida Princesa Isabel 183 (Copacabana), tel: 541-7522/ 542-8004. Open 8am–8pm.
Alô Rio (a tour information service which operates in English as well as Portuguese), tel: 542-8080. Open 8am–8pm.

TELEGRAM

Telegrams can be sent from any post office. You can send a telegram by telephone by dialing 135. Your hotel can arrange this. If you are a house guest, the operator can tell you how much will be charged on your host's phone bill.

FACSIMILE

Nearly all hotels have this service. There are also many office services bureaux, travel agents, post offices and other outlets. The charges for sending a fax vary widely.

Travel Packages

A variety of individual and group tours to Rio are available. Some are all-inclusive packages with transportation, food and lodging, excursions and entertainment thrown in; some include only international air transportation and hotel accommodation. Special tours to Rio for Carnival usually include tickets to the big samba parade and club balls. Other special interest tours are also organized. A travel agent will be able to supply you with information about different options being offered.

If you aren't in Rio on a tour which includes "everything" or if you are but would prefer something else to what is scheduled on a given day, arrange through your hotel or a local travel agent to join a variety of local tours. Air-conditioned buses take tour groups to Corcovado, Sugarloaf and other lookout points. On city tours, you visit the Botanical Gardens and Tijuca National Park and there's also soccer at Maracanã stadium.

Day tours on the water include visits to Paquetá Island and the Paradise Island Tour. A half or full day outing can be booked on the Bateau Mouche, Tuesday–Sunday and on holidays. The morning cruise sails out of the bay to visit the islands that you see from the beach in Ipanema and Leblon. The after-noon cruise tours the bay, including a stop at Paquetá. The full day cruise offers both routes with lunch included. The boat leaves Praça 15 (downtown). Spanish Cuisine, Sol e Mar, Av. Nestor Mozeira 11 (Botafogo), tel: 543-1663.

Gray Line, tel: 512-9919, offers many tours, the most unusual of which are a helicopter ride over the city and a thrilling day of river rafting in the mountains.

H. Stern Jewelers offer a tour of their workshops at their headquarters in Ipanema. Rua Visconde de Pirajá 490, tel: 259-7442.

The Roteiros Culturais historic walking tours (in English) of the older parts of the downtown Centro district can be arranged for groups through **Blumar**, Rua Visconde de Pirajá 550, downstairs 107/109, tel: 511-3636. Evening tours will take you to a samba show, where diner is often included. Or visit Afro-Brazilian spiritualist rites. Day trips out of Rio by bus can be taken to beach towns in both directions – Búzios, Cabo Frio etc. up the coast and Angra dos Reis, Paraty, Pedro de Guaratiba and Itacuruçá down the coast – or to the mountain towns of Petrópolis and Teresópolis.

If you want to venture further afield, you can take a tour to another part of Brazil from Rio. There are day trips by plane to Brasília or the Iguaçu falls, or tours to the Amazon and Pantanal, the south, the northeast or the colonial cities of Minas Gerais. In the peak season there may be a wait, so make reservations beforehand.

Ocean cruises out of Rio go south to Buenos Aires and up in the Caribbean, calling at Brazilian ports. These are organized by Linea C and Oremar. Make reservations well in advance. The camping Clube do Brasil (Rua Senador Dantas 75, 29th floor. Tel: 210-3171) organizes trekking tours in remote scenic areas.

Embassies and Consulates

Addresses and telephone numbers for consulates in Rio de Janeiro are listed below. It's a good idea to call before visiting – diplomatic missions frequently do not keep normal business hours. If you're on business, your consulate's commercial sector can be helpful.
Australia: Avenida Rio Branco 1, Suite 810. Tel: 518-3351
Canada: Rua Lauro Muller 116, Suite 2707. Tel: 542-7593.
UK: Praia do Flamengo 284, 2° andar (Flamengo). Tel: 553-3223.
USA: Av. Pres. Wilson, 147 (Centro). Tel: 292-7117.

Emergencies

MEDICAL SERVICES

Should you need a doctor while in Rio, the hotel you are staying at will be able to recommend reliable professionals who often speak several languages. Many of the better hotels have a doctor on duty. Your consulate will also be able to supply you with a list of physicians who speak your language. Clínica Gaudino Campos, Avenida Nossa Senhora De Copacabana 492, tel: 548-9966.

Check with your health insurance company or travel agent before traveling to make sure your insurance plan covers any medical service necessary while abroad.

Emergency Hospitals
Miguel Couto, Rua Bartolomeu, Mitre 1108. Tel: 274-2121.
Rocha Maia, Rua General Severiano 91, Botafogo. Tel: 295-2121.
Sousa Aguiar, Praça da República 111, Centro. Tel: 296-4114 or 221-2121.
Ambulance: dial 192.
Fire brigade: dial 193.

Drugstores
Prescription drugs are available in abundance – frequently without a prescription – and you may find old favorites that have been banned for

years in your home country. Bring a supply of prescription drugs that you take regularly. Aspirin, antacids, bandaids, sunscreen, etc. are easily available. Many pharmacies stay open until 10pm and there are 24-hour drugstores in several parts of town.

Drugstores offer a variety of cosmetics, including many familiar brands. Sanitary napkins and tampons can be found in any drugstore or supermarket. Always open are the Farmácia Piaui (Av. Ataulfo de Paiva 1283-A in Leblon, tel: 274-7322; Rua Barata Ribeiro 646-B in Copacabana, tel: 548-7445), the Drogaria Cruzeiro (Av. N.S. de Copacabana 1212 in Copacabana, tel: 267-1421) and the Farmácia do Leme (Av. Prado Junior 237-A in Copacabana, tel: 275-3847).

Getting Around

On Arrival

BY TAXI

Until you get your bearings, you are better off taking a special airport taxi for which you pay in advance at the airport at a fixed rate, set according to your destination. There will be less of a communication problem, no misunderstanding about the fare and even if the driver takes you around by the "scenic route," you won't be charged extra for it. If you decide to take a regular taxi, check out the fares posted for the official taxis so that you'll have an idea of the normal rate.

BY BUS

A special airport bus service provides transportation from Rio's International Airport, passing through the downtown business district (Centro) and then on to the domestic Santos Dumont airport or looping by the major beach hotels in Copacabana, Ipanema, Leblon, São Conrado and out to Barra da Tijuca. Ask at the airport information desk whether your hotel is on the route. Another option is to take the special bus to the in-town Santos Dumont airport and take a taxi.

BY CAR

If you're really adventurous, you can rent a car at either one of the airports. Some of the top class hotels will send a driver to pick you up at the airport – it's best to make arrangements beforehand when you make your room reservations.

BY AIR

For travel within Brazil, the major airlines are Transbrasil, Varig, Vasp and Tam, with several other regional carriers which service the smaller cities. All four of the larger lines fly extensive routes throughout the country and have ticket counters at the airports and ticket offices in other cities. Tickets can also be purchased at travel agencies, often at hotels, and reservations can be made by phone or telex. Unless you want to play things by ear, it is easiest to make reservations at home through your travel agent, before traveling.

Different lines have similar prices for the same routes, although it's hard to say what these are, as prices are always changing.

There is a 20 percent discount for some night flights (*vôo econômico* or *vôo noturno*) with departures between midnight and 6am. Sometimes 50 percent discounts are offered for women on these night flights. Most routes will have a night flight by one or another of the major airlines.

Transbrasil and Varig also offer an airpass, which must be purchased outside Brazil. It costs US $440 (mid-1995 price), is valid for 21 days and allows you to visit four cities (not including your starting point in Brazil). Extra stops are US $100 each. Ask your travel agent about this option – it is a good deal if you plan to travel extensively within Brazil.

The large airlines also cooperate in a shuttle service between Rio and São Paulo (with flights every half hour), Rio and Brasília (flights every hour) and Rio and Belo Horizonte (usually about 10 flights per day). Although you may be lucky, a reservation is a good idea.

On domestic flights checked baggage is limited to 44 lb (20 kg) and internationally accepted norms apply for hand luggage.

An air taxi service is also available to fly anywhere in the world. Enquire at the airport or make arrangements through a travel agent or your hotel.

Be sure to verify from which airport your flight leaves, if the city has more than one. Your hotel will be able to help you with such arrangements and provide transportation to the airport.

BY RAIL

Except for overcrowded urban commuter railways, trains are not a major form of transportation in Brazil and rail links are not extensive. If you have the time, the night train is one of the nicest ways to travel between Rio and São Paulo. Reserve in advance (tel: 263-9856). The train leaves at 11.30pm and arrives at 8am. You can enjoy dinner in the diner car or in your sleeper compartment.

BY BUS

Comfortable, on-schedule bus services are available to all parts of Brazil and to several other South American countries from Rio. For the foreigner, buses are inexpensive.

Remember that distances are long and bus rides can take days. You might prefer to break a long journey with a stop along the way. Various comfort levels are available. On the six-hour ride between Rio de Janeiro and São Paulo, for example, you can either take the regular bus, with upholstered, reclining seats, or the more expensive *leito* sleeper, with wider and fully reclining seats with foot rests, as well as coffee and soft drinks aboard.

At busy times like holidays, buses on the Rio-São Paulo line depart at the rate of one per minute. On other routes, there may be one bus per day (such as the Rio-Belém route, a 52-hour trip) or just one or two per week. You can purchase your ticket in advance through a travel agent or at the bus station.

If you're on a flexible holiday schedule, try to avoid the weekend exodus when *cariocas* escape to the resort cities up and down the coast and in the mountains. Traffic bogs down and the bus depot becomes impossibly crowded, especially during the school holidays (December–February and July).

Public Transport

BY BUS

Only a small percentage of Brazilians can afford cars, so public transportation is used a great deal. Special air-conditioned buses (known as a *frescão*) connect residential areas to the downtown business district. One line links Rio's two commercial airports and another runs from the international airport out to Barra da Tijuca, passing by the beach hotels in Copacabana, Ipanema, Leblon and São Conrado. The *frescões* stop at regular bus stops. As you get on, you will be handed a ticket.

Take a seat and an attendant will come around to collect your fare – which will be modest by Western standards. Your hotel can help provide information about bus routes, but most hotels discourage tourists from riding anything but the special buses.

Another special bus line, the *jardineira*, follows the beaches from Leme to São Conrado (through Copacabana, Ipanema and Leblon). White posts mark where the *jardineiras* stop along the way. The open sides (giving the buses the appearance of an old-fashioned street car) and slower pace allow you to take in the sights.

The regular buses are very cheap. Get on through the back door (often quite a high step up) and after paying the *trocador*, who will give you change, move through the turnstile. It's a good idea to have your fare ready – several people may board at your stop and all have to get through the turnstile before they can sit down. This is a favorite bottleneck for pickpockets who can jump out the back door as the bus takes off.

If you travel standing, be sure to hold on tight. Although many Rio bus drivers are friendly and helpful, some are particularly inconsiderate of passengers, jamming on the brakes suddenly, careening around corners. Signal when you want to get off by pulling the cord (some buses have buttons) and exit through the front door. Robberies do occur, even on crowded buses, in broad daylight. If you ride the regular city buses, try to avoid the rush hour when passengers on certain lines are packed in tighter than the proverbial sardines in the can. Don't carry valuables, keep your camera inside a bag and shoulderbags in front of you, avoid calling attention to yourself by speaking loudly in a foreign language. In short, be discreet.

BY TAXI

Taxis are probably the best way for visitors to get around in Rio. Of course, it's easy to get "taken for a ride" in a strange city. Whenever possible, take a taxi from your hotel where someone can help you tell the driver where you want to go. Radio taxis that you order by phone are slightly more expensive, but safer and more comfortable.

Although the drivers of the yellow cabs you flag down on the street won't actually rob you, some occasionally try to overcharge or take you the long way around. Try to find out about how much you should expect to pay for a given destination – most trips will be just a few dollars. Airport taxis charge exorbitant rates by Brazilian terms, but you will probably find fares relatively low compared to North America or Europe.

You can book a regular taxi (no extra fee) from Cooper-Transpa, tel: 593-2598. For a radio taxi (percentage above meter) call Coopertramo, tel: 560-2022. For a special taxi (pre-set rate) call Cootramo, tel: 560-0500; or Transcoopass, tel: 590-6891.

Private Transport

CAR RENTAL

Cars are easily rented in Rio. Both **Avis** and **Hertz** operate in Brazil while the two largest Brazilian national chains are **Localiza** and **Nobre**. There are also other good local companies. Rates will vary depending on the type of the car. Some companies charge a flat daily rate, while others charge for mileage. Payment can be charged on major international credit cards. Some companies will charge extra if you rent a car in one city and hand it back in another. If you plan to drive one way only between cities, it's best to rent from one of the two largest chains which have more branches.

Arrangements can be made at the airport as you arrive, through your hotel or at the agencies. An international driver's license facilitates matters, but you can rent a car with your driver's license from home. For a relatively modest fee, you can hire a driver along with the car.

Driving in Brazil may be chaotic compared to what you are used to. Rio drivers are notorious for their erratic lane changing, in-town speeding and disregard for pedestrians and other drivers on the road. Be on the defensive and expect the unexpected. Parking can be difficult downtown. A good solution is to park your car at the Botafogo subway station and take the underground into town. Wherever you park in Rio, always lock the car and never leave anything visible inside the car. Even if you don't think of it as valuable, some Brazilians might.

It seems wherever you park, within seconds a freelance car "guard" will appear, either offering to keep an eye on your car in the hopes of receiving a tip or actually demanding that you pay him in advance for his (dubious) vigilance. The equivalent of US 40 to 50 cents is sufficient. It's best to pay or risk finding some slight damage to the car upon your return.

The Metrô

Rio de Janeiro has an excellent, though not extensive, subway service, with bright, clean, air-conditioned cars. The metrô is one of the easiest way for a tourist to get around without getting lost. Maps in the stations and in each car help you find your way without having to communicate in Portuguese. Lines run out from the city center and service is further extended by bus links, with train-bus combination tickets. Buses which are an extension of subway lines are marked *integração*.

Rio's two lines reach out from downtown only as far south as Botafogo and as far as the northern suburb of Irajá, with stops near the Sambódromo and Maracanã soccer stadium. Bus link-ups extend service on both ends. The Rio subway runs daily from 6am–11pm.

There is just one price for a single (*unitário*) ticket, even if you transfer from one line to another. There are round-trip (*ida e volta*) and multi-fare tickets as well as different combination tickets with buses (*metrô-ônibus*). Tickets are sold in the stations and on the *integração* buses and prices are clearly posted. (*Entrada* = entrance; *saida* = exit).

The highways, especially the interstates, are quite good, but are crowded with many trucks which slow down traffic on winding, climbing stretches in the mountains. If you plan to travel much by road in Brazil, buy the Quatro Rodas (Four Wheels) Brazil road guide, complete with road maps and itineraries, available at most newsstands.

Water Transport

There are regular ferryboat services across the bay to Niteroi and to the bay islands of Paquetá and Governador from the Praça Quinze (XV) station downtown. Both services use huge double-decker ferries and hydrofoils (*aerobarcos*).

A visit to Paquetá makes a nice outing – the regular boat takes 90 minutes, the hydrofoil 15 minutes. The ferries run all day until 11.30pm. Hydrofoils run from 10am–4pm Monday–Friday, 8am–5pm on Saturday, Sunday and holidays. Sailboats, yachts, schooner-like *saveiros* and speed boats can be rented at Marina da Gloria, Aterro do Flamengo (tel: 205-6716). Ocean cruises are organized out of Rio to Buenos Aires and the Caribbean, with stops along Brazil's coast, by Linea C and Oremar. Book well in advance.

Where to Stay

Choosing a Hotel

There is no shortage of good hotels in Rio de Janeiro. High quality international-standard hotels have multilingual staff prepared to help you find what you want and need. Many hotels have their own travel agencies. We list here only a selection of the best hotels in town, in which all rooms have private baths with hot showers, air conditioning, telephone, television and refrigerator-bar. Rates include breakfast and a 10 percent service charge is added on to the bill. But there are less expensive hotels.

You can rent a furnished apartment for just a few days up to several months. Look in the classified advertisements section of the *Jornal do Brasil* or *O Globo* under *Imóveis* (real estate) – *Aluguel* (rental) – *Temporada* (short-term). There are also several decent apartment-hotels in Rio.

It is always best to make reservations well in advance, especially during Carnival or on a major holiday, when hotels are full of Brazilian tourists as well as visiting foreigners. Travelers often come to get away from the Northern Hemisphere winter and Brazilians also travel more during the summer school holidays in January and February, as well as in July. Even if you are traveling to an area that you think is off the usual international tourist route, beware; local facilities there may be saturated with Brazilians.

If you are venturing away from the usual places visited by tourists, for which no hotels are listed here, you will find the *Quatro Rodas Guia Brasil* road guide useful. Available on newsstands, it has road maps and listings including hotels, restaurants and local attractions for 715 Brazilian cities. Although available only in Portuguese, it uses a system of symbols with explanations in English and Spanish.

In smaller towns with fewer options, some of the hotels indicated here offer more modest accommodations. Cheaper hotels cost as little as $15–$20 for a couple. They are usually clean with polite service, but you will most likely have to communicate in Portuguese. It's always a good idea to ask to see the room before deciding to take it.

Hotels in Rio

THE VERY BEST

These hotels have swimming pools and saunas, some of the city's top restaurants, beauty parlors, jewelers, shops, travel agencies, medical personnel, satellite dish antennas (to receive television programs from the US), secretarial services, telex and facsimile and ample facilities for conventions and banquets.

Caesar Park
Av. Vieira Souto 460, Ipanema
Tel: 525-2525
Fax: 521-6000
Telex: (21) 21204
Reservations, toll-free: 0800-210 789
On the beach in Ipanema. Beautiful view from the sundeck, poolside bar on the roof. Tea room, babysitters. Petronius restaurant specializes in seafood and has a sushi bar.
Inter-Continental Ri
Av. Pref. Mendes de Morais 222, São Conrado
Tel: 322-2200
Fax: 322-5500
Toll-free: 0800-118 003
Besides being on the beach, it also has a fabulous view of the surrounding green mountains. Three tennis courts, gymnasium and discotheque nightclub. Barber shop, baby-sitters, car rentals. Restaurants include gourmet Monseigneur and branch of Alfredo's of Rome.
Meridien
Av. Atlântica 1020, Leme
Tel: 275-9922
Fax: 541-6447
Telex: (21) 23183
Reservations, toll-free: 0800-111 554
On the Leme end of Copacabana beach. Has its own cinema and nightclub. Also a barber shop, car rental. Its rooftop Saint-Honoré restaurant is one of Rio's finest.
Sofitel Rio Palace
Av. Atlântica 4240, Copacabana.
Tel: 525-1232
Fax: 525-1200
Toll-free: 0800-210 740
At Ipanema end of Copacabana beach. Nightclub, English-style bar with live music. Babysitters, tea room, car rental. Cassino Atlântico shopping mall is on the ground and basement levels. Le Pré Catalan restaurant is one of the best in Rio.

FIVE-STAR HOTELS

These hotels, which have also earned the Brazilian tourism board, Embratur's maximum five-star rating, are well-served in terms of bars and restaurants, have boutiques and jewelers, beauty parlors and saunas.

Copacabana Palace
Av. Atlântica 1702, Copacabana.
Tel: 548-7070
Fax: 235-7330
Toll-free: 0800-211 533
Elegant old building on the beach in Copacabana, a relic of the casino days. Pleasant poolside restaurant, art gallery and theater, medical service, barber shop, babysitters, secretarial service and telex.
Everest Rio
Rua Prudente de Morias 1117, Ipanema
Tel: 532-2282
Fax: 521-3198
Toll-free: 0800-244 485
One block off the beach in Ipanema, in Rio's most fashionable restaurant and shopping area. Barber shop. Rooftop pool with view.

Marina Palace
Rua Delfim Moreira 630, Leblon.
Tel: 259-5212
Fax: 259-1644
On the beach in Leblon. Satellite TV.

Rio Othon Palace
Av. Atlântica 3264, Copacabana
Tel: 522-1522
Fax: 522-1697
Toll-free: 0800-210 799. On Copacabana beach, has a pool, barber shop, babysitting, secretarial and telex services. Rooftop Skylab bar has a great view; chic basement. Also the Studio C nightclub.

Rio Sheraton
Av. Niemeyer 121, Vidigal
Tel: 274-1122
Fax: 239-5643
Toll-free: 0800-118 003
On its own little beach halfway between Leblon and São Conrado. Barbecue house, tennis courts and three swimming pools on seaside grounds. Satellite dish antenna, car rental, travel agency, medical staff, babysitters, secretarial and telex services. Banquet and conference facilities.

LUXURY HOTELS

Leme Othon Palace
Av. Atlântica 656, Leme
Tel: 275-8080
Fax: 275-8080
Toll-free: 0800-118 998
On the beach. Beauty parlor, meeting rooms.

Luxor Copacabana
Av. Atlântica 2554, Copacabana.
Tel: 548-2245
Fax: 255-1858
Reservations, toll-free: 0800-165 322
On the beach. Jewelers.

Marina Rio
Av. Delfim Moreira 696, Leblon
Tel: 239-8844
Telex: (21) 30224
On the beach. Meeting rooms for small groups.

Praia Ipanema
Av. Vieira Souto 706, Ipanema
Tel: 239-9932
Fax: 239-6889
On Ipanema beach. Rooftop pool,

beauty parlor, meeting rooms.

Sol Ipanema
Av. Vieira Souto 320, Ipanema
Tel: 523-0095
Fax: 521-6464
Small rooftop pool, beauty parlor and satellite dish antenna.

ALSO EXCELLENT

California Othon
Av. Atlântica 2616, Copacabana.
Tel: 257-1900
Toll-free: 0800-210 799
Good beachfront location. Beauty parlor.

Gloria
Rua do Russel 632, Gloria 222
Tel: 555-7272
Fax: 555-7282
Toll-free: 0800-213 077
Near downtown and close to the Marina da Gloria. Pool, sauna, beauty parlor, tea room, theater, convention facilities, handicraft shop.

Ipanema Inn
Rua Maria Quitéria 27, Ipanema
Tel: 523-6092
Fax: 511-5094
Low-priced hotel with small but comfortable rooms. Close to beach.

Luxor Continental
Rua Gustavo Sampaio 320, Leme
Tel: 275-5252
Fax: 541-1946
Toll-free: 0800-165 322
One block from beach in Leme. Boutique, jewelers, small meeting room.

Miramar Palace
Av. Atlântica 3668, Copacabana
Tel: 521-1122
Fax: 521-3294
Toll-free: 0800-232 211
On Copacabana beach. Tea room, convention facilities, jeweler.

Ouro Verde
Av. Atlântica 1456, Copacabana.
Tel: 543-4123
Fax: 543-4776
Small hotel on beach in Copacabana. Traditional, high quality Ouro Verde restaurant.

Luxor Regente
Av. Atlântica 3716, Copacabana
Tel: 523-4212
Fax: 267-7693

Toll-free: 0800-213 073
On Copacabana beach. Convention facilities, jeweler, sauna. Excellent Forno e Fagão restaurant.

Trocadero
Av. Atlântica 2064, Copacabana.
Tel: 257-1834
Toll-free: 0800-210 799
On Copacabana beach. Moenda restaurant specializes in Brazilian food.

Hotels Outside Rio

The following is a list of hotels in other cities in the state of Rio de Janeiro.

ANGRA DOS REIS

Hotel do Frade/Portogalo
Reservations tel: (021) 511-5394
Fax: 259-7195
Reservations for both hotels can be made at Rua Marques De São Vicente 124.

BÚZIOS

Auberge de l'Hermitage
Baia Formosa
Tel: (024) 623-1148
Reservations in Rio: (021) 232-0478.

Pousada Casas Brancas
Morro Humaitá, 10
Tel: (024) 623-1458/2147
Fax: 623-2147

Pousada La Chimere
Praça Eugênio Honold 36, Praia dos Ossos
Tel/fax: (024) 623-1108
Reservations in Rio: (021) 220-2129.

Pousada nas Rocas
Ilha Rasa, Marina Porto Buzios
Tel: (024) 629-1303
Fax: (024) 629-1120
Toll-free: 0800-240 640
Reservations in Rio: (021) 223-0001.

CABO FRIO

Ponta de Areia
Av. Espadarte 184, Caminho Verde,

Ogiva
Tel/fax: (024) 643-2053
Pousada Porto Pero
Av. dos Pescadores 2002
Tel/fax: (024) 643-6565
Pousada Portoveleiro
Av. dos Espardartes 129, Caminho
Verde, Ogiva
Tel/fax: (024) 647 3081

ITACURUÇÁ

Hotel do Pierre
Itacuruçá Island
Tel: (021) 688-1560
Jaguanum
Jaguanum Island
Reservations in Rio: (021) 237-5119.

ITATIAIA

Cabanas de Itatiaia
Parque Nacional, km. 8
Tel: (024) 352-1328
Fax:352-1566
Hotel do Ypê
Parque Nacional, km. 13
Tel/fax: (024) 352-1453
Simon
Parque Nacional, km. 13
Tel: (024) 352-1122
Rio Reservations: (021) 262-8829

NOVA FRIBURGO

Bucsky
Estrada Niteroi-Nova, Friburgo, km.
76.5, Mury
Tel: (024) 522-5052
Fax: 22-9769
Telex: (021) 32243
Garlipp
Estrada Niteroi-Nova, Friburgo, km.
70.5, Mury
Tel/fax: (024) 542-1330
Mury Garden
Estrada Niteroi-Nova, Friburgo, km.
70, Mury
Tel: (024) 542-1120
Park Hotel
Al. Princesa Isabel, Parque São
Clemente
Tel/fax: (024) 522-0825
Sans Souci
Rua Itajai, Sans Souci

Tel/fax: (024) 522-7752
Telex: (024) 534348

PARATI

Pousada do Ouro
Rua Dr. Pereira, 145
Tel: (024) 371-2045
Fax: (024) 371-1311
Reservations in Rio: (021) 221-2022.

PETRÓPOLIS

Casa do Sol
Estr. Rio-Petrópolis, km. 115,
Quitandinha
Tel/fax: (024) 243-5062
Riverside Parque
Rua Hermogêneo Silva, 522, Retiro
Tel: (024) 231-0730
Fax: (024) 243 2312
Toll-free: 0800-248 011

RESENDE

River Park
Avenida Nova Resende 262
Tel: (024) 355-3344
Fax: (024) 354-7314

TERESÓPOLIS

Rosa Dos Ventos
Estr. Teresópolis Nova Friburgo, km.
22.6
Tel: (021) 742-8833
Fax: (021) 742-8174
Telex: (021) 34958
São Moritz
Estr. Teresópolis Nova Friburgo, km.
36
Tel/fax: (021) 641-1115
Reservations tel: (021) 239-4445.

Motels

If traveling by car, you should be
aware that motels in Brazil are not
what you're used to at home:
rooms, usually garishly decorated
and outfitted with mirrors, private
pools and round beds, are rented
out by the hour for amorous trysts.

Campgrounds

If you are interested in camping,
contact the **Camping Clube do
Brasil** at their national
headquarters in Rio de Janeiro, at
Rua Senador Dantas 75, 29th floor
(tel: 210-3171). There are several
campgrounds on the outskirts of
Rio. The **Casa do Estudante do
Brasil**, located at Praça Ana Amelia
9, 8th floor, Castelo, in downtown
Rio (tel: 220-7223) has a list of
hostels in 10 Brazilian states,
including several in Rio, which are
registered with the International
Youth Hostel Federation and charge
just a few dollars. Despite the
name, there is no age restriction.

Where to Eat

What to Eat

There are restaurants to suit every taste and budget in Rio, where you can get a meal at practically any time of the night. A big meal early in the morning, however, may be more difficult to find. Breakfast usually consists of café com leite (hot coffee with milk), bread and sometimes fruit. Lunch is the heaviest meal of the day and you might find it very heavy indeed in the hot climate. Supper can be quite late.

Traditional Brazilian cuisine is tastily seasoned, usually not peppery. In a country as large and diverse as Brazil, there are, naturally, regional specialties, some of which can be sampled in Rio restaurants. Rio itself does not have a special cuisine, but borrows recipes from other regions and from around the world. The staple diet for working class cariocas is rice and (usually black) beans, supplemented by some kind of meat and vegetables. A typical lunch in a modest restaurant is rice, beans, French fries and a thin slice of beef steak (bife).

If there is one dish that is truly carioca, it would be black bean feijoada. Although feijoada is popular in Brazil, in Rio it is something of an institution for Saturday lunch. Many consider the best feijoada in town to be served at the **Domus Aurea** (only during events) and **Tiberius** restaurants in the Caesar Park hotel in Ipanema. Other good places to try this local favorite (only served on Saturday) are **Moenda**, **Sal e Pimenta**, **Atlantis** and **Monte Carlo**.

Although travel books will encourage you to get out of your hotel and sample the local fare, in Rio, it just so happens that many of the top restaurants are located in hotels. This includes not only the excellent French and "international" cuisine, but also excellent Brazilian food.

Cuisine from the mountainous state of Minas Gerais is heavy on pork and beans. Some of the restaurants specializing in Brazilian cuisine have such offerings as: tutu (mashed black beans thickened with manioc meal) or feijão tropeiro (fradinho beans, bacon and manioc meal). Minas Gerais also produces delicious pork sausage and queijo minas, a fresh, white, bland cheese served with fruit paste for dessert.

While barbecued meats are not unique to Brazil, the way in which they are served is. Originating in Brazil's south where the gaucho cowboys roast meat over an open campfire, churrasco is popular all over the country and foreign visitors are usually delighted with the churrascaria barbecue restaurants. Those that specialize in the rodizio system offer all the meat you can eat for a set price. But it's not just one type or cut of beef.

Waiters come round to your table with skewers of chicken, pork, sausage and several cuts of beef. Choose what looks best to you and it is sliced right onto your plate. They keep coming back, so don't worry that you'll miss anything. Meanwhile, your table is loaded with a variety of side dishes.

As you would expect in a seaport city, there is plenty of seafood. Most "international" restaurants have many fish, shrimp and other seafood offerings on their menus. The Portuguese restaurants also serve a great deal of seafood (although the bacalhau, dried salted codfish, is imported from colder seas). One of the tastiest local varieties of fish is the badejo sea bass, with firm, white meat. Peixe a Brasileira, which many restaurants include in the menu, is a fish stew served with pirão (manioc root meal cooked with broth from the stew to the consistency of porridge).

Rio's very best restaurants are French. French chefs at such

Bahian Cuisine

The most unusual variety of Brazilian food is the style of cooking from the northeastern state of Bahia, which has a strong African influence. Bahian cuisine uses a lot of seafood, prepared with coconut milk and dendê palm oil. Bahian food can be very hot, although restaurants usually serve the pimenta sauce separately. If you do like it hot, ask for hot malagueta pepper sauce which many restaurants prepare themselves, often jealously guarding the recipe.

Favorite dishes from Bahia include: vatapá (fresh and dried shrimp, fish, ground raw peanuts, coconut milk, dendê oil seasonings thickened with bread into a creamy mush); moqueca (can be made of fish, shrimp, crab meat or a mixture of seafood in a dendê and coconut milk sauce); xinxim de galinha (a chicken fricassee with dendê oil, dried shrimp and ground raw peanuts); caruru (a shrimp-okra gumbo with dendê oil); babá de camarão (cooked and mashed manioc root with shrimp, dendê oil and coconut milk); and acarajé (a patty made of ground beans fried in dendê oil and filled with vatapá, dried shrimp and pimenta).

In Rio, restaurants serving Bahian specialties include: **Moenda** and **Yemanjá**. A stand at the handicraft fair on Praça General Osório in Ipanema on Sundays also sells Bahian food. Most seafood restaurants also include at least one or two Bahian dishes, most often a moqueca.

A modest restaurant in Santa Teresa, **Bar do Arnaudo**, serves food from the northeast. The specialty is dried, salted beef (carne seca or carne do sol).

elegant establishments as **Le Saint Honoré**, **Claude Troisgros** and **Clube Gourmet** include tropical ingredients in their imaginative creations.

Fast food is available at almost every corner in Rio. You will see the familiar golden arches of **McDonald's** which have sprouted up in several neighborhoods. The biggest chain of fast food stores is **Bob's**. **Gordon's** in Copacabana has good sandwiches.

There is a Brazilian alternative, which is worth trying: the *salgadinho*. These little pastries, filled with beef, chicken, cheese, shrimp, *palmito*, etc., can be tiny, and are usually served as hors d'oeuvres at a reception or to go with a drink at a bar.

There are little lunch counters with a variety of these snacks and some of the best can be bought at the bakeries, which you can either take home or eat standing up at the counter, along with a fruit juice or soft drink.

Also at the bakery, try *pão de queijo*, a cheesy quick bread. *Pastelarias*, which specialize in *pasteis* (two thinly-rolled layers of pasta-like dough with a filling sealed between and deep-fried), almost always offer *caldo de cana* or sugar cane juice as well. Instead of French fries, try *aipim* frito, deep-fried manioc root, to go with beer.

Pizza parlors are to be found all over town. The **Mister Pizza** chain probably has the largest number of outlets. Many of the sidewalk restaurants along the beach will serve a cheesy and often quite doughy pizza.

Many Brazilian desserts are made with fruit, coconut, eggs and milk. *Compotes* and thick jams, often served with mild cheese, are made out of many fruits and even squash and sweet potatoes. Avocado is also used as a dessert, mashed or whipped up in the blender with sugar and lemon juice. There are wonderful tropical fruit sherbets and ice creams. Coconut appears in many desserts and candies – sidewalk vendors sell molasses-colored and white *cocadas*.

Portuguese-style egg yolk desserts are delicious, especially *quindim* (a rich, sweet egg yolk and coconut custard). *Doce de leite* is a Brazilian version of caramel, made by boiling milk with sugar, often served with cheese. *Pudim de leite* is a very common dessert, a pudding made with sweetened condensed milk and caramel syrup. Manioc is used in the dessert *bolo de aipim*, a stiff pudding made out of the grated root and coconut.

Sweet shops sell a variety of *docinhos*, or candies and cakes, pies, etc. One of the most special desserts, (and after a large meal on a hot day, perhaps the most appropriate) is tropical fruit – there's always something exotic and delicious in season.

Where to Eat

BRAZILIAN

Academia Da Cachaça
Rua Conde de Bernadote, 26, Leblon
Tel: 239-1542
Open: Monday 4.30pm–last customer, Tuesday to Sunday 11am–last customer. Major credit cards. A small restaurant, always crowded. Specialty dishes with *carne-seca* (dried meat).

Bar do Arnaudo
Rua Almirante Alexandrino 316, Santa Teresa
Tel: 252-7246
Open: Tuesday to Saturday noon–10pm, Sunday noon–8pm. Credit cards: American Express. Specialties of the Northeast in the quaint Santa Teresa hillside district. A favorite order is dried salted beef (*carne de sol*) and manioc root. There can be a long wait on weekends, but reservations are not accepted.

Botequim
Rua Visconde de Caravelas, 184, Botafogo
Tel: 286-3391
Open: Monday to Sunday, 11.30am until the last customer. Major credit cards. There are tables to eat and drink all over the place: in the main building, on the terrace and in the

small garden. The food is typical Brazilian, simple but very tasty. Try the meat dishes and, of course, the *feijoada*.

Escondidinho
Beco dos Barbeiros 12, A & B, Centro
Tel: 242-2234
Open: 11am–6pm, closed: Saturday and Sunday. No credit cards. Full menu of Brazilian food plus each day's special: *muqueca*, *feijoada*, *cozido*, *sarapatel*, chicken in blood sauce, specialties from Minas Gerais.

Flor Do Leblon
Rua Dias Ferreira 521-A, Leblon
Tel: 294-2849
Open: Monday to Sunday 11am–2am. Credit cards: Diners. A simple but very popular restaurant. During the weekends the restaurant spills onto the side-walk to accommodate all the hungry customers. Minced meat dish is a must.

Maria Thereza Weiss
Rua Visconde Silva 152, Largo do IBAM, Botafogo
Tel: 539-1098
Open: noon–1am, closed: Monday. Major credit cards. Maria Thereza Weiss is well known in Brazil for her books on Brazilian cooking. Restaurant in big old house serves selection of Brazilian dishes and traditional international fare as well as an array of traditional Brazilian desserts. A shop outside also sells pastries, sweet snacks and cakes to go.

Moenda
Av. Atlântica 2064, Copacabana (Hotel Trocadero)
Tel: 257-1834
Open: daily noon–midnight. Major credit cards. Brazilian dishes and Bahian specialties. Waitresses in Bahian garb will explain the ingredients. Good *feijoada*. View of Copacabana beach.

Villa Riso
Estrada da Gávea 729, São Conrado
Tel: 322-1444
Open: Tuesday to Sunday 12.30–4pm. Brazilian specialties served on the veranda of an 18th-century plantation house – only for groups as part of Villa Riso's colo-

nial tour. Call direct or go through your hotel.

Yemanjá
Rua de Visconde de Pirajá 128-A, Ipanema
Tel: 247-7004
Open: Tuesday to Friday 6pm–midnight, Sunday to Saturday noon–midnight. Major credit cards. Well-prepared *bahian* dishes such as *acarajé, vatapá, caruru* and *muquecas* are served.

CHINESE AND JAPANESE

Centro China
Rua Alice 88, Laranjeiras
Tel: 558-5398
Open: Tuesday to Friday noon–3pm, 7–11pm, Saturday and Sunday noon–4pm, 7pm–midnight. All credit cards. Good Chinese food. Owner, Ming, is from Shanghai. Shark's fin soup, tofu, sweet and sour pork. View of the lagoon.

Grande Muralha
Av. Maracaná 987, Suite 3073
Tel: 568-6389
Open: Monday to Saturday noon–3pm, 7–11.30pm, Sunday noon–10.30pm. No credit cards. Peking and Cantonese cuisine at moderate prices.

Madame Butterfly
Rua Barâo da Torre 472, Ipanema.
Tel: 267-4347
Open: Monday to Sunday noon–2am. Major credit cards. A sophisticated restaurant with some outstanding sushi. Frequented by the rich and beautiful *cariocas*.

Miako
Rua do Ouvidor 45, upstairs, Centro
Tel: 232-6640
Open: Monday to Saturday 11.30am–3pm, closed: Sunday. Credit cards: American Express. One of Rio's best Japanese restaurants. *Sushi, sashimi, teppanyaki, tanuki-udon, tempura.* Downtown location.

Sushi Leblon
Rua Dias Ferreiras 256, Leblon
Tel: 274-1342
Open: Tuesday to Saturday 7pm–1am, Sunday 1pm–midnight. Major credit cards. *Sushis, sashimis* and *saké* animate this

arty hangout. Some dishes created by the restaurant like the hot *maki* are now legends among Japanese food lovers.

Tanaka
Rua Bartolomeu Mitre 112, Leblon
Tel: 259-5491
Open Tuesday to Sunday 7pm–2am. No credit cards. Tanaka is one of the most successful sushi restaurants in Rio. Today the owner of Tanaka has four other restaurants in the city and everybody knows that his sushi is simply the best.

CHURRASCARIAS (BARBECUE)

Carretão
Rua Siqueira Campos 23, Copacabana
Tel: 236-3435
Open: 11am–midnight. *Rodizio*-style barbecue, top quality meats and side dishes.

O Casarão
Av. Niemeyer 121, Vidigal (Rio Sheraton Hotel)
Tel: 274-1122
Open: noon–4pm, 7pm–midnight. Major credit cards. For a fixed price, help yourself at the barbecue pit and salad bar in a small restaurant in the hotel grounds. Lovely sea breezes.

Majorica
Rua Senador Vergueira 11/15, Flamengo
Tel: 205-6820
Open: noon–midnight. Credit cards: American Express. Good quality barbecued meats – choose the cut you want from the pit if you like. Pleasant, cozy decor.

Mariu's
Av. Atlântica 290B, Leme
Tel: 542-2393
Open: 11.30am–12.30am. Major credit cards. *Rodizio*-style barbecue. Fine meats, large variety of excellent side dishes, efficient service, used to dealing with foreigners. On the beach in Leme.

Palace
Rua Rodolfo Dantas 16, Copacabana
Tel: 541-6748
Open: 11am–2am. Credit cards:

Only some are accepted. Good barbecued meats served *rodizio*-style at a fast pace. Next to Copacabana Palace.

Pampa
Av. das Américas 5150, Barra da Tijuca (Carrefour supermarket)
Tel: 325-0861
Open: 11.30am–11.30pm. Credit cards: Visa, Diners. *Rodizio* service with quality cuts of meat.

Plataforma
Rua Adalberto Ferreira 32 Leblon
Tel: 274-4022
Open: 11am–3am. Major credit cards. Large barbecue house with international menu as well. Upstairs, the Plataforma I samba show.

Porcão
Rua Barão da Torre 218, Ipanema
Tel: 522-0999
Open: 11am–1am; Av. Armando Lombardi 591, Barra da Tijuca. Tel: 493-3355. Open: 11am–1am. Credit cards: Major ones. Traditional *rodizio*-style barbecue restaurants, one in Ipanema and one in Barra da Tijuca. Large groups are not a problem here.

Porcão
Av. N.S. de Copacabana, 1144, Copacabana
Tel: 523-1497
Open: 11.30am–1am. Major credit cards. *Rodizio or à la carte* barbecue plus international menu.

T-Bone
Rua Laura Müller 116, Botafogo (Shopping Rio Sul)
Tel: 275-7895
Open: 11am–11pm. Most major credit cards are accepted. Take a break from shopping – good barbecue steak house right in the mall.

FRENCH

Le Bec Fin
Av. N.S. de Copacabana 178A, Copacabana
Tel: 542-4097
Open: Monday to Saturday 7pm–2am, Sunday noon–5pm, closed Wednesday. All major credit cards accepted. Classic French cuisine in deluxe restaurant with im-

peccable service. One of Rio's most traditional. Pleasant piano music.

Café de la Paix
Av. N.S. de Copacabana 178A, Copacabana
Tel: 275-9922
Open: 7pm–3am. Major credit cards. Charming art nouveau decor, informal. High quality French food. Afternoon tea. On Saturday, *feijoada* and Brazilian buffet are offered. On the beach.

Le Champs Élysées
Av. Presidente Antônio Carlos 58, 12th floor (maison de France), Centro
Tel: 220-4713
Open: noon–5pm, closed: Saturday and Sunday. Credit cards: American Express. Attractive downtown restaurant with French country cooking, upstairs from the French consulate. Great rooftop view of Sugarloaf.

Claude Troisgros
Rua Custódio Serrão 62, Jardim Botânico
Tel: 537-8582
Open: Monday to Friday noon–3.30pm and 7.30pm–12.30am, Saturday 7.30pm–12.30am. Major credit cards. One of Rio's finest restaurants, in pretty house on quiet street. Chef Trosgros introduce native fruits and vegetables into his imaginative nouvelle cuisine recipes. Order *à la carte* or be daring and try the surprise *menu confiance*. Reservations only.

Clube Gourmet
Rua General Polidoro 186, Botafogo
Tel: 295-3494
Open: noon–3pm, 8.30pm–1am. No lunch on Saturday. Major credit cards. Unusual Brazilian ingredients also turn up in the French recipes here. Informal atmosphere despite its elegance. Choose one dish from each of four-courses, from the full gourmet menu at dinner for a set price.

Garcia & Rodrigues
Av. Ataulfo de Paiva 1251, Leblon
Tel: 512-8188
Tuesday to Saturday 1pm–3pm and 8pm–midnight, Sunday 1pm–6pm, Monday 8pm–midnight. Major credit cards. One of the stars of the carioca gastronomic sky. Choose wine from the cellar from the excellent wine list.

Ouro Verde
Av. Atlântica 1456, Copacabana (Hotel Ouro Verde)
Tel: 543-4123
Open: 12.30pm–past midnight. Major credit cards. Classic French food. Discreetly elegant. Long-standing tradition. Also international menu. On the beach.

Le Pré Catelan
Av. Atlântica 4240, Copacabana (Rio Palace Hotel)
Tel: 525-1160
Open: Monday to Saturday 7.30pm–11.30pm. Major credit cards. Lovely *belle époque* dining room. French nouvelle cuisine with surprises, impeccable service. Branch of the Paris original, supervised by Gaston Lenotre. Reservations are recommended.

Le Saint Honoré
Av. Atlântica 1020, 37th floor, Leme (Hotel Meridien)
Tel: 546-0880
Open: 7pm–midnight. Closed Sunday. Major credit cards. Imaginative nouvelle cuisine. *Prix fixe* set menu at lunch, à la carte for dinner. Dinner only on Saturday. Elegant decoration, fabulous view of Copacabana, superb eating.

Traiteurs De France
Av. Nossa Senhora de Copacabana 386, Copacabana
Tel: 548-6440
Open Monday to Sunday noon–5pm. No credit cards. One of the best restaurants for French cuisine in the city but unfortunately it closes early. Haddock sweetened with paprika and duck in a sauce seasoned with ginger and honey are two of many irresistible dishes on the menu.

INTERNATIONAL

Alcaparra
Praia do Flamengo 150, Flamengo
Tel: 557-7236
Open: Monday to Sunday noon until last client. Major credit cards. Atmosphere is slightly formal but the food is excellent, especially the fish dishes. Try the chicken with spinach and mushrooms.

Antonino
Av. Epitácio Pessoa 1244, Lagoa
Tel: 523-3791
Open: noon–2am. Credit cards accepted. View across Lagoa to the mountains beyond. Classic menu, high quality food. Piano bar on ground floor. Reservations necessary for evenings (try to get a window seat).

Atlantis
Av. Atlântica 4240, 1st floor, Copacabana (Rio Palace Hotel)
Tel: 525-1232
Open: noon–4pm and 8pm–11pm. Major credit cards. Window seats and outdoor tables have beautiful view of Copacabana beach. Seafood buffet Friday, Saturday *feijoada*, New York Sunday brunch. Live music at night.

Café do Teatro
Av. Rio Branco, Centro (Teatro Municipal)
Tel: 262-4164
Open: 11am–4pm, closed: Saturday and Sunday. Major credit cards. Assyrian decor à la Cecil B. DeMille. On the ground floor of the opera house. Varied menu with specials.

Colombo
Rua Gonçalves Dias 32-36, Centro
Tel: 232-2300
Open: 11am–6pm, Saturday tea room only: 9am–1pm, closed: Sunday. Major credit cards. Lovely *belle époque* restaurant dating from 1884. Stained glass skylight, background piano. Downstairs, turn-of-the-century mirrored tearoom. Copacabana beach: Fifty years younger than the original downtown establishment.

Florentino
Av. General San Martin 1227, Leblon
Tel: 274-6841
Open: noon–2am. Major credit cards. Small, intimate dining area upstairs. Downstairs, a cozy bar. Many fish dishes. Elegant, fashionable spot. Reservations necessary.

Guimas
Rua José Roberto Macedo Soares
5, Gávea
Tel: 259-7996
Open: noon–1am. No credit cards.
Small, charming. Popular with the
art set. Always busy but won't take
reservations.

Hippopotamus
Rua Barão da Torre 354, Ipanema
Tel: 247-0351
Open: 11pm until at least 4am.
Credit cards accepted. The "Hippo"
is an exclusive private club for
members (and their guests) only.
But five-star hotels can make reservations for their guests. Sophisticated and elegant. Good food, good
service. The chef is French and his
specialty is fish. Bar and discotheque. Crowded on weekends.

The Lynx
Rua Teixeira de Melo 31, Ipanema
Tel: 522-9796
Open: Monday to Friday 7pm–2am,
Saturday to Sunday noon–2am. Major credit cards. International menu
and crowd. The menu is creative
and the food made with caprice.
House specialty is grilled codfish,
with purée of spinach and sauce
with mint.

Monte Carlo
Rua Duvivier 21, Copacabana
Tel: 541-4097
Open: noon–2am. Credit cards
accepted. Traditional menu also
includes Brazilian favorites.
Saturday *feijoada*; *cozido* on Sundays. Comfortable bar. Reservations recommended on the
weekend.

Nino
Rua Domingos Ferreira 242A,
Copacabana
Tel: 255-9696
Open: noon–2am; Praia de Botafogo
228, Botafogo. Tel: 551-8597, 399-
0018. Open: noon–2am. Credit
cards accepted at all branches.
Food is always good, service efficient. Downtown restaurant popular
at lunch. Many Brazilian dishes on
the menu. Same high standards at
all branches.

Pérgula
Av. Atlântica 1702, Copacabana
(Copacabana Palace Hotel)
Tel: 255-7070

Open: 11.30am–3.30pm,
7pm–1am. Major credit cards.
Elegant restaurant in historic
Copacabana Palace. Over sixty
years old. Good meats, good service.

ITALIAN

Alfredo di Lello
Av. Prefeito Mendes de Moraes
222, São Conrado (Hotel Inter-
Continental)
Tel: 322-2200
Open: noon–3pm, 7.30–11pm.
Major credit cards. Rio's branch of
the famous Alfredo of Rome, one of
only three outside Italy. The house
specialty is Fettuccine al Alfredo.

Amacord
Rua Maria Quitéria 136, Lagoa
Tel: 287-0335
Open Monday to Sunday noon until
the last client. Major credit cards. A
light and colorful environment with
sophisticated clientele. Specialties
on the menu are lamb in rosemary
sauce and risotto made of shrimps
and pineapple, salads are the best
in town.

Carpaccio & Cia
Rua Dias Ferreira 571 A, Leblon
Tel: 274-8142
Open Monday to Friday 6pm–1am,
Saturday to Sunday noon–1am. Major credit cards. Over 50 different
carpaccios and other Italian dishes
on the menu. Reasonable prices, always crowed and definitely the
place to go if you want to mix with
the famous of Rio.

Da Brambini
Av. Atlântica 514, Leme
Tel: 275-4346
Open Monday to Sunday noon–2am.
Major credit cards. A small
restaurant with only 38 seats. Its
wise to make a reservation. House
specialties are dishes from the
north of Italy.

Enotria
(Fashion Mall), Estrada Da Gávea
899, 2nd floor
Tel: 322-6064
Open: noon–4pm and
7pm–12.30am. Major credit cards.
Many consider Enotria Rio's best
Italian restaurant. Owner Danio

Braga is certainly one of the city's
foremost authorities on wines and
the restaurant boasts one of the
best-stocked wine cellars in town.
Excellent northern cuisine. Reservations necessary for this small, cozy
eatery.

La Mole
Rua Dias Ferreira 147, Leblon
Tel: 294-0699

Rua Marquês
De Valença 74 (Tijuca)
Tel: 284-1599
Rua Armando Lombardi 175 (Barra)
Tel: 494-2625
Open: 11am–1am. Major credit
cards. Familiar pasta dishes,
pizzas, steaks, chicken. Nothing
fancy, but food is reliable and inexpensive. You may have to wait for a
table.

Quadrifoglio
Rua JJ Seabra 19
Tel: 294-1433
Open: noon–3pm, 8pm–1am. No
credit cards. Homey, small restau-
rant with delicious pastas and other
Italian classics. Reservations are a
good idea.

Satiricon
Rua Barão da Torre 192, Ipanema
Tel: 521-0627
Open: noon–2am, Monday
6pm–2am. Credit cards: only some
are accepted. Pasta and Italian recipes featuring seafood.

Pizza Palace
Barão da Torre 340, Ipanema
Tel: 521-1289
Open Monday to Sunday noon until
the last client. Major credit cards.
Cheap and well-prepared Italian
food. The menu offers seafood and
traditional Portuguese dishes.
Young clientele.

NORTH AMERICAN AND BRITISH

USA Today
Rio Sul, Rua Lauro Muller 116,
Botafogo
Tel: 543-6845
Open Monday to Sunday
11am–11pm. Major credit cards.
Restaurant is decorated in the
colors of the American flag. The
dishes are beef and hamburgers.

The Lord Jim Pub
Rua Paul Redfern 63, Ipanema
Tel: 259-3047
Open: Tuesday to Friday 3pm–7pm.
No credit cards. The ground floor
recreates a country pub. English
home cooking served on the
second and third floors. Great complete afternoon tea service (reservation needed for tea).

PORTUGUESE

Adegão Português
Campo de São Cristóvão 212-A,
São Cristóvão
Tel: 580-7288
Open: noon–11pm, Sunday
noon–9pm. Major credit cards. Authentic Portuguese cuisine – ozido,
bacalhau, octopus, roast suckling
pig, Portuguese desserts. Located
on the square where the Northeastern Fair is held on Sunday.

Antiquarius
Rua Aristides Espinola 19, Leblon
Tel: 294-1049
Open: noon–2am
Major credit cards. An attractive
restaurant decorated with antiques.
Alenteja recipes, lighter than most
Portuguese cuisine. Good bacalhau
dishes, many lusitanian seafood
dishes, fabulous Portuguese desserts. Also "international"
selections. The Sunday cozido is
considered by some to be the best
in town. Reservations
recommended for dinner.

Ponto de Encontro
Rua Barata Ribeiro 750-B,
Copacabana
Tel: 255-9699
Open: noon–2am. Major credit
cards. Portuguese and international
cuisine served in cozy wood-pan-
eled dining room. Shop next to entrance sells pastries, Portuguese
sweets and take-home food.

Penafiel
Rua Senhor dos Passos 121,
Centro
Tel: 224-6870
Open: 11am–3.30pm, closed:
Saturday and Sunday. No credit
cards. Unsophisticated. Run by the
same family since it opened in
1912. Plain but good Portuguese

cooking, you may have to wait for a
table. On pedestrian street in the
Saara shopping district downtown.
Desserts are Brazilian (try out the
banana-cheese Mineiro com Botas).

SEAFOOD

Alba–mar
Praça Marechal Ancora 184/186
(near Praça XV, downtown)
Tel: 240-8428/8378
Open: 11.30am–10pm, closed:
Sunday. Credit cards: American
Express. Near the port and terminal
for the ferry boats, housed in the
sole remaining tower of what was
once a municipal market, has beautiful view of the bay. Fish is the
specialty, but also an international
menu. Busy at lunch, but not at
night.

Barracuda
Marina da Gloria (Parque do
Flamengo)
Tel: 265-4641
Open: noon–midnight, Sunday
noon–6pm. Major credit cards. Pic-
turesque location at the marina.
Popular with the business crowd.
Seafood and international. Reserva-
tions essential for lunch.

A Cabaça Grande
Rua do Ouvidor 12, Centro
Tel: 509-2301
Open: noon–4pm, closed:
weekends. Credit cards accepted.
Traditional downtown seafood
restaurant, serves some of the tastiest fish in Rio. Try the house
specialty: seafood soup.

Cândido's
Rua Barros de Alarcão 352, Pedra
de Guaratiba
Tel: 417-2674
Open: noon–6pm, weekends
noon–9pm. Credit cards: Diners.
This outstanding fish and seafood
restaurant is actually out of Rio and
lunch here could be included in an
outing to the fishing village of Pedra
de Guaratiba. Sophisticated eating
in a relaxed atmosphere.
Reservations essential for the
weekend. If possible go on a week-
day.

Grottammare
Rua Gomes Carneiro 132, Ipanema

Tel: 522-3186
Open: 6pm–1am, weekends
noon–1am. Major credit cards.
Fresh grilled, poached seafood.
Restaurant has its own fishermen
and you can choose your fish and
have it made to order. Good service, large portions. Also serves
meat and pasta dishes. Make reservations.

A Marisqueira
Rua Barata Ribeiro 233,
Copacabana
Tel: 547-3920
Open: daily 11am–1am; Rua Gomes
Carneiro, Ipanema. Tel: 267-9944.
Closed: Monday. Major credit cards.
Traditional restaurant specializing in
a variety of good seafood. Also
serves other meats.

Pax Delícia
Rua Maria Quitéria 99, Ipanema
Tel: 247-4191
Open: Monday 6pm–midnight,
Tuesday to Sunday noon–midnight.
Major credit cards. Nice view to the
green plaza Praça da Paz. The dish-
es with salmon, shrimp and lobster
are all delicious and well prepared.
The menu is famous for its
desserts.

Petronius
(only for events) Av. Vieira Souto
460, Ipanema (in the Hotel Caesar
Park)
Tel: 287-3122
Open: 7pm–1am, Saturday
noon–4pm. Major credit cards.
Elegant restaurant, with excellent
service, exquisite cuisine. View of
Ipanema beach, piano music.

Quatro Sete Meia (476)
Rua Barros de Alarcão 476, Pedra
de Guaratiba
Tel: 417-1716
Open: Wednesday to Sunday
noon–6pm, closed Monday to
Tuesday. Some credit cards. Also
out in Guaratiba. Small, simple restaurant near the sea. Excellent seafood. Reservations absolutely
necessary.

Satyricon
Rua Barão da Torre 192, Ipanema
Tel: 521-0627
Open: Tuesday–Sunday 7pm–2am,
Monday 6pm–2am. Major credit
cards. One of the most
sophisticated restaurants in Rio

decorated with tanks of fishes and seafood waiting to be picked for the table. Expensive but worth it. Grilled fish with salad is a must.

Shirley
Rua Gustavo Sampaio 610, Leme
Tel: 275-1398
Open: noon–1am. No credit cards. Tasty Spanish and Portuguese seafood recipes. Small, modest and always busy, there is usually a wait for a table and reservations are not accepted. Have a seafood snack while waiting.

Sol e Mar
Av. Reporter Nestor Moreira 11, Botafogo
Tel: 543-1663
Open: 11am–3pm. Major credit cards. Bayside seafood restaruant with view across the water of Sugarloaf, sail-boats. Very pleasant, also an outdoor cocktail area.

Tia Palmira
Caminho do Souza 18, Barra de Guaratiba
Tel: 410-8169
Open: 11.30am–6pm, closed: Monday. Some credit cards. Modest restaurant out in Barra de Guaratiba has a set menu offering a sampling of various seafood specialties and fruit desserts. Indoor/outdoor dining areas. No reservations accepted.

Vice-key
Av. Monsenhor Ascâncio 535, Praça do O, Barra da Tijuca
Tel: 493-1683
Open: noon–2am. No credit cards. Live lobsters, crayfish, oysters raised in tanks – really fresh. Colonial setting.

RESTAURANTS WITH A VIEW

Alba–mar
Downtown, on the bay near the ferry station and the port. (*See listing under Seafood*).

Antonino
On the Lagoa Rodrigo de Freitas lagoon. (*International*).

Atlantis
Terrace restaurant in Rio Palace Hotel. On the beach in Copacabana. (*See listing under International*).

Le Champs Élysées
Downtown restaurant with view of bay, Sugarloaf. (*See listing under French*).

Restaurante Morro Da Urca
Av. Pasteur 520
Urca (at the cable car station)
Tel: 295-2397
Open: daily noon–7pm. Credit cards accepted. On the top of Morro da Urca, the first station on the cable car trip up to Sugarloaf. View of southern residential areas, downtown, the bay, its bridge and surrounding mountains. International cuisine. Accommodates large groups easily.

Os Esquilos and A Floresta
Both in the Tijuca Forest Park. Look on the map of the park roads. Located in the parking lot near the *Cascatinha* waterfall as you enter the park. Traditional home cooking served in old colonial houses with open veranda surrounded by the lush green forest. Fireplace for chilly days. Afternoon tea service. Just as pretty – and even greener – on a rainy or foggy day.

Os Esquilos
Tel: 492-2197
Open: noon–6pm. Some credit cards.

A Floresta
Tel: 492-5358
Open: 11am–9pm. No credit cards.

Moenda
In the Hotel Trocadero, Copacabana. (*See listing under Brazilian*).

Petronius
(for events only) in the Caesar Park, on the beach in Ipanema. (*See listing under Seafood*).

Quatro Sete Mei (476)
Near the water at Pedra de Guaratiba fishing village. (*See listing under Seafood*).

Rive Gauche
1484, Lagoa
Tel: 522-0645
Open: 8pm until the last customer leaves. Credit cards accepted. Elegant restaurant with view of the Rodrigo de Freitas lagoon and green mountains beyond. International menu. Live music in the bar Monday–Saturday. Popular Biblos Bar nightclub on ground floor.

Le Saint Honoré
Spectacular view of Copacabana and Leme beaches from the 37th floor of the Meridien Hotel. (*See listing under French*).

Sol e Mar
on the bay near the Yacht Club. (*See listing under Seafood*).

Tiberius
Av. Vieira Souto 460, 23rd Floor, Ipanema (Caesar Park Hotel)
Tel: 525-2525
Open: 8am–10pm. Major credit cards. View of Ipanema and Leblon beaches and the mountains beyond Leblon from the 23rd floor of Caesar Park Hotel in Ipanema. Open all day serving breakfast, lunch, afternoon tea and dinner. International menu includes light snacks as well as full meals. Buffet in town. *Feijoada* served on Saturday is one of the best in town. Opens onto rooftop, where you can have a drink and admire the view.

Cafés

The best way to get to know Rio and the *carioca* way of life is to start a conversation with the locals. It is sometimes complicated because of the language but on the other hand Brazilians love to get involved in a good conversation. Nice places to meet and talk to the *cariocas* are in the cafés in Ipanema:

Armazén Do Café
Rua Maria Quitéria 77
Tel: 522-5039.

Felice Caffé
Rua Gomes Carneiro 30
Tel: 522-7749.

Le Panetier
Rua Vinicius De Moraes 121
Tel: 521-0824.

Letras & Expressões
Café Ubaldo, Visconde de Pirajá 276
Tel: 521-6110.

Drinking Notes

Brazilians are great social drinkers and love to sit for hours talking and often singing with friends. During the hottest months, this will usually be in open air restaurants where most of the people will be ordering *chopp*, cold draft beer, perfect for the hot weather. Brazilian beers are really very good. There may be some confusion when ordering – although *cerveja* means beer, it usually refers to bottled beer only.

Brazil's own unique brew is *cachaça*, a strong liquor distilled from sugar cane, a type of rum, if you will, but with its own distinct flavor. Usually colorless, it can also be amber. Each region boasts of its locally produced *cachaça*, also called *pinga*, *cana* or *aguardente*, but traditional producers are the states of Minas Gerais, Rio de Janeiro, São Paulo and the northeastern states, where sugar cane has long been a cash crop.

Out of *cachaça*, some of the most delightful drinks are concocted. The most popular is the **caipirinha** which can be considered the national drink: lime, crushed in a glass (peel, and all), sugar, ice and *cachaça*: perfect in its simplicity. Variations of this drink are made using vodka or rum, but you should try the real thing. Some bars and restaurants mix their *caipirinhas* sweeter than you may want – order yours *com pouco açucar* (with a small amount of sugar) or even *sem açucar* (without sugar).

Batidas, as the name suggests, are beaten in the blender or shaken and come in as many varieties as there are types of fruit in the tropics. Basically fruit juice with *cachaça*, some are also prepared with sweetened condensed milk. Favorites are *batida de maracujá* (passion fruit) and *batida de coco* (coconut milk) – exotic flavors for visitors from cooler climates. When imbibing *batidas*, don't forget that the *cachaça* makes them a potent drink, even though they taste just like fruit juice.

Straight *cachaça* or beer is what the working class Brazilian will drink in the neighborhood *botequins*, little bars where you drink standing up at the counter. Some of these will serve *cachaça* steeped with herbs – the resulting infusion is considered to be "good for what ails you." The *botequins* are quite often filled with

men, and while women are not barred and won't usually be hassled, they may not feel comfortable about being the only female in this male stronghold. And a single female foreigner will be more than obvious.

Try the Brazilian **wines**. Produced in the cooler southern states, they are quite good. Restaurants offer a selection of the best – ask the *maître d'* for help in ordering what you like. *Tinto* is red, *branco* is white and *rosé* is the same; *seco* is dry and *suave*, which actually means soft, refers to the sweetness of the wine. Excellent wines imported from Argentina and Chile are not expensive in Brazil, so you may want to take advantage of this. The usual variety of spirits are available, both *importado* (imported) and *nacional* (domestic). There are no good Brazilian whiskeys and imports are very expensive. Some familiar brands are produced locally – you will know by the price.

Among the non-alcoholic beverages, fresh fruit juices are a real treat. Any hotel or restaurant will have three or four types but the snack bars specializing in **suco de fruta** have an amazing variety. The fruits on display – guavas, mangoes, pineapples, passion fruit, persimmons, tamarind, fruits that even if their names were translatable you would never have heard of, as well as the more familiar apples, melons, bananas and strawberries – are as tasty as they are colorful.

They will also whip up a glass of lemonade for you or squeeze a plain old orange. All juices are made fresh for each order. Delicious fruit milkshakes called **vitaminas** make a nutritious snack. Most common are the *mista* or mixed fruit – usually papaya and banana with a touch of beetroot to give it a pretty color; *banana com aveia*, which is banana and raw oatmeal; and *abacate* which is made from avocado. These make great breakfast accompaniments.

If you've never sipped coconut water – the water from the green

fruit – you can stop at a street vendor, often a trailer near the beach. Restaurants or bars that serve **água de coco** will usually hang the cocos near the door (pronounced like *cocoa*; if you want hot chocolate, ask for chocolate *quente*, otherwise you'll probably get a coconut). The top is lopped off and you drink the clear, colorless juice with a straw. After drinking the water, you can ask to have the coco split open so that you can eat the soft, gelatin-like flesh inside the shell.

Another tropical treat is the juice of sugarcane, which is squeezed and served at snack bars that advertise **caldo de cana**. Street vendors use a little crank wringer. This juice, as is to be expected, is sweet and filling, and has a pleasant, subtle flavor.

Among soft drinks, you will find the familiar Coca-Cola and Pepsi products as well as domestic brands. A uniquely Brazilian soft drink is **guaraná**, flavored with a small Amazon fruit. Quite sweet, but good, it is a favorite with children.

Bottled mineral water is available everywhere, both carbonated (*com gás*) and plain (*sem gás*), and it's best for visitors to stick to it. Although water in the cities is treated, people further filter it in their homes and if you are a houseguest, you will no doubt be served **agua filtrada**. Not drinking unfiltered tap water is a question of common sense.

If you are traditional and can't do without your morning tea, never fear. Tea is grown in Brazil and many of the fancier hotels and restaurants can offer you an English brand. Try the indigenous South American **mate** (pronounced "ma-tchee") tea. The black version is drunk as a refreshing iced tea; the green, called *chimarrao*, is sipped through a silver straw with a strainer at the lower end; in Brazil's far south it's a gaucho tradition.

Last, but certainly not least, is the coffee for which Brazil is justly famous. **Café** is roasted dark, ground fine, prepared strong and taken with plenty of sugar. Coffee with hot milk (*café com leite*) is the breakfast beverage throughout Brazil. Other than at breakfast, it is served black in tiny demitasse cups and never with a meal.

The *cafezinhos* or "little coffees" will be offered the visitor to any home or office. They are served piping hot at any *botequim* and are the traditional and, you will agree, perfect ending to every meal.

If you want to take ground coffee back, you can buy it at the airport, vacuum-packed to last longer, or pick it up at any supermarket or bakery.

Attractions

Culture

MUSEUMS

Museums sometimes close for restoration for long periods – often several years. Check to make sure the museum is open before traveling long distances.

Ethnology
Museu do Folclore Edison Carneiro (Folk Museum), Rua do Catete 181, Catete. Tel: 285-0441. Open: Tuesday to Friday 11am–6pm, Saturday, Sunday and holidays 3–6pm.
Museu do Indio (Indian Museum), Rua das Palmeiras 55, Botafogo. Tel: 286-8799. Open: Tuesday to Friday 10am–5.30pm, closed: for lunch, noon–2pm.
Museu do Negro (Negro Museum), Rua Uruguaiana 77, Centro. Tel: 242-4492. Open: Monday to Friday 8am–5pm.

History
Museu da República (Museum of the Republic), Rua do Catete 153, Flamengo. Tel: 285-6350. Open: Tuesday to Friday noon–5pm, Saturday to Sunday 2pm–6pm. Good Folklore Museum in same building.
Museu Histórico Nacional (National Historical Museum), Praça Rui Barbosa, Centro. Tel: 240-9529. Open: Tuesday to Friday 11am–5pm, Saturday, Sunday and holidays 2–5pm.
Museu Histórico e Diplomático, Av. Marechal Floriano 196, Centro. Tel: 253-2828. Open: Tuesday, Wednesday, Friday 1.15–4.15pm.
Museu Casa de Rui Barbosa (Rui Barbosa House), Rua São Clemente 134, Botafogo. Tel: 537-0036.

Open: Tuesday to Friday 1–4pm.
Museu Histórico da Cidade (City Historical Museum), Estr. Santa Marinha, Gávea (inside the Parque da Cidade). Tel: 512-2353. Open: Tuesday to Friday 9am–5pm, Saturday and Sunday 11am–5pm.

Performing Arts and Music
Museu da Imagem e do Som (Museum of Image and Sound – Popular Music), Praça Rui Barbosa 1, Centro (near Praça XV de Novembro). Tel: 262-0309. Open: Monday to Friday 1–6pm.
Museu Villa-Lobos, Rua Sorocaba 200, Botafogo. Tel: 226-3845. Open: Monday to Friday 10am–5pm.
Museu Carmen Miranda, Parque do Flamengo (across from Av. Rui Barbosa no. 560). Tel: 551-2597. Open: Monday to Friday 1–4pm.

Science and Technology
Museu Nacional (National Museum), Quinta da Boa Vista, São Cristóvão. Tel: 567-6316. Open: Tuesday–Sunday 10am–4pm.
Museu do Trem (Train Museum), Rua Arquias Cordeiro 1046, Engenho de Dentro. Tel: 269-5545. Open: Tuesday–Friday 10am–noon, Saturday and Sunday 1–5pm.

Art
Museums have permanent collections of Brazilian and international art and exhibitions are held periodically.
Museu Chácara do Céu, Rua Murtinho Nobre 93, Santa Teresa. Tel: 232-1386. Open: Tuesday to Saturday noon–5pm, Sunday 1–5pm.
Museu Nacional de Belas Artes (National Museum of Fine Arts), Av. Rio Branco 199, Centro. Tel: 240-9869. Open: Tuesday to Friday 12.30–6pm, Saturday, Sunday and holidays 3–6pm.
Museu do Açude, Estr. do Açude 764, Alto da Boa Vista. Tel: 237-9367. Open: Thursday to Sunday 11am–5pm.
Museu de Arte Moderna (Modern Art Museum), Av. Infante D. Henrique 85, Parque do Flamengo. Tel: 210-2188. Open: Tuesday to

Sunday noon–6pm.

Museu International de Arte Naif do Brazil (MIAN), Rua Cosme Velho 561, Cosme Velho. Tel: 205-8612. Open Tuesday to Friday 10am–6pm, Saturday to Sunday noon–6pm.

Museu de Arte Contemporânea (Museum of Contemporary Art), Mirante da Boa Viagem, Ingá Niterói. Tel: 620-2400. Open: Tuesday to Sunday 11am–7pm, Saturday 1–9pm.

ART GALLERIES & CULTURAL CENTERS

The majority of cultural centers and galleries in Rio show contemporary Brazilian art, and now and then, international art. Art galleries are concentrated in Ipanema and the cultural centers in the center of the city. Newspapers have listings of current exhibitions.

Centro Cultural Banco do Brazil, Rua Primeiro de Março 66, Centro. Tel: 216-0626. Open: Tuesday to Sunday 10am–10pm.

Casa França-Brasil, Rua Visconde de Itaboraí 78, Centro. Open: Tuesday to Sunday 10am–8pm. Tel: 253-5366.

Espaço Cultural dos Correios, Rua Visconde de Itaboraí 20, Centro. Tel: 563-8770. Open: Tuesday to Sunday noon–8pm.

Paço Imperial, Praça XV de Novembro 48, Centro. Tel: 533-4407. Open: Tuesday to Sunday noon–6.30pm.

Centro Cultural Helio Oiticica, Rua Luís de Camões 68 Praça Tiradentes. Tel: 232-2213. Open: Tuesday to Friday noon–8pm, weekend 11am–5pm.

Galeria LGC Arte Hoje, Rua do Rosário 38, Centro. Tel: 263 7353. Open: Tuesday to Sunday noon–7pm.

Galeria Paulo Fernandes, Rua do Rosário 38, Centro. Tel: 253-8582. Open: Tuesday to Sunday noon–7pm.

Galeria Cohn Edelstein, Rua Jangadeiros 14, Ipanema. Tel: 523-0549. Open: Monday to Friday 11am–8pm.

Galeria Anna Maria Niemayer, Shopping da Gávea, Rua Marquês de São Vincente 52, Gávea. Tel: 239-9144. Open: Monday to Friday 10am–9pm, weekend 10am–6pm.

CONCERTS

Music is definitely Brazil's forte. A variety of musical forms has developed in different parts of the country, many with accompanying forms of dance. While the Brazilian influence is to be heard around the world (especially in jazz), what little is known of Brazilian music outside the country is just the tip of the iceberg. Take in a concert by a popular singer (look under "Shows" in the newspaper) or ask your hotel to recommend a nightclub with live Brazilian music: *bossa nova*, *samba*, *choro* and *seresta* are popular in Rio.

If you are visiting at Carnival, you will see and hear plenty of music and dancing in the streets, mostly *samba*, but also *frevo* and *axé*. There are also shows all year long, designed to give tourists a taste of Carnival and of Brazilian folk music and dance. If you like what you hear, get some records or tapes to take home with you.

The classical music and dance season runs after Carnival through December, centered at the **Teatro Municipal** (on Praça da Veiga, downtown, tel: 544-2900). Many concerts are also held at the nearby **Sala Cecilia Meireles** (Largo da Lapa 47, tel: 224-4291) and there are many other auditoriums and small recital halls where performances are held. Rio's symphony is the *Orquestra Sinfonica Brasileira*.

The Teatro Municipal's own orchestra accompanies the ballets and operas held there. Besides presentations by local talent, Rio is included in world concert tours by international performers. Look under "*música*" in the newspapers; both classic ballet and modern dance presentations are listed under "*dança*."

THEATER

In order to enjoy most theater performances, you really would have to understand the language. Rio de Janeiro has a busy season which runs from after Carnival through November.

CINEMA

Some Brazilian cinema is very good – Brazil has, in fact, exported films quite successfully to North America and Europe. Without a knowledge of Portuguese, however, you may well wait and see exports back home with subtitles in your language. But the majority of films shown in Rio are foreign-made, mostly American, all in the original language with Portuguese sub-titles. Check out what's playing under the "*cinema*" heading in the local papers. Over the last couple of years, cinemas showing quality films and arthouse movies have opened up in Rio. Many serve as meeting points and also have bookshops, bars and cafés:

CineClube Laura Alvim, Av. Viera Souto 176, Ipanema.

Estação Botafogo, Rua Voluntários da Patria 88, Botafogo.

Estação Unibanco, Rua Voluntários da Patria 35, Botafogo.

Palácio, Rua do Passeio 40.

Nightlife

The night buzzes in Rio. The action starts late: dinner is never before 9pm and shows begin at 10pm or later. Nightclubs don't begin to warm up until midnight and you may be surprised by the sunrise on your way out.

PUBS AND BARS

Many bars around town also serve lunch and have live music. The best include:

Antonino, Av. Epitácio Pessoa 1244 on the Lagoa. Tel: 523-3549.

Blue Angel, Rua Júlio de Castilhos 15 B, Copacabana. Tel: 227-1810.
Bofetada Up, Farme De Amoedo 87 A, Ipanema. Tel: 522-9526.
Chico's, Av. Epitácio Pessoa 1560 on the Lagoa. Tel: 523-3514.
Equinox, Rua Prodente de Morais 729, Ipanema. Tel: 247-0580.
Garota Ipanema, Rua Vinicius de Moraes 49, Ipanema. Tel: 523-3787.
Harry's Bar, Av. Bartolomeu Mitre 450, Leblon. Tel: 259-4043.
Jazzmania, Av. Rainha Elisabeth 769, Ipanema. Tel: 227-2447.
Lord Jim Pub, Rua Paul Redfern 63, Ipanema. Tel: 259-3047.
Mariu's, Av. Atlântica 290, Leme. Tel: 542-2393.
Mistura Fina, Rua Garcia d'Avila 15, Ipanema. Tel: 259-9394.
Mostarda, Av. Epitácio Pessoa 980 990, Lagoa. Tel: 523-1747.
The Cattleman, Av. Epitacio Pessoa 846 on the Lagoa. Tel: 239-2863.

Popular bars with live music for dancing include:
Café Nice, Av. Rio Branco 277 (downstairs), Centro. Tel: 240-3871.
Carinhoso, Rus Visconde de Pirajá 22, Ipanema. Tel: 523-0302.
Sobre as Ondas, Av. Atlântica 3432 (upstairs), Copacabana. Tel: 522-1296.
Vinicius, Av. N.S. de Copacabana 39, Copacabana. Tel: 513-4757.
Vogue, Rua Cupertino Durão 173, Leblon. Tel: 274-4145.

If you're not up to a wild night on the town, have a quiet drink at one of the sidewalk restaurants along the beach and enjoy the sea breeze. Many of the top beachfront hotels have quiet rooftop bars with fabulous views where you can enjoy a nightcap. Try the **Skylab** on the 30th floor of the Rio Othon Palace (Av. Atlântica 3264 on Copacabana beach. Tel: 522-1522 ext 8187) or the **Ponte de Comando** at the top of the Miramar Palace (Av. Atlântica 3668, Copacabana. Tel: 247-6070), both open till 2am.

DISCOS AND NIGHTCLUBS

If you want something a little livelier, there are many nightclubs and discotheques. The social set hang out at the fashionable private clubs, such as:

Hippopotamus, Rua Barão da Torre 354, Ipanema. Tel: 247-0351. Two of the trendiest nightclubs are **Provisório** (Barão da Torre 368, Ipanema. tel: 522-1460) and the punk hangout, **Crepúsculo de Cubatão** (Rua Barata Ribeiro 543, Copacabana. Tel: 235-2045). Other popular spots include:
The Ballroom, Rua Humaitá 110. Tel: 537-7600.
Biblos, Av. Epitácio Pessoa 1484, Lagoa. Tel: 522-0645.
Casa Rosa, Rua Alice 550, Laranjeiras. Tel: 558-8332.
Caligula, Rua Prudente de Morais 129, Ipanema. Tel: 287-1369.
Circus Disco, Rua Gen. Urquiza 102, 2nd floor, Leblon. Tel: 274-7895.
El Turf, Jockey Club, Praça Santos Dumont 31, Gávea. Tel: 274 1444.
Fundição Progresso, Rua dos Arcos, Lapa. Tel: 220-5070.
Fun Club, Shopping Rio Sul, Rua Lauro Muller 116, Botafogo.
Greenwich Village Art Beer, Av. Sernambetiba 4462, Barra da Tijuca. Tel: 433-3441.
Help, Av. Atlântica 3432, Copacabana.
Ilha Dos Pescadores, Estrada da Barra Tijuca 793, Barra da Tijuca. Tel: 494-3485.
Kalesa, Rua Sacadura Cabral 61 Praça Mauá. Tel: 263-5289.
La Dolce Vita, Av. Min. Ivan Lins 80, Barra da Tijuca. Tel: 399-0105.
Mariuzinn, Rua Paul Pompéia 102, Copacabana. Tel: 247-8849.
Mikonos, Rua Cupertino Durão 177, Leblon. Tel: 294-2293.
Mistura Fina, Estr. da Barra da Tijuca 1636, Itanhangá. Tel: 399-3460.
West Side, Av. do Pepé 646, Barra da Tijuca. Tel: 389-0760/493-3489.
Zoom, Largo de São Conrado 20,

São Conrado. Tel: 322-4179.

Rio has many nightclubs with strip tease and sex shows. In Copacabana they're concentrated at the **Leme** end, around **Av. Princesa Isabel**, **Av. Prado Junior** and **Praça do Lido** square, bordered by Av. N.S. de Copacabana, and the beach drive Av. Atlântica between Rua Ronald de Carvalho and Rua Belford Roxo. Less classy are the **Praça Mauá** bars near the port and the nightclubs along **Rua Mem de Sá** in Lapa, which feature transvestites.

Gafierias
Gafierias are traditional old-fashioned dance halls with live music. The **Asa Branca** (Av. Mem de Sá 17, Lapa. Tel: 224-2342) is a modern version and often features a popular singer. More authentic gafierias are:
Elite, Rua Frei Caneca 4, upstairs, Centro. Tel: 232-3217.
Estudantina, Praça Tiradentes 79, Centro. Tel: 232-1149.

Live Concerts & Shows
The two big names for live concerts by Brazilian and international pop singers are **Canecão** (Av. Wenceslau Brás 215, Botafogo. Tel: 543-1241) and **Metropolitan** (Via Parque Av. Ayrton Senna 3000, Barra da Tijuca. Tel: 283-3773). Concerts are also periodically scheduled for **Morro da Urca** (first station half-way up to Sugarloaf, tel: 541-3737) and the **Maracanãzinho** stadium (Rua Prof. Eurico Rabelo, São Cristóvão. Tel: 568-9962). International superstars occasionally fill the giant **Maracanã** soccer stadium next door (at the same telephone number).
Many singers give shows in the **João Caetano** theater on Praça Tiradentes, downtown (tel: 221-1223). Informal concerts (rock, jazz, popular Brazilian music) are held in the **Parque da Catacumba** on the Lagoa (tel: 287-8293) – be prepared to sit on the grass. Especially during the summer season there are often concerts and shows on the beaches. Big

stars giving special performances at Teatro Municipal, Canecão and the Metropolitan usually perform for free on Rio's beaches. Shows with Brazilian music, rock and pop on a smaller scale can be found all around the city. Some of the best places are:

Hipódromo Up, Praça Santos Dumont 108, Gávea. Tel: 294-0095.

Rock in Rio Café, Barra Shopping, Av. das Américas 4666, Barra da Tijuca. Tel: 431-9500.

Teatro Rival, Rua Alvaro Alvim 33, Centro. Tel : 532-4192.

Terraço Rio Sul, Shopping Rio Sul, Rua Lauro Muller 116, Botafogo. Tel: 545-7281.

And the **Circo Voador** (near the Arches in Lapa) schedules a variety of shows, with room to dance along. Pop concerts are listed in the newspapers under "shows."

Samba

Brazil is the land of samba and if you miss the biggest samba show of all, Carnival in Rio, there is plenty of samba to be heard and seen all year long. If you want to improve your style before getting on the dance floors, there are private classes which welcome gringos:

Casa de Dança Carlinhos de Jesus, Rua da Passagem 145, Botafogo. Tel: 541-6186.

Centro de Dança Jaime Arôxa, Rua Sâo Clemente 155, Botafogo. Tel: 266-2615.

Companhia de Dança Aérea, Rua Arnaldo Quintela 43, Botafogo. Tel: 542-8239.

After lessons you may want to visit some of the following samba clubs:

Cordâo da Bola Preta, Av. Treze de Maio 13, Centro. Tel: 240-8049.

Helênico, Rua Itapiru 1305, Rio Comprido. Tel: 273-6448.

Nega Fulô, Rua Conde de Irajá 132, Botafogo. Tel: 266-6294.

Clube do Samba, Estrada da Barra da Tijuca 65, Barra da Tijuca. Tel: 399-0892.

Labaredo, Estrada da Barra da Tijuca 65, Barra da Tijuca. Tel: 399-1582.

There are popular samba shows for tourists. The best way to visit them is to go as part of a group tour. Ask your hotel about reservations.

Scala-Rio, Avenida Afrânio de Melo Franco 296, Leblon. Tel: 239-4448.

Plataforma 1, Rua Adalberto Ferreira 32, Leblon. Tel: 274-4022.

You can also visit a Carnival parade rehearsal at one of the **samba schools**. Most groups rehearse in the poorer suburbs or near *favelas*, and it is advisable to arrange a visit through your hotel.

Sport

Participant Sports

Private clubs are big in Brazil and besides the socializing, this is where most upper and middle class Brazilians practice sports. Although you can usually visit as a guest, some of these sports facilities can be found in top class hotels.

AQUATIC SPORTS

As to be expected in a tropical seaside city, a variety of aquatic sports can be enjoyed in Rio. Ocean swimming is refreshing in the hottest months. The waves that break on Rio's ocean beaches are quite strong and it's difficult to do any actual "swimming" – it's more like playing in the waves. The water in the bay is too polluted for swimming, yet the bay beaches are just as crowded as the sea. Several of the hotels and almost all the private clubs have swimming pools. There are no public pools in Rio.

If you're interested in sailing, surfing, windsurfing, fishing or scuba diving, go to the **Marina da Glória**, on the Aterro do Flamengo in Gloria, right in town (tel: 205-6716). Sail-boats, yachts, speed-boats and schooner-like Brazilian *saveiros* can be rented, complete with fishing equipment and crew starting around $100 a day. Resort hotels in small beachtowns near Rio also have boats, surf and windsurf boards, diving equipment and instructors. Popular spots for diving near Rio are the "Sun Coast," east of Rio (Cabo Frio, Búzios) and the "Green Coast" to the south and west (Angra dos Reis, Parati) where the water is calm and breathtakingly clear.

TENNIS AND GOLF

The Rio Sheraton, Inter-Continental Rio and Nacional Rio hotels have tennis courts. There are few public courts, as the game is played mostly at clubs.

Golf is not a popular sport in Brazil, but Rio has two beautiful courses at the **Gávea** and **Itanhangá** golf clubs. Although exclusive, you can arrange through your hotel to play as a visitor for about $17 (excluding rental of equipment). The mountain towns of Petrópolis and Teresópolis each have a country club and you can also play at the seaside city of Angra dos Reis.

HANG GLIDING

Hang gliding is popular. Gliders leap off the Pedra Bonita peak and soar in circles like hawks on the air currents before landing on the beach at São Conrado. Inexperienced flyers can go tandem with an instructor.

Contact the **Associação de Vôo Livre** at Avenida Prefeito Mendes de Morais (Praia do Pepino), tel: 322-0266. If you prefer to just watch, go to the end of the beach at São Conrado on a Sunday.

JOGGING

Joggers have some beautiful places to keep in shape while in Rio. The wide sidewalks along the beach in Leme, Copacabana, Ipanema and Leblon have the "distance" marked in kilometers. Other favorite spots for *carioca* runners are around the Rodrigo de Freitas lagoon, along the parkway in Flamengo and up in the Floresta da Tijuca national park. Rio has its own marathon which attracts international contenders.

OTHER ACTIVITIES

If you enjoy climbing, you won't need to leave the city. There are many peaks to climb, including Rio's landmarks, Sugarloaf and Corcovado. Excursion clubs arrange outings to areas outside Rio where you can go mountain climbing, spelunking, white-water canoeing and kayaking and sailing. Rapids shooting and rubber rafting excursions can be arranged through the hotels. Contact **Centro Excursionista do Rio de Janeiro** (Av. Rio Branco, 277/805, Centro. Tel: 220-3548).

There are beautiful hiking trails in the **Floresta da Tijuca** national park, all unmarked. For more information on hiking and camping, contact the **Camping Clube do Brasil**. They rent trailers and organize treks. Hunting is forbidden by law throughout Brazil.

Spectator Sports

SOCCER (FUTEBOL)

This is *the* sport in Brazil, a national passion that unites all ages and classes. During World Cup season, the country comes to a halt as everyone tunes in to watch the Cup matches on TV. If you're a soccer fan, arrange through your hotel to see a professional game – there are organized tours.

The boisterous fans are often as interesting to watch as the game itself at Rio's giant **Maracanã Stadium** which squeezes in crowds of up to 180,000. There is rarely any violence, but it is recommended that you get a reserved seat (around $5–8) rather than sitting in the packed bleachers (about $1.50). Most weekend afternoons or in the early evening, you can see a "sandlot" match between neighborhood teams on the beaches or in the parks (also the venues for volleyball matches).

HORSE RACING

Horse racing is popular and you can watch and bet at races almost every Monday and Friday evening and Saturday and Sunday afternoon. The most important race

Capoeira

Capoeira is a uniquely Brazilian sport. The tradition has been kept alive chiefly in Salvador, Bahia, but there are also academies in Rio de Janeiro, where tourists can either observe or take part in classes. The best known of these is the Associação de Capoeira Mestre Bimba, Rua das Laranjeiras 1, Terreiro de Jesus. Originally a form of ritual fight practiced by African slaves, *capoeira* has evolved into a stylized fight-dance, with its own accompanying rhythms and music, using the feet a great deal to strike out and requiring graceful agility. Presentations are included in folk dance or samba shows – enquire at your hotel. There are occasional performances by street groups, for example at the entrances to the Mercado Modelo in Cidade Baixa.

in Brazil, the Grande Premio do Brasil sweepstakes, is held at Rio's 35,000-spectator racetrack (Praça Santos Dumont, 31, Joquei. Tel: 259-0144) on the first Sunday in August.

MOTOR RACING

Brazil's Formula I Grand Prix is now held in São Paulo, but there is still plenty of motorsport in Rio at the autodrome in Glória.

Language

The Bare Minimum

Portuguese, not Spanish, is the language of Brazil. If you have a knowledge of Spanish, it will come in handy – you will recognize many similar words and most Brazilians understand Spanish. Although many upper-class Brazilians know at least some English or French and are eager to practice on the foreign visitor, don't expect the man on the street to speak your language. A foreigner's effort to learn the local language is always appreciated.

You can easily get by in English at large hotels and fancy restaurants. However, if you like to wander around on your own, a pocket dictionary would be helpful.

First names are used a great deal in Brazil. In many situations in which English-speakers would use a title and surname, Brazilians often use a first name with the title of respect. *Senhor* for men (written Sr. and usually shortened to *Seu* in spoken Portuguese) and *Senhora* (written *Sra*) or *Dona* (used only with first name) for women. If João Oliveira or Maria da Silva calls you Sr. John, rather than Mr. Jones, then you should address them as Sr. João and Dona Maria.

There are three second-person pronoun forms in Portuguese. Stick to *você*, equivalent to "you". O *senhor* (for men) or *a senhora* (for women) is used to show respect for someone of a different age group or social class or to be polite to a stranger.

As a foreigner, you won't offend anyone by using the wrong form of address. If you are learning when to use the formal or informal style, copy how others address you.

In some parts of Brazil, mainly the northeast and the south, *tu* is used a great deal. Originally, in Portugal, *tu* was used similarly to the German "Du," among intimate friends and close relatives, but in Brazil, when this form is used, it is equivalent to *você*.

If you are staying longer and are serious about learning the language, there are Portuguese courses for non-native speakers. Meanwhile, here are some essential words and phrases.

Addresses

Alameda (abbreviated Al.) = **lane**.
Andar = **floor, story**.
Av. or *Avenida* = **avenue**.
Centro = the central downtown business district, also frequently referred to as *a cidade* or the city.
Cj. or *Conjunto* = a suite of rooms or sometimes a group of buildings.
Estrada (abbreviated Estr.) = road or highway.
Largo (Lgo.) = **square or plaza**.
Praça (Pça.) = **square or plaza**.
Praia = **beach**.
Rodovia (Rod.) = **highway**.
Rua (abbreviated R.) = **street**.
Sala = **room**.
Sobreloja = mezzanine.

Ordinal numbers are written with a ° sign after the numeral, so that 3° *andar* means 3rd floor. The federal interstate highways are written with a BR in front of the number, for example, BR-101, which follows the Atlantic coast. *Ramal* (pronounced 'ha-maul') = telephone extension.

Politeness

Please/Thank you (very much)/*Por favor*/*(muito) Obrigado* (or *obrigada*, for a woman speaking)
You're welcome ("its nothing")/*De nada*
Excuse me (to apologise)/*Desculpe*
Excuse me (to take leave or get past someone)/*Com licença*

Greetings

Tudo Bem (all's well) is one of the most common forms of greeting: a person asks, "*Tudo bem?*" and the other replies, "*Tudo bem.*" This is also used to mean "OK," "all right," "will do," or as a response when someone apologizes, indicating, as it were, "That's all right, it doesn't matter."

Good morning/*Bom dia*
Good afternoon/*Boa tarde*
Good evening, good night/*Boa noite*
How are you?/*Como vai?*
Well, thank you/*Bem, obrigado*
Hello (to answer the telephone)/*Alô*
Hello (greeting)/*bom dia, boa tarde*
Hi, hey!/*Oi* (informal greeting also used to get someone's – like the waiter's – attention)
Goodbye (casual and common)/*Tchau* Goodbye ("until soon")/*até logo*
Goodbye (similar to "farewell")/*adeus*

My name is.../*Meu nome é...*
I am.../*Eu sou...*
What is your name?/*Como é seu nome?*
It's a pleasure (when introduced)/*É um prazer* (or frequently) *prazer*
Good! Great!/*Que bom!*
Health! (common toast)/*Saúde!*
Do you speak English?/*Você fala inglês?*
I don't understand/*Não entendo*
I didn't understand/*Não entendi*
Do you understand?/*Você entende?*
Please repeat more slowly/*Por favor repete, mais devagar*
What do you call this (that)?/*Como se chama isto (aquilo)?*
How do you say...?/*Como se diz...?*

Nouns/Pronouns

Who?/*Quem?*
I/*Eu*
We/*Nós*
You (singular)/*Você*
You (plural)/*Vocês*
He, She, They/*Ele, Ela, Eles, Elas*
My, Mine (depending on gender of object)/*Meu, Minha*

Our, Ours/*Nosso, Nossa* (depending on gender of object)
Your, Yours/*Seu, Sua* (depending on gender of object)
His or Her, Hers, Their or Theirs/*Dele, Dela, Deles* (also *Seu, Sua* in all three cases)

Getting Around

Where is the...?/*Onde é...?*
beach/*a praia*
bathroom/*o banheiro*
bus station/*a rodoviária*
airport/*o aeroporto*
train station/*a estação de trem*
post office/*o correio*
police station/*a delegacia de polícia*
ticket office/*a bilheteria*
marketplace/*o mercado/a feira*
embassy/*a embaixada*
consulate/*o consulado*

Where is there a...?/*Onde é que tem...?*
currency exchange/*uma casa de câmbio*
bank/*um banco*
pharmacy/*uma farmácia*
(good) hotel/*um (bom) hotel*
(good) restaurant/*um (bom) restaurante*
bar/*um bar*
snack bar/*uma lanchonete*
bus stop/*um ponto de ônibus*
taxi stand/*um ponto de taxi*
subway station/*uma estação de metrô*
service station/*um posto de gasolina*
newsstand/*um jornaleiro*
public telephone/*um telefone público*
supermarket/*um supermercado*
shopping center/*um shopping center*
department store/*uma loja de departamentos*
boutique/*uma boutique*
jeweler/*um joalheiro*
hairdresser/*um cabeleireiro*
barber/*um barbeiro*
laundry/*uma lavanderia*
hospital/*um hospital*

Do you have...?/*Tem...?*
I want...please./*Eu quero...por favor.*

I don't want.../*Eu não quero...*
I want to buy.../*Eu quero comprar...*

Where can I buy...?/*Onde posso comprar...?*
cigarettes/*cigarro*
film/*filme*
a ticket for.../*uma entrada para...*
a reserved seat/*um lugar marcado*
another (the same)/*um outro igual*
another (different)/*um outro differente*
this, that/*isto, aquilo*
something less expensive/*algo mais barato*
postcards/*cartões postais*
paper/*papel*
envelopes/*envelopes*
a pen/*uma caneta*
a pencil/*um lápis*
soap/*sabonete*
shampoo/*xampu*
toothpaste/*pasta de dente*
sunscreen/*filtro solar*
aspirin/*aspirina*

I need.../*Eu preciso de...*
a doctor/*um médico*
a mechanic/*um mecânico*
transportation/*condução*
help/*ajuda*

How much?/*Quanto?*
How many?/*Quantos?*
How much does it cost?/*Quanto custa?, Quanto é?*
That's very expensive/*É muito caro*
A lot, (also very), many/*Muito, Muitos*
A little, few/*Um pouco, um pouquinho/poucos*

Numbers

1/*um*
2/*dois*
3/*três*
4/*quatro*
5/*cinco*
6/*seis* (or often *meia*, meaning "half" for half dozen)
7/*sete*
8/*oito*
9/*nove*
10/*dez*
11/*onze*
12/*doze*
13/*treze*

14/*quatorze*
15/*quinze*
16/*dezesseis*
17/*dezessete*
18/*dezoito*
19/*dezenove*
20/*vinte*
21/*vinte e um*
30/*trinta*
40/*quarenta*
50/*cinqüenta*
60/*sessenta*
70/*setenta*
80/*oitenta*
90/*noventa*
100/*cem*
101/*cento e um*
200/*duzentos*
300/*trezentos*
400/*quatrocentos*
500/*quinhentos*
600/*seiscentos*
700/*setecentos*
800/*oitocentos*
900/*novecentos*
1,000/*mil*
2,000/*dois mil*
10,000/*dez mil*
100,000/*cem mil*
1,000,000/*um milhão*

Commas and periods in numbers in Portuguese are used so that one thousand is written 1.000 and one and a half (1.5) is written 1,5.

Opposites

Yes, no/*Sim, não*
More, less/*Mais, menos*
Large, small/*Grande, pequeno*
Larger, smaller/*Maior, menor*
Expensive, inexpensive/*Caro, barato*
Warm, cool/*morno, frio*
Hot, cold/*quente, gelado*
With, without/*com, sem*
First, last/*Primeiro, ultimo*
Good, well/*Bom, bem*
Better, best/*Melhor, o melhor*
Bad, worse, worst/*Ruim, Pior, o pior*
Far, near/*Longe, perto*
Fast, slow/*Rápido, devagar*
Right, left/*Direita, esquerda*
Here, there/*Aqui, lá*
Now, later/*Agora, depois*

Time

Hours of the day are numbered from "zero hour" to 24, but can also be referred to as being in the morning (*da manhã*), in the afternoon (*da tarde*) or at night (*da noite*), so that 8pm could be referred to as *vinte horas* (literally 20 hours, written 20) or as *oito* (eight) *horas da noite*.

When?/*Quando?*
What time is it?/*Que horas são?*
Just a moment please/*Um momento, por favor*
What is the schedule? (bus, tour, show, etc.)/*Qual é o horário?*
How long does it take?/*Leva quanto tempo?*

Hour, day/*Hora, dia*
Week, month/*semana, mês*
At what time?/*A que horas?*

At 1, at 2, at 3/*A uma hora, as duas horas, as três horas*
An hour from now/*Daqui a uma hora*
Which day?/*Que dia?*
Yesterday/*Ontem*
Today/*Hoje*
Tomorrow/*Amanhã*

This week/*Esta semana*
Last week/*a semana passada*
Next week/*a semena que vem*

Monday/*Segunda-feira*, **often written 2a**
Tuesday/*Terca-feira*, **3a**
Wednesday/*Quarta-feira*, **4a**
Thursday/*Quinta-feira*, **5a**
Friday/*Sexta-feira*, **6a**
Saturday/*Sábado*
Sunday/*Domingo*
The weekend/*O fim de semana*

Transportation

Taxi, bus, car/*Taxi, ônibus, carro*
Plane, train, boat/*Avião, trem, barco*
A ticket to.../*Uma passagem para...*
I want to go to.../*Quero ir para...*
How can I get to...?/*Como posso ir para...?*
Please take me to.../*Por favor, me leve para...*
Please call a taxi for me./*Por favor, chame um taxi para mim.*
What is this place called?/*Como se chama este lugar?*
How long will it take to get there?/*Leva quanto tempo para chegar lá?*
Please stop here. Stop!/*Por favor pare aqui. Pare!*
Please wait./*Por favor, espere*
I want to rent a car./*Quero alugar um carro.*
What time does the ... leave?/*A que horas sai o ... ?*
Where does this bus go?/*Este ônibus vai para onde?*
Does it go via ... ?/*Passa em ... ?*
Departure tax/*Taxa de embarque*
I want to check my luggage./*Quero despachar minha bagagem.*

I want to store my luggage./*Quero guardar minha bagagem.*

At the Hotel

I have a reservation./*Tenho uma reserva.*
I want to make a reservation./*Quero fazer uma reserva.*
A single room/*Um quarto de solteiro*
A double room/*Um quarto de casal*
With air conditioning/*Com ar condicionado*
I want to see the room./*Quero ver o quarto.*
Suitcase/*Mala*
Bag, purse/*Bolsa*
Room service/*Serviço de quarto*
Key/*Chave*
The manager/*O gerente*

Money

Cash/*Dinheiro*
Do you accept credit cards?/*Aceita cartão de crédito?*
Can you cash a traveler's check?/*Pode trocar um traveler's check? (cheque de viagem)*
I want to exchange money./*Quero trocar dinheiro.*

What is the exchange rate?/*Qual é o câmbio?*
The bill, please./*A conta, por favor.*
I want my change, please./*Eu quero meu troco, por favor.*
I want a receipt./*Eu quero um recibo.*

At the Restaurant

Waiter/*Garçon*
Maitre d'/*Maitre*
I didn't order this./*Eu não pedi isto.*
Is service included?/*Está incluido o serviço?*
The menu/*O cardápio*
The wine list/*A carte de vinhos*

Breakfast/*Café da manhã*
Lunch/*Almoço*
Supper/*Jantar*
The house specialty/*A especialidade da casa*
Mineral water (carbonated)/*Água mineral com gás*
Mineral water (still)/*Água mineral sem gás*
Coffee/*Café*
Tea/*Chá*
Beer/*Cerveja*
White wine/*Vinho branco*
Red wine/*Vinho tinto*
A soft drink, juice/*Um refrigerante, suco*
An alcoholic drink, a cocktail/*Um drink/Um cocktail*
Ice/*Gelo*

An appetizer, a snack/*Um tira-gosto, um lanche*
Beef/*Carne*
Pork/*Porco*
Chicken/*Frango*
Fish/*Peixe*
Shrimp/*Camarão*

Well done/*Bem Passado*
Medium rare/*Ao ponto*
Rare/*Mal Passado*

Vegetables/*Verduras*
Salad/*Salada*
Fruit/*Fruta*
Rice/*Arroz*
Potatoes (Frenchfried)/*Batatas (Fritas)*
Beans/*Feijão*
Soup/*Sopa*

Bread/*Pão*
Butter/*Manteiga*
Toast/*Torradas*
Eggs/*Ovos*

Sandwich/*Sanduiche*
Pizza/*Pizza*
Dessert/*Sombremesa*
Sweets/*Doces*

A plate/*Um prato*
A glass/*Um copo*
A cup/*Uma xícara*
A napkin/*Um guardanapo*
Salt/*Sal*
Pepper/*Pimenta*
Sugar/*Açucar*

Further Reading

Other Insight Guides

Of the almost 200 titles in the *Insight Guides* series, the books which highlight destinations in this region include: *Insight Guides* to *Brazil, Chile, Ecuador, Peru, Argentina, Buenos Aires* and *Venezuela*. There is also an overall guide to the world's most surprising continent, *Insight Guide: South America*.

Rainforest enthusiasts will be interested in *Insight Guide: Amazon Wildlife*, which vividly captures in expert text and glorious photography the flora and fauna of the region.

ART & PHOTO CREDITS

All photography by JOHN MAIER JR. except for:

Robert Harding Picture Library 121
Tony Stone Worldwide 14/15, 16/17, 18/19
Vange Millet, Courtesy of Museu Nacional de Belas Artes 22/23, 26
Vange Millet, Courtesy of Museu **Paulista USP** 24
Vange Millet, Courtesy of Aceno Galeria de Arte 27
Vange Millet 28, 29, 30, 31

Maps Berndtson & Berndtson
Visual Consultant V. Barl
Map Production Polyglott Kartographie, Berndtson & Berndtson Publications
© 1999 Apa Publications GmbH & Co. Verlag KG (Singapore branch)

Index

Numbers in italics refer to photographs

The World of Insight Guides

400 books in three complementary series cover every major destination in every continent.